Praise for

GETHSEMANE, GC
and the GARDEN

"Karl G. Maeser said, 'A true teach cannot help being one.' Those words desc and in this book he teaches at his best. testimony he shares have been gained ov dedicated discipleship. Each chapter is help us all more fully appreciate and app

—Brad Wilcox, BYU professor, *Atonement* and

"With his head and heart, Ed Pinegar has created many manuscripts that are i But never before was he fully prepared message on the Savior as portrayed in thi ship and inspiration, he has brought to message on the life and mission of the Sa to partake liberally of the spiritual feast pared. When you reach the last page, you rejoice that you know the Savior better a

—George and Susa

GETHSEMANE, *Golgotha,* *and the* GARDEN TOMB

GETHSEMANE, *Golgotha,* *and the* GARDEN TOMB

the SACRIFICE *of the* EXALTED SON *of* GOD

ED J. PINEGAR

CFI
An imprint of Cedar Fort, Inc.
Springville, UT

ISBN 13: 978-1-4621-1765-9

Published by CFI, an imprint of Cedar Fort, Inc.
2373 W. 700 S., Springville, UT 84663
Distributed by Cedar Fort, Inc., www.cedarfort.com

Library of Congress Cataloging-in-Publication Data

Pinegar, Ed J., author.
Gethsemane, Golgotha, and the Garden Tomb: the sacrifice of the exalted Son of God / Ed J. Pinegar.
pages cm
Includes bibliographical references.
ISBN 978-1-4621-1765-9 (hardback w/dustjacket : alk. paper)
1. Atonement--Church of Jesus Christ of Latter-day Saints. I. Title.
BX8643.A85P56 2015
232'.3--dc23

2015027445

Cover design by Shawnda T. Craig

Edited and typeset by Jessica B. Ellingson

Printed in China

10 9 8 7 6 5 4 3 2 1

Printed on acid-free paper

CONTENTS

ACKNOWLEDGMENTS

It is with gratitude that I express my appreciation for all the wonderful friends and editors that have made this work possible: my dear friends Richard Allen, Alonzo Gaskill, Don Parry, and Jack Welch, who have mentored me and taught me much. To Eschler Editing I express my gratitude. Thanks to McKell Parsons, Jessica Ellingson, and the staff at Cedar Fort; the book is better for all their efforts. And to my sweetheart, Pat, who always is so supportive of my time spent hunched over the computer, typing with my three fingers, I am forever grateful. It is because of the grace, goodness, and mercy of our Father in Heaven and His Beloved Son, Jesus Christ, that make life eternal possible through the suffering and sacrificing Christ, who brought about the infinite Atonement.

INTRODUCTION

It is a difficult undertaking to write and describe the events of our beloved Savior's suffering and sacrificing in order to complete the infinite Atonement. Never have I attempted such a delicate and tender subject concerning my beloved Savior Jesus Christ. He is my Savior and Redeemer. He has paid the price for you and me. He did all of this because He loves us with a perfect love. He suffered, bled, and died so we might not only be forgiven of our sins but also have everlasting life, even life eternal. He has put us beyond the reach of death and hell—even the monster Satan himself—if we choose to follow and obey Him. I remind myself that this is all made possible by the grace of God and the Lord Jesus Christ, who was ever seeking to please His Father.

The Lord Jesus Christ, the Beloved Son of God the Father, came to earth to do the will of His Father. The Father's will was fulfilled through His Only Begotten Son in the flesh. He is the Anointed One—the Messiah. He became the Christ. He fulfilled the infinite Atonement through His suffering, sacrificing in Gethsemane, enduring crucifixion on the cross at Golgotha, and coming forth in His triumphal Resurrection from the Garden Tomb. He established the kingdom of God, which was built upon His gospel. He sought only to please His Father in all that He did (see John 8:28–29). The Savior can do only what the Father has shown Him to do and commanded Him to do. Christ, ever the obedient and submissive Son, gave His will to His Father: "Thy will be done." Jesus was lifted up on the cross that He might draw all mankind unto Him, that they—you and I—might partake of the love of God through the infinite Atonement.

The gospel is not only the good news that Christ would come and provide the way of life and life eternal; it is literally the plan of exaltation, even the plan of happiness. We can partake of the gospel of Jesus Christ as we come unto Him. The gospel is the foundation of the Church and kingdom of God, which through the greater priesthood would provide the life-saving and exalting ordinances and covenants. One of the Lord's purposes in making the ultimate sacrifice of the Atonement was to *draw* us to Him, for He, Christ the Anointed One, is the only way back to the Father. There is no other way (see John 14:6). The power to *draw* near to the Lord is brought about by the enabling power of the Atonement according to the power of the Father. We are not only attracted to the Lord but motivated as well. Our gratitude should swell within our beings, and the love of God, the fruit of the tree of life, will fill our souls. We will be happy. If you have never been acquainted with gratitude, you will never know happiness. Happiness can only be found in receiving and acting upon the infinite Atonement of the Savior Jesus Christ. The Lord Jesus Christ, because of doing the will of the Father, provides the opportunity to give all humankind the opportunity to return to our Father and find peace and rest. We must come unto Him. This phrase occurs over and over again in the scriptures. This is not a casual invitation. This is the ultimate request of the Lord and Redeemer of the world. No better example is found than when the Savior said, "Behold, I stand at the door, and knock: if any man hear my voice, and open the door, I will come in to him, and will sup with him, and he with me" (Revelation 3:20). Not only does the Savior invite us to come, He literally comes to us and knocks at our hearts, inviting us to come unto Him. If we open our hearts, the Lord will be with us. Can there be any greater expression of love than that? I think not. Our Savior is offering us life eternal. As we begin to understand and appreciate these supernal and empowering truths, our hearts should be full of gratitude and we will "come unto Christ, and be perfected in Him" (Moroni 10:32).

The Savior was required to suffer in such agony and sacrifice all, including the horrific death on the cross at Golgotha. His suffering was immeasurable and infinite. "And being in an agony [which means, by definition, intense emotion, great pain and anguish, even suffering to that of preceding death] he prayed more earnestly: and his sweat was as it were great drops of blood falling down to the ground" (Luke 22:44). No one in all of history has been known to sweat blood from every pore. This condition in medical terms is called hematidrosis. This can only occur under extreme stress. The stress that the Lord suffered was for every sin committed upon the earth since the beginning of time. This is incomprehensible for the finite mortal mind, for only a God could comprehend and have the power to suffer so greatly. And Christ the Lord did. He suffered infinitely. He suffered more than any human soul has ever suffered. He suffered in every facet possible, physically, emotionally, intellectually, and spiritually, as only the Son of God, the great Jehovah, the Creator of heaven and earth could suffer. No mortal mind can comprehend His suffering. Our finite mortal minds cannot grasp, comprehend, or even begin to understand the suffering of the Lord.

When I begin to try to understand and appreciate the suffering of my Savior with my little mind, I am overwhelmed with gratitude and thanksgiving. Gratitude is what the Lord wants us to feel. Our gratitude begins to draw us to Him. As the scriptures indicate, "that I [the Lord through His suffering, sacrificing, and completing the infinite Atonement] might draw all men unto me" (3 Nephi 27:14). It is gratitude that lets the love of God (the giving of His Son so we might have everlasting life) into our hearts. Surely this is why we were admonished by Moroni to ponder about the Lord and His goodness in our lives. Gratitude must be felt in order to accept the Atonement into our lives. If it were not so, we could not have the love of God within our souls and thus enjoy happiness for which the love of God was designed to bring.

To help us better understand and appreciate the suffering of the Lord, He describes His own suffering and the consequences of those who do not "come unto Him" and repent and partake of His infinite Atonement. The Lord is seeking desperately to help us understand the ultimate power and effect of the Atonement and what is expected of us in order for it to empower our lives. He said, "Therefore I command you to repent—repent, lest I smite you by the rod of my mouth, and by my wrath, and by my anger, and your sufferings be sore—how sore you know not, how exquisite you know not, yea, how hard to bear you know not. For behold, I, God, have suffered these things for all, that they might not suffer if they would repent; but if they would not repent they must suffer even as I; which suffering caused myself, even God, the greatest of all, to tremble because of pain, and to bleed at every pore, and to suffer both body and spirit—and would that I might not drink the bitter cup, and shrink—Nevertheless, glory be to the Father, and I partook and finished my preparations unto the children of men" (D&C 19:15–19). This scripture helps me grasp the significance of the Atonement. We cannot be casual about this ultimate gift that required so much. My heart aches and my eyes glisten as I share my feelings of what my beloved Savior has done for me and for all of us. He has saved the world! His grace is sufficient. It is that grace that, when accepted, can propel us forward to good works, for thus we were created to do so (see Ephesians 2:8–10). If our hearts could feel of His ultimate sacrifice for us, surely we would change. Oh how we ought to pray for a broken heart and contrite spirit so that we can feel of His ultimate sacrifice and goodness and be motivated through gratitude to do good. Then we would "press forward with a steadfastness in Christ, having a perfect brightness of hope, and a love of God and of all men. Wherefore, if ye shall press forward, feasting upon the word of Christ, and endure to the end, behold, thus saith the Father: Ye shall have eternal life" (2 Nephi 31:20). This steadfastness in Christ is expressed through our repentance. This is the premise for the test of life. This is why the prophets were exhorted to "preach nothing save it were repentance and faith on the Lord, who had redeemed his people" (Mosiah 18:20). For it is through repentance that we apply the infinite Atonement to our lives and receive the forgiveness of sins.

Our gratitude to the Lord will increase as we come to understand and appreciate the suffering and sacrificing Christ endured for our sins and the sins of the world and to provide the way back to the presence of our Father. This, in fact, is the premise of this book. As we come to better understand and appreciate the suffering and sacrificing of Christ the Lord, we will come to feel a deep gratitude for the love of God, which will reach into the depths of our souls, and we will change. It is this premise that we will revisit time and again, so that the atoning sacrifice of the Lord will take root in our souls. It is this gratitude, the catalyst of all growth and change that will truly draw us to our Savior and will propel us to make positive changes in our lives.

As a father, mission president, temple president, and priesthood leader, I have seen countless examples of how the Atonement has transformed people's lives. I will share those experiences throughout the book. I have witnessed the healing of souls. I have seen a change of heart. I have seen sins literally removed from their very being. I have seen guilt swept away. I have seen forgiveness cleanse the soul of a victim of abuse. I have seen behavior change as gratitude for the Savior brought commitment into their lives. I have seen commitments made and covenants kept by the enabling power of the Atonement. I have witnessed and participated in the nurturing power of our Savior through His infinite Atonement. I bear witness that the Lord's Atonement is not only the center of the gospel of Jesus Christ but also the center and strength of our very lives. As we come to understand and appreciate our beloved Savior Jesus Christ and His immeasurable suffering and sacrifice which led to the infinite Atonement, then and only then can we really begin to become even as He is. Thus gratitude is the reason for this book, gratitude for the goodness and mercy of God the Father and our Savior Jesus Christ.

Chapter 1

GOD *the* FATHER *and* GOD *the* SON

God the Father, Elohim, our Heavenly Father, is the Father of our spirits (see Hebrews 12:9). He is over all things, and it is His perfect plan of exaltation that we voted for and that is in place today. We are spiritually begotten of our Heavenly Father. All things are done according to the will of God the Father, "the will of the Son being swallowed up in the will of the Father" (Mosiah 15:7; see also John 5:19, 30). It is the ultimate power of God that is given to Christ, and "by the power of the Father he hath risen again" (Mormon 7:5), "giving the Son power to make intercession for the children of men" (Mosiah 15:8). The Father's power is indeed the power and authority of the priesthood by which all things are done on the earth in the name of His Beloved Son, and it is "according to the power of the Father I [Christ] will draw all men unto me" (3 Nephi 27:15). As the Lord was baptized, it is made clear that He had power from His Father: "And he received all power, both in heaven and on earth, and the glory of the Father was with him, for he dwelt in him" (D&C 93:17). Note the phrase for he [God] dwelt in him [Christ]. This same principle was exemplified when Jesus was anointed: "How God anointed Jesus of Nazareth with the Holy Ghost and with power: who went about doing good, and healing all that were oppressed of the devil; for God was with him" (Acts 10:38). The Savior went about doing good, for "God was with Him." We pray to the God of all power, our Heavenly Father, in the name of His Beloved Son, Jesus Christ. He is our Heavenly Father.

God the Son is the Father's Only Begotten Son in the flesh. He also acts as the Father for and in behalf of the Father. The term *Father* is a name, a title, and a role. Jehovah, the promised Messiah, even Christ the Lord, has been given many descriptions, titles, and roles. Three specific examples explain His Fatherhood.

As the firstborn Son in the spirit, Jehovah is Christ, the Father of heaven and earth. Jehovah, who is Christ the Lord, is "*the Father of heaven and earth, the Creator of all things* from the beginning; and his mother shall be called Mary" (Mosiah 3:8; emphasis added; see also Ether 4:7; Alma 11:39).

Christ also becomes our Father as we are spiritually begotten by Him—*as we covenant with Him, we are spiritually begotten of Him, becoming His sons and daughters, and are we are reborn:* "And now, because of the covenant which ye have made ye shall be called the children of Christ, his sons, and his daughters; for behold, this day he hath spiritually begotten you; for ye say that your hearts are changed through faith on his name; therefore, ye are born of him and have become his sons and his daughters" (Mosiah 5:7). The premortal Christ, Jehovah, speaking to the brother of Jared, said, "Behold, I am Jesus Christ. *I am the Father and the Son*. In me shall all mankind have life, and that eternally, even they who shall believe on my name; and they shall become my sons and my daughters" (Ether 3:14–15; emphasis added; see also Mosiah 15:1–4).

The premortal Christ, Jehovah, becomes the Father as He acts for God the Father by what we call divine investiture. He literally speaks and acts for and in behalf of God the Father with all His power and authority. Jehovah is the God of the Old Testament. He was and is the one speaking and acting for and in behalf of God the Father, for they truly are *one* in all things. And the Lord Jesus Christ said, "I and my Father are one" (John 10:30; see also 3 Nephi 20:35; D&C 50:43) The Lord speaks of Himself being the "Great I Am" when He said, "Listen to the voice of Jesus Christ, your Redeemer, the Great I Am, whose arm of mercy hath atoned for your sins" (D&C 29:1). And again He said, "Thus saith the Lord your God, even Jesus Christ, the Great I Am, Alpha and Omega, the beginning and the end, the same which looked upon the wide expanse of eternity, and all the seraphic hosts of heaven, before the world was made" (D&C 38:1; see also D&C 39:1). Who is this *Great* I Am? "And God said unto Moses, I am that I am: and he said, Thus shalt thou say unto the children of Israel, I am hath sent me unto you" (Exodus 3:14). We see that Christ the Lord is indeed the Great I Am of the Old Testament, acting for His Father with divine investiture. The Lord made mention of this in John when He said, "Verily, verily, I say unto you, Before Abraham was, I am" (John 8:58).

The Savior—ever so humble and reverent to His Father, the God over all things—said, "I go unto the Father: for my Father is greater than I" (John 14:28). The Savior said, "I am come in my Father's name" (John 5:43). Jesus always sought to please His Father: "Then said Jesus unto them, When ye have lifted up the Son of man, then shall ye know that I am he, and that I do nothing of myself; but as my Father hath taught me, I speak these things. And he that sent me is with me: the Father hath not left me alone; for I do always those things that please him" (John 8:28–29). The Lord Jesus Christ was ever the benevolent Son of God who did the Father's will in all things as He became the Christ, the Savior and Redeemer of all mankind.

As I speak of our Heavenly Father and our Elder Brother, even Jesus Christ the Lord, special feelings come into my heart. God the Father, Elohim, is my Father. I am His boy. Forgive me as I use the Aramaic term *Abba*, which means Daddy or Papa. You see, I often feel that way toward my Heavenly Father, as I will explain. Following the death of my father on Mother's Day in 1947, my relationship with my Heavenly Father deepened. I sought to know Him and to please Him. My prayers were still reverent but became more familial. I knew He was my real Father—the Father of my eternal spirit. I was His son, just like all of us are the sons and daughters of Almighty God. The magnitude of this truth coming into my soul gave me a power of self-worth, and words can hardly describe my feelings toward my Heavenly Father and my divine nature. I, like you, have a divine destiny. I have come on a special assignment and journey to learn how to become like my Savior and my Father. My Elder Brother, the Savior of the world, my empowering example, has shown you and me the way home to our Father. He has not only shown us the way, He has made the way through His ultimate sacrifice, which has brought forth the infinite Atonement, which empowers our lives. Our Savior came so that we might be perfected and made complete as we come unto Him. Our Savior has sought to do the will of the Father, to please Him, and to bless His brothers and sisters. This knowledge makes my heart tender and my love for my Savior deepens. My personal Savior fills my soul with overflowing love and gratitude, and yet in my weakness I cry out with Nephi, "O wretched man that I am! Yea, my heart sorroweth because of my flesh; my soul grieveth because of mine iniquities. I am encompassed about, because of the temptations and the sins which do so easily beset me" (2 Nephi 4:17–18). Why can't I be better when I want to be better? We all want to be better. I, like you, want to be like my Savior, but I fall short so much of the time. In my weakness, I draw even closer to my Father and my Savior because I know that in my humility and by exercising faith, They will strengthen me through the Savior's enabling Atonement. They will strengthen all of us. We can become better. We can be made perfect. Time is on our side, and with a willing heart, we will plug along like the old "workplugs"—the horses that pulled the "drags" and the wagons with their heavy-laden load. We will make it. We can be like Ammon, and in the strength of the Lord, we can do all things. We love our Heavenly Father and our Savior, and we can choose to go forward, seeking to do Their will and build up the kingdom of God.

Chapter 2

The ANOINTED ONE

THE ANOINTED ONE—THE PROMISED MESSIAH AND CHRIST

To understand the purpose of God the Father's perfect plan, it is important to recognize that His Beloved Son, as the Anointed One, would carry out all of His Father's work here upon the earth. It is through His Anointed One that the infinite Atonement as well as the establishment of the kingdom of God here upon the earth will be completed. It is through Christ that the power of God, the holy priesthood, can bless all the children of God so that they might partake of eternal life.

Of the term *Messiah* we read that it is "an Aramaic word meaning 'the anointed.' It occurs only in Dan. 9:25–26 and John 1:41; 4:25 (Messias). Used as the title of an office, it denotes the King and Deliverer whose coming the Jews were eagerly expecting. In the New Testament the deliverer is called the Christ, which is the Greek equivalent of Messiah, and Jesus the Messiah is called Jesus the Christ, Jesus Christ, or Christ Jesus" (Bible Dictionary, "Messiah").

In the beautiful words of our Savior, He describes His purpose as the Anointed One: "My meat is to do the will of him that sent me, and to finish his work" (John 4:34). "For I came down from heaven, not to do mine own will, but the will of him that sent me" (John 6:38). And why did the Father send His Son? "That I might be lifted up upon the cross; and after that I had been lifted up upon the cross, that I might draw all men unto me" (3 Nephi 27:14).

Christ was obedient to His Father. These scriptures need to be internalized so that we realize how completely the Lord accepted His assignment to carry out the work of His Father—our immortality and eternal lives. What do we learn from this? This willingness of the Savior to do the will of His Father is an example for us to follow. This is why we work with all our heart, might, mind, and strength. This is why we learn our duties. This is why we sacrifice our all. This is why we dedicate our lives to bringing souls to Christ. Yielding our wills to God's is the only real gift we can give. Our agency will never be violated; thus, when we have anything to give of ourselves, it will always have to do with giving our will. This can be simply expressed by being obedient to the commandments of God.

The Savior was anointed to come to this earth to redeem mankind from their lost and fallen state and to pay for all of our sins. The payment has been made! We will suffer for our sins if we do not repent. We came to this earth to prove ourselves worthy of returning to the presence of the Father: "And we will prove them herewith, to see if they will do all things whatsoever the Lord their God shall command them" (Abraham 3:25). Earth life is all about repenting and making the mighty change—for all have sinned (see Romans 3:23). Therefore, we do the will of God. We will repent and call upon Him in the name of His Son forevermore (see Moses 5:8). We, like our Savior, seek to do the will of God by keeping the commandments of God. Christ was the perfect example in all things. He was and is the promised Messiah.

We who have received our endowments have been anointed to become as explained in the *Encyclopedia of Mormonism*:

> The washings and anointings of the biblical period have a parallel today in The Church of Jesus Christ of Latter-day Saints. In response to a commandment to gather the saints and to build a house "to prepare them for the ordinances and endowments, washings, and anointings," these ordinances were introduced in the Kirtland Temple on January 21, 1836. In many respects similar in purpose to ancient Israelite practice and to the washing of feet by

> Jesus among his disciples, these modern LDS rites are performed only in temples set apart and dedicated for sacred purposes. . . . The anointing of a person or object with sacred ointment represents sanctification and consecration, so that both become "most holy" unto the Lord. In this manner, profane persons and things are sanctified in similitude of the messiah (Hebrew "anointed one"), who is Christ (Greek "anointed one"). (Donald W. Parry, "Washings and Anointings," in *Encyclopedia of Mormonism*, ed. Daniel H. Ludlow 5 vols., 1992, 4:1551)

The goodness of God is always evident as He is seeking to give us all things so that we can become empowered to go about doing good. Recognizing the goodness of God and His desires to give every promised blessing possible to His children brings closeness and a relationship that causes us to have a greater knowledge of God. This is a major purpose in being endowed in the holy temple. Anointings refer to a preparation for as well as a pronouncement of blessings to consecrate, to become holy and sanctified, as noted in Leviticus 8:10–12 and Exodus 30:29. Every moment of our lives from premortal life to the resurrection and beyond was and is part of the perfect plan of God the Father. This humbles my soul and teaches me of my Father's love and concern for every aspect of my life. His work is you and me. This is what He does. This perfect example is for us as parents too. We were anointed—set apart if you will—to become like our Heavenly Parents.

Isaiah is quoted extensively in the New Testament and the Book of Mormon, and our Savior said of him, "I give unto you that ye search these things diligently; for great are the words of Isaiah" (3 Nephi 23:1). Abinadi, in his pleading and empowering sermon, quoted Isaiah when he spoke prophetically of the Messiah (he also quoted Isaiah 53). And so to be obedient to the Lord, we shall search the words of Isaiah, which speak messianically of the suffering of our beloved Savior. We will carefully go through this chapter of Isaiah that speaks prophetically of our suffering Savior, which will help us understand and appreciate the coming forth of our Messiah, Christ the Lord. Thus the personal commentary will help us appreciate Isaiah's words, which are precious to our souls if we understand and apply them to our lives.

I plead guilty that when reading the scriptures at times—and particularly Isaiah, whose poetic writing style can at times feel daunting to decipher—I sometimes simply read without feeling. And in that I do err. As I wrote the little commentary to bring insight to my soul (and hopefully yours), I was filled with gratitude for my beloved Savior. I am grateful for a prophet of God who was to prophesy of the coming of the Messiah and was specific as to the things He would do. This is the purpose of Isaiah's messianic treatise concerning our Savior in Isaiah 53. As we go verse by verse, hopefully we will come to understand and appreciate the suffering and sacrificing Christ so that our gratitude will be deepened and our lives changed forever.

THE MESSIANIC PROPHESY OF OUR SAVIOR—ISAIAH CHAPTER 53

1. Who hath believed our report? and to whom is the arm of the Lord revealed?

Who will believe Isaiah's words of this coming Messiah? I believe. The arm of God's power was revealed as Christ performed many miracles:

> But though he had done so many miracles before them, yet they believed not on him:
>
> That the saying of Esaias the prophet might be fulfilled, which he spake, Lord, who hath believed our report? and to whom hath the arm of the Lord been revealed?
>
> Therefore they could not believe, because that Esaias said again,
>
> He hath blinded their eyes, and hardened their heart; that they should not see with their eyes, nor understand with their heart, and be converted, and I should heal them. (John 12:37–40)

Surely God does not blind the eyes of men as Paul taught: "In whom *the god of this world hath blinded the minds* of them which believe not, lest the light of the glorious gospel of Christ, who is the image of God, should shine unto them" (2 Corinthians 4:4; emphasis added). People choose to harden their hearts, as demonstrated throughout the Book of Mormon (see in index "hardheartedness"). The arm or power of God will be revealed to all mankind, for He is the Healer; the Messiah is to be the Redeemer of all of God's children, Jew and Gentile alike. The coming Messiah brings about the salvation of mankind, and we are to work out our own salvation (judged by our works) through the Lord and His empowering Atonement. The grace of God is revealed in the arm of the Lord to those who seek the Lord and come unto Him. "For by grace are ye saved through faith; and that not of yourselves: it is the gift of God: not of works, lest any man should boast. For we are his workmanship, created in Christ Jesus unto good works, which God hath before ordained that we should walk in them" (Ephesians 2:8–10). The God's anointed Son enables us to do everything here upon the earth. God assisted His Son to do good: "Who [Christ] went about doing good . . . for God was with him" (Acts 10:38). We likewise go about doing good, having been "created in Christ Jesus" unto good works. We are empowered by the Lord, for He is our strength in the arm of His power (see 2 Nephi 28:32; Jacob 2:25; Mosiah 12:24; Alma 29:10; 3 Nephi 16:20).

Whom and what will we believe? We believe those we love, trust, and respect. As we exercise our faith, we can believe in what they say, knowing that it is the word of God. This is why we believe the prophets of God and those who speak by the power of the Holy Ghost: "And whatsoever they shall speak when moved upon by the Holy Ghost shall be scripture, shall be the will of the Lord, shall be the mind of the Lord, shall be the word of the Lord, shall be the voice of the Lord, and the power of God unto salvation" (D&C 68:4). In a quiet moment in the temple of our God, I was sitting next to a prophet of God, and we discussed those sacred things that can be discussed in the Lord's holy house. I inquired of him concerning something we had discussed, and he taught me a transcending truth when he said, "Let us just sit quietly and listen to the Spirit, and we shall be taught." I closed my eyes, felt the Spirit, and felt that the transcending truths we had discussed were true. The arm of the Lord was revealed.

The arm of the Lord is revealed constantly as His power is exerted here upon the earth to bless the children of God. The Lord, ever giving His support to His prophets and others, reminded them while they were in His service, "Verily, thus saith the Lord unto you, my friends Sidney and Joseph, your families are well; they are in mine hands, and I will do with them as seemeth me good; for in me there is all power. Therefore, follow me, and listen to the counsel which I shall give unto you" (D&C 100:1–2). We rely on the arm of the Lord. The tender mercies of the Lord are what Moroni asked us to ponder (see Moroni 10:3). Each of us can sit for a moment and recall them in our own lives. I can remember the cold and dark night when a light rain fell and the temperatures plummeted. I could not see the black ice while I was driving merrily along. The freeway was busy, and cars were going at high speeds as allowed. Then it happened. In a flash, my car was turning and turning, and lights were everywhere in my eyes. I cried out, "Father, help me." That's all I could say. All of a sudden, I found myself in the grassy median headed the right way. My heart was in my throat, and I was panting, but I was safe. I offered another silent but lengthy prayer of gratitude and continued on my way home. I have learned never to judge another's tender mercy, for each of us receive them in different ways. Sometimes the tender mercy is a wonderful opportunity for growth that we thank our Heavenly Father for at a later time.

2. For he shall grow up before him as a tender plant, and as a root out of a dry ground: he hath no form nor comeliness; and when we shall see him, there is no beauty that we should desire him.

The Jews were expecting and hoping for a liberator with power and might from their oppression—but this was not the case. The Messiah came unseemly as a tender plant from dry ground, as the babe of Bethlehem, and He "increased in wisdom and stature, and in favour with God and man" (Luke 2:52). There was nothing available from Jewish leaders, for they were not a flowing well of the word of God, but rather they were desolate, apostate, and without any nourishing power; they were "of a dry ground." His strength was from His Father. He looked like others without the pomp, power, or majesty of the world but as the humble Son of God, the Eternal Father. And thus the Lord always looks upon our hearts and not on the outward appearance of man. Where we are from, the apparent position or station we hold, or the clothes we wear will not exalt or empower us, but rather the submissiveness of our soul to the will of God.

3. He is despised and rejected of men; a man of sorrows, and acquainted with grief: and we hid as it were our faces from him; he was despised, and we esteemed him not.

The scriptures verify Isaiah's words, "Who, when he was reviled, reviled not again; when he suffered, he threatened not; but committed himself to him that judgeth righteously" (1 Peter 2:23). The Jews openly despised Him: "And because they turn their hearts aside, saith the prophet, and have despised the Holy One of Israel, they shall wander in the flesh, and perish, and become a hiss and a byword, and be hated among all nations" (1 Nephi 19:14). He was indeed rejected: "And he began to teach them, that the Son of man must suffer many things, and be rejected of the elders, and of the chief priests, and scribes, and be killed, and after three days rise again" (Mark 8:31). And in all of His suffering and sacrificing of fulfilling His infinite Atonement, He knew sorrow and grief so He would know how to succor His people:

> And he shall go forth, suffering pains and afflictions and temptations of every kind; and this that the word might be fulfilled which saith he will take upon him the pains and the sicknesses of his people. And he will take upon him death, that he may loose the bands of death which bind his people; and he will take upon him their infirmities, that his bowels may be filled with mercy, according to the flesh, that he may know according to the flesh how to succor his people according to their infirmities. (Alma 7:11–12)

Even in all of His goodness, the Jews rejected Him because of hardheartedness, jealousy, and, for those in power, fear of losing their apostate honors of men. They could not see in Him what was foretold, for they did not understand the scriptures: "Search the scriptures; for in them ye think ye have eternal life: and they are they which testify of me" (John 5:39; see also Topical Guide, "Jesus Christ, Prophecies about"). In wickedness, people see what they choose to see. As we seek to serve and help others in the strength of the Lord, is there any burden so hard that we wouldn't stand up to persecution? As the old saying goes, "No good deed ever goes unpunished." The great Apostle Peter understood: "For this is thankworthy, if a man for conscience toward God endure grief, suffering wrongfully. For what glory is it, if, when ye be buffeted for your faults, ye shall take it patiently? but if, when ye do well, and suffer for it, ye take it patiently, this is acceptable with God" (1 Peter 2:19–20). So often, even within the Church, one can be judged or criticized wrongly for doing good. And for that we may suffer and even ask why. Remember in those trying times that we are "acceptable with God." What greater approval do we need than to know we are pleasing our Heavenly Father? Why would we turn our faces away from someone for fear that through association our peers might be judgmental and draw negative impressions?

I remember in school that there were those who were made fun of and ridiculed by others for being different or not being part of "the group." They were often the new kids at the school. When the boys sought to show off their power, they surrounded the new boy and proceeded to beat him up. There was no one there to help. Others turned their eyes away as if to hide from the wrongdoing. There was no refuge for the offended even though the boy had done no wrong. There was pain for the young boy, but to those who stood by—their conscience would be seared with the memory of not standing up for the downtrodden and abused they should have cared for.

4. Surely he hath borne our griefs, and carried our sorrows: yet we did esteem him stricken, smitten of God, and afflicted.

The suffering and sacrificing of Christ was part of the infinite Atonement. In New Testament times, people judged others according to their afflictions, thinking that it was due to their sins and misdeeds. This is exemplified in John where we read, "And as Jesus passed by, he saw a man which was blind from his birth. And his disciples asked him, saying, Master, who did sin, this man, or his parents, that he was born blind? Jesus answered, *Neither hath this man sinned, nor his parents*: but that the works of God should be made manifest in him" (John 9:1–3; emphasis added). Thus Isaiah explained that likewise, because of all our Savior's grief and sorrows, the people of His day thought that God, as a just punishment, was literally smiting Him.

The power of false traditions can hurt even the unsuspecting. Oh that judging another could be purged from our souls, yea even the thought of judging flee from our heart and mind. That sin brings a tremendous load of garbage to carry throughout our lives. Remember, "Judge not, that ye be not judged. For with what judgment ye judge, ye shall be judged: and with what measure ye mete, it shall be measured to you again" (Matthew 7:1–2). Even when we think we are right and speak with a voice of authority to defend it, correcting another may not be the right thing to do. Being "right" may not be the right thing, but loving-kindness is always right, for charity never faileth.

5. But he was wounded for our transgressions, he was bruised for our iniquities: the chastisement of our peace was upon him; and with his stripes we are healed.

The doctrine of the Atonement is made clear that the Lord, our Savior and Redeemer, was wounded (with pain and suffering) and bruised (beaten, scourged, and made to sweat blood) for our sins. Justice and mercy were fulfilled through the Atonement. The Savior's suffering and sacrifice as He worked out the Atonement gave us peace and rest if we but repent: "Whosoever repenteth, and hardeneth not his heart, he shall have claim on mercy through mine Only Begotten Son, unto a remission of his sins; and these shall enter into my rest" (Alma 12:34). We are healed through Christ. We are taught so beautifully through the scriptures that we can learn vicariously without the actual experience because we have taken the word of God into our very souls. We, by the power of the word, can not only learn the truth but also be edified and uplifted to greater heights. The word has the power to change our lives (see Alma 31:5). Alma stands as an example of one who received this heavenly gift of the Atonement and did find peace in his very soul: "And it came to pass that I was three days and three nights in the most bitter pain and anguish of soul; and never, until I did cry out unto the Lord Jesus Christ for mercy, did I receive a remission of my sins. But behold, I did cry unto him and I did find peace to my soul" (Alma 38:8). Alma's example is magnificent and empowering in realizing the infinite power of the Atonement. We can see vicariously through the eyes and heart of Alma the enabling power of the Atonement.

6. All we like sheep have gone astray; we have turned every one to his own way; and the Lord hath laid on him the iniquity of us all.

In mortality, all of us are in a fallen state. We have all sinned. At one time or another, we have not kept the commandments, and thus we have separated ourselves from God and need help. The Lord fully understood and willingly took upon Himself our sins that justice might be honored. If we repent, through the great plan of redemption, we can be forgiven and return to the presence of our Father through the mercy, grace, and goodness of the Lord. As a bishop, I have witnessed this in my own life and in the lives of countless numbers of the children of God. I have seen tears of sorrow turn to tears of joy as the burden of sin has been lifted through the Atonement of Christ. The words of so many echo the words of Enos, "My guilt is gone" (see Enos 1:6), and the words of Alma, "I was harrowed up by the memory of my sins no more" (Alma 36:19). All of us can partake of this transcendent gift that only Christ can give. When we have been forgiven, we feel the blessings of forgiveness of sins. Gratitude is forever written in our hearts as our sins are swept away.

7. He was oppressed, and he was afflicted, yet he opened not his mouth: he is brought as a lamb to the slaughter, and as a sheep before her shearers is dumb, so he openeth not his mouth.

Our Beloved Savior knew His lot. He had agreed to this selfless act of redemption for all mankind. As He struggled in Gethsemane, He yet said, "Thy will be done." Isaiah's prophecy was fulfilled. He accepted His assignment as the Savior and Redeemer without debate or confrontation from his accusers: "And when he was accused of the chief priests and elders, he answered nothing. Then said Pilate unto him, Hearest thou not how many things they witness against thee? And he answered him to never a word; insomuch that the governor marvelled greatly" (Matthew 27:12–14). The prophecy was fulfilled. What was foretold actually happened. Isaiah knew and stands as a prophetic seer to help us understand our beloved Savior and all He went through for the sake of mankind.

8. He was taken from prison and from judgment: and who shall declare his generation? for he was cut off out of the land of the living: for the transgression of my people was he stricken.

The Sanhedrin illegally tried the Savior in the night. Christ's generation or posterity shall be as numbered as the grains of sand, for we are, through covenant, His children. We have been spiritually begotten as His sons and His daughters: "And now, because of the covenant which ye have made ye shall be called the children of Christ, his sons, and his daughters; for behold, this day he hath spiritually begotten you; for ye say that your hearts are changed through faith on his name; therefore, ye are born of him and have become his sons and his daughters" (Mosiah 5:7). Our Savior's life was cut short in mortality as He suffered death so that we might be saved and receive immortality and eternal life. It is interesting in the scriptures how many times we are encouraged to repent and turn back to Christ. Why isn't a few times enough? Why do the Lord and His prophets speak of it hundreds of times? The Lord uses repetition to insure that we do not forget and to reemphasize the importance of the principle. And this is why the Atonement, the suffering, and the sacrificing of Christ are repeated over and over again. This is why we partake of the sacrament weekly. Never think that the Lord is redundant when He or His prophets remind us concerning eternal truths. The weakness and frailty of the mortal mind need reminding lest we fall away through forgetfulness. We are reminded again that the Lord was stricken for our sins.

9. And he made his grave with the wicked, and with the rich in his death; because he had done no violence, neither was any deceit in his mouth.

Christ was crucified between two thieves (the wicked) yet buried in the tomb of Joseph of Arimathea (the rich), and in all of this never was there violence, dishonesty, guile, or wrongdoing on His part. Christ also obtained richness in death in that "he that hath eternal life is rich" (D&C 6:7). Prophecy fulfilled. The scriptures testify of Christ in every way. In all of this, Isaiah made sure that we understood the depth of the character of our beloved Savior: "*Neither was any deceit in His mouth.*" The Lord was the example of purity. He never sought any pretense or deception in all His efforts to help people understand His divine nature and calling. He was meek and lowly and exhorted all to become meek and lowly (see Matthew 11:29; Alma 13:28).

10. Yet it pleased the Lord to bruise him; he hath put him to grief: when thou shalt make his soul an offering for sin, he shall see his seed, he shall prolong his days, and the pleasure of the Lord shall prosper in his hand.

Our Father was pleased that His Beloved Son was willing to suffer and go through such agony for the benefit of all of God's children. This statement often made me wonder, Why would the Father be pleased to see His Son suffer? The perfect plan of God the Father required the suffering of His Son to pay for the sins of all His children. The word *pleased* to see His Son's suffering simply meant that the Father was satisfied and content that His perfect plan had been followed and justice had been satisfied by the merciful act of His Son's Atonement. Heavenly Father's will was fulfilled by the hand of Christ (all that He did to fulfill the Atonement), and this pleased God the Father.

The Lord's seed are all those who come unto Christ and accept His Atonement. Through baptism, being born again, and covenants, we become the sons and daughters of Christ. Through the Atonement, the resurrection is made possible and all of God's children shall increase in their days. God the Father receives joy because of His obedient and righteous Son, even Christ the Lord, and His infinite Atonement being completed. Our Savior had submitted to the Father's will (see Matthew 26:39, 42, 44). The pleasure of God the Father shall prosper in the hand of His Son. As I pause to ponder those verses, I am again reminded of not only the work and glory of the Father but also the price He and our Savior had to pay for us to return to His presence. He knew His Son had to suffer to save His children. Our Father in Heaven is always thinking of His children and how He can bless our lives, and so does His Son—our beloved Savior. The tenderness and kindness of our loving Father and our Savior is continually being expressed if we can have eyes to see and hearts to feel.

11. He shall see of the travail of his soul, and shall be satisfied: by his knowledge shall my righteous servant justify many; for he shall bear their iniquities.

God the Father saw the "travail" of His Son's soul. The great effort and exertion of our Savior along with the pain and agony had paid the price for sin. Justice was content, for the debt had been satisfied. The conditions of the redemption of mankind had been fulfilled. The liability was gone. We become justified through faith in the Lord Jesus Christ, which increases our knowledge of God, knowledge of the mysteries of the kingdom, and empowering knowledge of all the ordinances and covenants we have entered into. These ordinances and covenants can exalt us and make all things right through the enabling power of the Atonement. Obedience and good works justify the righteous through the grace of our Savior Jesus Christ. This is why many are justified and not all, because they choose not to enter in to the Lord's ordinances and covenants to become justified and sanctified through Christ the Lord and by the power of the Holy Ghost. Amulek taught,

> And thus he shall bring salvation to all those who shall believe on his name; this being the intent of this last sacrifice, to bring about the bowels of mercy, which overpowereth justice, and bringeth about means unto men that they may have faith unto repentance.
>
> And thus mercy can satisfy the demands of justice, and encircles them in the arms of safety, while he that exercises no faith unto repentance is exposed to the whole law of the demands of justice; therefore only unto him that has faith unto repentance is brought about the great and eternal plan of redemption.
>
> Therefore may God grant unto you, my brethren, that ye may begin to exercise your faith unto repentance, that ye begin to call upon his holy name, that he would have mercy upon you. (Alma 34:15–17)

Amulek makes clear how faith unto repentance justifies us, and those who do not exercise faith unto repentance are exposed to the whole law and the demands of justice. The Savior has borne our iniquities if we but repent.

12. Therefore will I divide him a portion with the great, and he shall divide the spoil with the strong; because he hath poured out his soul unto death: and he was numbered with the transgressors; and he bare the sin of many, and made intercession for the transgressors.

He (Christ) shall divide the spoils (the portion given to the conquerors) with the strong (the obedient and devoted followers of Christ). And what are the spoils? Victory over death and hell, which makes possible eternal life. The spoils of the Atonement are everlasting life. We can, through our righteousness and the grace of God, receive all that the Father has. Paul reminds us, "And if children, then heirs; heirs of God, and joint-heirs with Christ; if so be that we suffer with him [we are persecuted for His namesake, we agonize for others and seek to help them, we do as He would do so that others may be blessed], that we may be also glorified together" (Romans 8:17). We take up our "cross" and follow Christ, whatever the price. We sacrifice all for the greater good. We offer ourselves as living sacrifice of service (see Romans 12:1–2). Why? Because we love our Heavenly Father and our Savior. Because the Messiah, or Christ, suffered and was "numbered with the transgressors." He was as if the transgressor, standing in for us—which He did. He made intercession for us through His atoning sacrifice. He was the propitiation for all of our sins (makes appeasement or satisfies the demands of justice). He made intercession for all mankind. He is our Advocate with the Father. He is the Mediator between God and men. He is the Resurrection and the Life. He is the Rock of our salvation.

In sum, Christ is the Anointed One, chosen from the beginning, to provide us a way back to the presence of God: "Jesus saith unto him, I am the way, the truth, and the life: no man cometh unto the Father, but by me" (John 14:6). He is the only way. There is no other way. And He stands knocking at the door, pleading for us to let Him into our lives that we might have eternal life (see Revelation 3:20).

IN SUMMARY

As I paused to ponder Isaiah's masterful dissertation on the Messiah, questions came to my mind. What did I think and ponder about when reading Isaiah's words concerning our beloved Savior? What passages stood out? Did I feel the intent that Isaiah had for writing them? Did gratitude enter my soul for the goodness of God and our beloved Savior? Pondering on the things of God is what we need to do as we read and feast upon the word of God in an effort to learn more about and come to understand the Atonement. We ponder the words so we can come to understand and appreciate their meaning. As we do so, we can be filled with gratitude and the love of God. This love will transform our hearts and give us an overwhelming desire to do good. Inspiration and revelation can be our reward for prayerful pondering, as demonstrated by Nephi and President Joseph F. Smith (see 1 Nephi 11–14; D&C 138).

As we search the scriptures and feast upon the word of God, we will see and feel the essence of our beloved Savior's work—He is the Redeemer of all mankind. The searching and feasting upon the word of God has made the Atonement real to me. The temple, the endowment, and all of the temple ordinances have brought understanding of our beloved Savior's Atonement. I see how the Atonement and the endowment are inseparably connected. This is because of the enabling power of the Atonement and the authority of the greater priesthood in administering the ordinances and covenants of the temple in concert, which can bring us back into the presence of our Father if we are faithfully obedient.

Jehovah was and is the promised Messiah, even Jesus Christ, the Son of God. It was through Him, the Anointed One, that all things would be done here upon the earth under the direction of the Father. I stand amazed of His infinite goodness and mercy He expressed throughout His life through His submissive obedience to the will of the Father. There are so many lessons to be learned again and again as we seek to know God our Father and our Savior Jesus Christ. This is not to know about but come to know Them, for this is life eternal (see John 17:3). And part of this knowledge is to understand why and what the Lord was praying for in the great intercessory prayer.

Chapter 3

The GREAT INTERCESSORY PRAYER

Prior to the great intercessory prayer and Gethsemane, the Lord went about preaching the gospel and ministering to the people. "Jesus came into Galilee, preaching the gospel of the kingdom of God, and saying, The time is fulfilled, and the kingdom of God is at hand: repent ye, and believe the gospel" (Mark 1:14–15). He in fact preached of His messiahship as He preached the gospel: "Jesus saith unto him, I am the way, the truth, and the life: no man cometh unto the Father, but by me" (John 14:6). As He ministered to the people (see Matthew 20:28; Mark 10:45), He went about healing all the people within His reach (see Matthew 4:23; 9:35; Luke 9:6, 11). And the Savior taught them the doctrine of the Father (see John 7:16). This doctrine, the celestial law, was the Savior's message in the Sermon on the Mount. This same message was given to the Nephites when the Lord taught them at the temple. This law and the teachings of the Savior replaced and fulfilled the law of Moses. The Lord then went among the people, teaching and healing them. He ministered to their every need. Then He offered the great intercessory prayer and prepared for Gethsemane.

This great intercessory prayer not only was a pleading Son's prayer to His Father but also was teaching the importance of the profound doctrine of being "one"—the great prayer of "oneness." This is such an important doctrine; without unity and oneness, the abundant blessings of the Holy Ghost cannot be ours. This boundless and pleading prayer by our Savior is an expression of

His love for us. It was the great high priestly prayer, an expression of the Intercessor, which is Christ the Lord. He is ever the Advocate, Mediator, Savior, and Redeemer, pleading for us. The Lord as an Intercessor intervenes for us and makes reconciliation for us (through the Atonement) so we can be worthy and able to return to our Father's presence. Everything the Savior does is for our eternal welfare. He cares for us and seeks that we might be "one" with the Father and the Son in unity, harmony, and purpose. This oneness and being "one with" Them is enabled by the Atonement. One of the first things the Lord taught upon His arrival on this continent was concerning contention: "For verily, verily I say unto you, he that hath the spirit of contention is not of me, but is of the devil, who is the father of contention, and he stirreth up the hearts of men to contend with anger, one with another. Behold, this is not my doctrine, to stir up the hearts of men with anger, one against another; but this is my doctrine, that such things should be done away" (3 Nephi 11:29–30). Contention is of the devil. The lack of contention as described in 4 Nephi 1:15–16 indicates that it was the love of God that brought this unity and harmony, where there was no contention. You note that if we have a spirit of contention, we are not of Him; we are not one with Him. This doctrine of being *one* is part of being exalted. This is why the Lord is pleading for us to be *one*. This is the At-*one*-ment: being one with God the Father and the Son. As the Lord was getting ready to suffer and sacrifice for us in order to complete the Atonement, He was teaching us through the great intercessory prayer the reason for the Atonement.

The Lord has on other occasions reminded us about this unity: "I say unto you, be one; and if ye are not one ye are not mine" (D&C 38:27). All the decisions in the highest quorums of the Church follow this principle of unity: "And every decision made by either of these quorums must be by the unanimous voice of the same; that is, every member in each quorum must be agreed to its decisions, in order to make their decisions of the same power or validity one with the other" (D&C 107:27). This doctrine of "oneness" and "unity" when lived stifles contention, and the fulness of the Holy Ghost can be manifested.

To better understand and appreciate the blessing of oneness and unity, we will take the great intercessory prayer verse by verse so we can see the great power in the Lord's pleading prayer and the transcending truths taught by it.

THE GREAT INTERCESSORY PRAYER—JOHN 17

1. These words spake Jesus, and lifted up his eyes to heaven, and said, Father, the hour is come; glorify thy Son, that thy Son also may glorify thee.

The great infinite and eternal Atonement is about to be fulfilled, and in so doing Christ shall be glorified (with power to carry out the Atonement) and be like unto the Father and be *one* with His Father. The Savior, for doing the Father's will, will glorify the Father. The Father's work and glory, which is the immortality and eternal life of His children, will be completed by His Son and bring glory to the Father. This type of *glory* refers to greatness, exaltations, honor, praise, majesty, triumphal power, and goodness. These descriptions define our Heavenly Father, for He is a personage of glory, and in this great work the Father is glorified. This form of glory is also connected to joy and rejoicing, which is always associated with the blessing of Heavenly Father's children. The Atonement is the ultimate power and blessing that can bring us back to God in a glorified state. And thus we see why we are the work and glory of our Father and Savior Jesus Christ, for in us our Father is glorified.

2. As thou hast given him power over all flesh, that he should give eternal life to as many as thou hast given him.

Our Heavenly Father gave His anointed Son the power to do all things: "And he hath power given unto him from the Father to redeem them from their sins because of repentance; therefore he hath sent his angels to declare the tidings of the conditions of repentance, which bringeth unto the power of the Redeemer, unto the salvation of their souls" (Helaman 5:11; see also 2 Nephi 2:8; Mosiah 5:15; Moroni 9:26). Remember, even though Christ carries out the work of God the Father, it is the Father who is still the Giver of all things to His Son and to us. The priesthood is the authority to act for God. The Atonement was foreordained by

God as part of the perfect plan to redeem His children. It was the Father who gave His Beloved Son (see John 3:16). It is the Father who gave the Lord the Holy Ghost and power to do all things (see Acts 10:38). It is the Father who provides and gives the Holy Ghost to us (see 3 Nephi 19:22). It is God the Father that gives us all He has according to our faithfulness as we are perfected through His Beloved Son, even Christ the Lord (see D&C 84:38). It is through Christ the Lord that we can receive eternal life and are brought back into our Father's presence. Who are those that are given from God the Father to His Son? The elect of God. "And ye are called to bring to pass the gathering of mine elect; for mine elect hear my voice and harden not their hearts" (D&C 29:7). The elect of God hear the voice of the Lord and harden not their hearts. The resurrected Lord declared to the righteous Nephites, "Ye are my sheep, and ye are numbered among those whom the Father hath given me" (3 Nephi 15:24; see also 3 Nephi 19:29; D&C 50:41; 84:63).

3. And this is life eternal, that they might know thee the only true God, and Jesus Christ, whom thou hast sent.

Eternal life, in the simplest terms, is God's life. God, as our Father, desires that His children should enjoy His kind of life, if they will only keep His commandments. In the Greek, this verse refers to a "sure" or "absolute" knowledge of God. Life eternal is brought about as we come to really know God and His Beloved Son. What does it take to know God? It is more than knowing about God; it is about actually knowing Him and having a relationship with Him and His Son so that They know us too. That is part of knowing. As the Lord stated, "Many will say to me in that day: Lord, Lord, have we not prophesied in thy name, and in thy name have cast out devils, and in thy name done many wonderful works? And then will I profess unto them: I never knew you; depart from me, ye that work iniquity" (3 Nephi 14:22–23; see also Matthew 7:23). We will better know our Father and our Savior as we understand and appreciate Their power, glory, love, goodness, mercy, and character and seek to become perfect like Them through our Savior Jesus Christ.

Heavenly Father loves us, desires our happiness, and seeks to guide us to eternal life as we consider the following:

- Heavenly Father's motives are based on a perfect love.
- Heavenly Father is perfect. He is perfect in His omniscience, omnipotence, and omnipresence, and with this knowledge we worship Him and follow all of His commandments. By so doing, we experience joy in worshipping and following all the commandments. Knowing the character of God and Christ, we can then exercise faith in Them (adapted from *Lectures on Faith*, 4).
- When we "know" God, we will desire to be like Him.
- We totally trust in God and "lean not" to our own understanding (Proverbs 3:5–6).
- We pray and commune with God. Through prayer, our relationship deepens and we come to know Him.
- As we become humble, we become able to see God: "The veil shall be rent and you shall see me and know that I am" (D&C 67:10). Then we will recognize our deep and total dependence upon Him. The grace and mercy of God are evidenced at every turn in our lives if we but take the time to look.
- Above all, we will come to know that we are the literal children of God the Father, with the divine capacity to receive all His blessings and enjoy a life like unto that of the Father and the Son. "The Spirit itself beareth witness with our spirit, that we are the children of God; and if children, then heirs; heirs of God, and joint-heirs with Christ" (Romans 8:16–17).
- It is through the knowledge of God and Christ that grace and peace are literally multiplied in us, because God has given us all things that pertain to godliness through Christ the Lord. It is through the great promises from our Father that we might be partakers of the divine nature of Christ and thus overcome the corruption of the world. We can do this as we diligently "add to [our] faith virtue; and to virtue knowledge; and to knowledge temperance; and

to temperance patience; and to patience godliness; and to godliness brotherly kindness; and to brotherly kindness charity" (2 Peter 1:5–7). With all of these virtues within our soul, we will have the knowledge of the Lord Jesus Christ and make "your calling and election sure" (2 Peter 1:10). Then we will enter into "the everlasting kingdom of our Lord and Saviour Jesus Christ" (2 Peter 1:11).

All of these blessings are enriched, enabled, and made possible and evident by the infinite and eternal Atonement. Everything is an appendage to Christ and His Atonement, which are inseparable. As we better understand the Atonement, we will better understand the character of God and our Savior and our total dependence upon Them. As our knowledge of the goodness of God and our Savior increases, so will our gratitude and thanksgiving. We will not offend God, because we will confess His hand in all things (see D&C 59:21). The Lord reminds us, "And he who receiveth all things with thankfulness shall be made glorious; and the things of this earth shall be added unto him, even an hundred fold, yea, more" (D&C 78:19). Yes, as we come to know God and our Savior Jesus Christ and see and feel Their tender mercy and goodness in our lives, we will "live in thanksgiving daily, for the many mercies and blessings which he doth bestow upon [us]" (Alma 34:38).

We will come to know God as we live the scripture, "If any man will do his will, he shall know of the doctrine, whether it be of God, or whether I speak of myself" (John 7:17). One of the best ways we come to know God and Jesus Christ is to come to Their holy house. "And this greater priesthood administereth the gospel and holdeth the key of the mysteries of the kingdom, even the key of the knowledge of God. Therefore, in the ordinances thereof, the power of godliness is manifest. And without the ordinances thereof, and the authority of the priesthood, the power of godliness is not manifest unto men in the flesh; for without this no man can see the face of God, even the Father, and live" (D&C 84:19–22). We see who They are and what They do. We witness firsthand the plan of exaltation unfolding before our eyes. We understand and experience Their character and Their purpose. With humility, we come to know our Father and our Elder Brother, even Christ the Lord. And with that knowledge, we stand with awe and reverence in Their presence and forever are indebted for the goodness and mercy. And with King Benjamin, we declare,

> For behold, if the knowledge of the goodness of God at this time has awakened you to a sense of your nothingness, and your worthless and fallen state—
>
> I say unto you, if ye have come to a knowledge of the goodness of God, and his matchless power, and his wisdom, and his patience, and his long-suffering towards the children of men; and also, the atonement which has been prepared from the foundation of the world, that thereby salvation might come to him that should put his trust in the Lord, and should be diligent in keeping his commandments, and continue in the faith even unto the end of his life, I mean the life of the mortal body—
>
> I say, that this is the man who receiveth salvation, through the atonement which was prepared from the foundation of the world for all mankind, which ever were since the fall of Adam, or who are, or who ever shall be, even unto the end of the world.
>
> And this is the means whereby salvation cometh. And there is none other salvation save this which hath been spoken of; neither are there any conditions whereby man can be saved except the conditions which I have told you.
>
> Believe in God; believe that he is, and that he created all things, both in heaven and in earth; believe that he has all wisdom, and all power, both in heaven and in earth; believe that man doth not comprehend all the things which the Lord can comprehend. (Mosiah 4:5–9)

We can see all these things in the sacred ordinances and covenants of the temple—the mysteries of the kingdom, the key to the knowledge of God, and the power of godliness manifested. This knowledge we can receive in Lord's holy house. We truly learn and see portrayed this great knowledge that will empower us. It gives us a true perspective of life. It gives hope when we feel discouraged. It brings into focus what matters most in life. It binds us by drawing us into sacred covenants. We come to see the Atonement as the empowering doctrine and enabling power of all things pertaining to the great plan of our Father, which is culminated in His holy house. The endowment and Atonement are inseparably connected. It is helpful to remember that the word *Atonement* means "to cover, to become at one," that is, to be reconciled to God, to be in harmony with God, and to return into the presence of the Father, and thus we will come to know Him. The endowment is a symbolic representation of the process by which we return to our Father's presence. You cannot speak of one without the other. Just as baptism accepts Christ and His Atonement, so likewise do the temple ordinances. Without all the temple ordinances, we cannot have the blessings of the Father: "And he that receiveth my Father receiveth my Father's kingdom; therefore all that my Father hath shall be given unto him" (D&C 84:38). In all of this we may be filled with gratitude. We truly want to "become." We not only want to know God but also seek to please God. We can go about doing good, because we have been anointed with power (through all the ordinances) and the Holy Ghost. We will truly know our Father and our Savior Jesus Christ.

4–5. I have glorified thee on the earth: I have finished the work which thou gavest me to do. And now, O Father, glorify thou me with thine own self with the glory which I had with thee before the world was.

The Savior taught the Father's doctrine and always acknowledged His supremacy. He sought only to do the will of the Father and to please Him. The Savior, knowing that His work is nearly finished, is praying as if the Atonement is completed. He seeks to return to His Father and partake of His glory. This is the very thing we seek. And this is why Christ suffered and died for us, so we may through obedience partake of eternal life and the glory of God, even the highest glory in the celestial kingdom of God.

6–8. I have manifested thy name unto the men which thou gavest me out of the world: thine they were, and thou gavest them me; and they have kept thy word. Now they have known that all things whatsoever thou hast given me are of thee. For I have given unto them the words which thou gavest me; and they have received them, and have known surely that I came out from thee, and they have believed that thou didst send me.

Christ did only those things that He saw the Father do and what the Father commanded Him to do. After praying to the Father (see Luke 6:12), the Savior called His Apostles from amongst His disciples. The Savior taught the people of His authority and power.

> Then answered Jesus and said unto them, Verily, verily, I say unto you, The Son can do nothing of himself, but what he seeth the Father do: for what things soever he doeth, these also doeth the Son likewise.
>
> For the Father loveth the Son, and sheweth him all things that himself doeth: and he will shew him greater works than these, that ye may marvel.
>
> For as the Father raiseth up the dead, and quickeneth them; even so the Son quickeneth whom he will.
>
> For the Father judgeth no man, but hath committed all judgment unto the Son:
>
> That all men should honour the Son, even as they honour the Father. He that honoureth not the Son honoureth not the Father which hath sent him.
>
> Verily, verily, I say unto you, He that heareth my word, and believeth on him that sent me, hath everlasting life, and shall not come into condemnation; but is passed from death unto life. (John 5:19–24)

The Savior, ever the benevolent Son of His Father, makes sure we know why He did what He did. He followed His Father, for the Father showed Him the things He needed to do. And in this perfect plan, God the Father is the author, and He did all things through His Son.

> Father, I thank thee that thou hast given the Holy Ghost unto these whom I have chosen; and it is because of their belief in me that I have chosen them out of the world.
>
> Father, I pray thee that thou wilt give the Holy Ghost unto all them that shall believe in their words.
>
> Father, thou hast given them the Holy Ghost because they believe in me; and thou seest that they believe in me because thou hearest them, and they pray unto me; and they pray unto me because I am with them. (3 Nephi 19:20–22)

It is important to know that the Son of God was only doing what His Father had requested Him to do. This not only gives Christ the authority but also shows He is teaching the grand principle of obedience, the first law of heaven. The Savior lives the same laws He requests us to live. God the Father foreordained all that is done here upon the earth. The Savior sought to fulfill His will in all things. He literally represents the Father in all things. And the Father always defers to Him when introducing Him: "Behold my Beloved Son, in whom I am well pleased, in whom I have glorified my name—hear ye him" (3 Nephi 11:7). God the Father sent His Only Begotten Son that we might have everlasting life (see John 3:16–17; 6:40; 10:36; 1 John 4:10).

9–10. I pray for them: I pray not for the world, but for them which thou hast given me; for they are thine. And all mine are thine, and thine are mine; and I am glorified in them.

This great pleading of the Lord is for His followers and those who have sought to do the will of God. And we, as we come to the Lord in righteousness, bring joy and happiness to our Savior. The Lord emphasized this as He prayed for His Nephite disciples:

> Father, I thank thee that thou hast purified those whom I have chosen, because of their faith, and I pray for them, and also for them who shall believe on their words, that they may be purified in me, through faith on their words, even as they are purified in me.
>
> Father, I pray not for the world, but for those whom thou hast given me out of the world, because of their faith, that they may be purified in me, that I may be in them as thou, Father, art in me, that we may be one, that I may be glorified in them. (3 Nephi 19:28–29)

This brings gravity to my soul. I can bring joy and glory to my Savior and Heavenly Father, or I can cause them sorrow and heartache. You see, we really are Their work and Their glory. They are glorified in us. This is what God and Christ do. Knowing the great love the Lord has for this work and His children, I am reminded of a passage that shows the heart of our Savior: "And it came to pass that the Lord of the vineyard wept, and said unto the servant: What could I have done more for my vineyard?" (Jacob

5:41). Our Savior's constant concern is for you and me. We can cause sorrow and suffering for our sins or joy and glory for our righteousness.

11–13. And now I am no more in the world, but these are in the world, and I come to thee. Holy Father, keep through thine own name those whom thou hast given me, that they may be one, as we are. While I was with them in the world, I kept them in thy name: those that thou gavest me I have kept, and none of them is lost, but the son of perdition; that the scripture might be fulfilled. And now come I to thee; and these things I speak in the world, that they might have my joy fulfilled in themselves.

The Savior was praying with the knowledge that He was soon to leave His mortal existence. Our being one with God the Father and our Savior Jesus Christ was His continual pleading throughout this great intercessory prayer. Our beloved Savior was praying for His beloved disciples and us. He wants us to enjoy a life like His and our Father's. This kind of life can only be perpetuated if we are one with the Father and the Son. Can there be a greater expression of love for us than this? I think not. This oneness with God and Christ is that we not only take upon ourselves the divine nature of Christ but also become perfected and complete through Christ and His Atonement. We have been commanded to become perfect (see 3 Nephi 12:48). So often people set aside perfection, but in reality that is exactly why we came to earth—to be made complete and perfect so we can receive all that the Father has. This is what our temple ordinances are all about. We have been promised eternal increase if we are faithful. And to be more exact, the scriptures teach, "Then shall they be gods, because they have no end; therefore shall they be from everlasting to everlasting, because they continue; then shall they be above all, because all things are subject unto them. Then shall they be gods, because they have all power, and the angels are subject unto them" (D&C 132:20). Our Savior reminds us that our joy is what brings joy to Him, for His joy is in us: "And he hath risen again from the dead, that he might bring all men unto him, on conditions of repentance. And how great is his joy in the soul that repenteth" (D&C 18:12–13). Our joy can in turn be fulfilled in helping others come unto Christ, as

Alma has repeatedly taught us: "And this is my glory, that perhaps I may be an instrument in the hands of God to bring some soul to repentance; and this is my joy" (Alma 29:9).

14. I have given them thy word; and the world hath hated them, because they are not of the world, even as I am not of the world.

The Savior gave His followers His very self, the word of God, the gospel, the way and the truth, the ordinances and covenants—for this is the good news, the way to the tree of life and life eternal. And this is how we are to live as well:

> And I now give unto you a commandment to beware concerning yourselves, to give diligent heed to the words of eternal life.
>
> For you shall live by every word that proceedeth forth from the mouth of God.
>
> For the word of the Lord is truth, and whatsoever is truth is light, and whatsoever is light is Spirit, even the Spirit of Jesus Christ.
>
> And the Spirit giveth light to every man that cometh into the world; and the Spirit enlighteneth every man through the world, that hearkeneth to the voice of the Spirit.
>
> And every one that hearkeneth to the voice of the Spirit cometh unto God, even the Father. (D&C 84:43–47)

We must cling to and hold fast to the iron rod, the word of God, that we may return to our Father: "Yea, we see that whosoever will may lay hold upon the word of God, which is quick and powerful, which shall divide asunder all the cunning and the snares and the wiles of the devil, and lead the man of Christ in a strait and narrow course across that everlasting gulf of misery which is prepared to engulf the wicked—And land their souls, yea, their immortal souls, at the right hand of God in the kingdom of heaven, to sit down with Abraham, and Isaac, and with Jacob, and with all our holy fathers, to go no more out" (Helaman 3:29–30). And Nephi taught us,

> And I said unto them that it was the word of God; and whoso would hearken unto the word of God, and would hold fast unto it, they would never perish; neither could the temptations and the fiery darts of the adversary overpower them unto blindness, to lead them away to destruction.

> Wherefore, I, Nephi, did exhort them to give heed unto the word of the Lord; yea, I did exhort them with all the energies of my soul, and with all the faculty which I possessed, that they would give heed to the word of God and remember to keep his commandments always in all things. (1 Nephi 15:24–25)

As we see, the word of God is needed, and it is powerful in our lives. As Alma explains, "And now, as the preaching of the word had a great tendency to lead the people to do that which was just—yea, it had had more powerful effect upon the minds of the people than the sword, or anything else, which had happened unto them—therefore Alma thought it was expedient that they should try the virtue of the word of God" (Alma 31:5).

There is no better way to teach the word of God than by the word of God. You have just been treated to what the Lord has said about what He has given us—the word of God. I have read this section many times, and I have come to realize even more how repetition deepens my understanding and commitment. I was on a speaking assignment with Brother Robert Matthews, one of the scholars instrumental in working on the cross-references and footnotes in the scriptures. I asked what he had been doing the past week, and he said, "I have read every scripture that pertains to prayer." I asked what was the result after the repetition of reading all these scriptures. He said, "I have an overwhelming desire to pray." We smiled, as we both understood the profound statement of what he had learned through repetition.

The previous verses are not my words but the words of God. Those were quintessential passages indicating the power of the word of God. We are to live them. Once in a discussion about a scripture, a student responded, "Oh yes, I remember reading that scripture once." Now, here is something that the Lord expects of us in regard to the scriptures. It is not reading, studying, or searching the scriptures, but as Nephi said, we are to "feast upon the words of Christ" (2 Nephi 32:3; see also 2 Nephi 31:20). There is a difference. Nephi expects us to take them into our souls, to liken them to our lives, and to live them (see 1 Nephi 19:23). The word of God will feed our spirits, and we will be told all things what we should do (see 2 Nephi 32:3). Remember, our Savior's words are the words of His Father. As I write, I reflect on my life as a younger man, oblivious to the power of the word. I plead guilty for not understanding or appreciating the word. I seek forgiveness and pray that what I have written will help us all cleave to the word of God.

There is another way to consider the word of God. The Lord said He had given them "thy word." In John we read, "In the beginning was the Word, and the Word was with God, and the Word was God. The same was in the beginning with God. All things were made by him; and without him was not any thing made that was made. In him was life; and the life was the light of men" (John 1:1–4). The word is indeed Christ the Lord, for "the Word was made flesh, and dwelt among us, (and we beheld his glory, the glory as of the only begotten of the Father,) full of grace and truth" (John 1:14). The word is described later by John in the book of Revelation: "And he was clothed with a vesture dipped in blood: and his name is called The Word of God" (Revelation 19:13). And again in the First Epistle of John: "For there are three that bear record in heaven, the Father, the Word, and the Holy Ghost: and these three are one" (1 John 5:7). Is this not a grand metaphor teaching us deeper truths that help us understand the word of God? Christ is the word of God. We live through Him and hold fast to His words—the words of eternal life, of which He is the "the author and finisher of our faith" (Hebrews 12:2).

When we see a scripture quoted or referenced, it is like a special experience to "look," and as we "look," transcending truths are revealed to us from feasting and pondering on the word of God. This is exactly what happened to Nephi when the Holy Spirit and an angel—"Angels speak by the power of the Holy Ghost; wherefore, they speak the words of Christ" (2 Nephi 32:3)—of the Lord taught him to "look," and he "looked" and saw the tree of life vision (see 1 Nephi 11–14). Remember the great experience of President Joseph F. Smith: "I sat in my room pondering over the scriptures; and reflecting upon the great atoning sacrifice that was made by the Son of God, for the redemption of the world; and the great and wonderful love made manifest by the Father and the Son in the coming of the Redeemer into the world; that through his atonement, and by obedience to the principles of the gospel, mankind might be saved" (D&C 138:1–4). And what was the result of this pondering prayerfully the word of God? A revelation from God. "As I pondered over these things which are written, the eyes of my understanding were opened, and the Spirit of the Lord rested upon me, and I saw the hosts of the dead, both small and great" (D&C 138:11). The Lord expects us to not treat lightly His word, for this is how we are to live. The Lord condemned the whole Church for treating lightly the things they had received:

> And your minds in times past have been darkened because of unbelief, and because you have treated lightly the things you have received—
>
> Which vanity and unbelief have brought the whole church under condemnation.
>
> And this condemnation resteth upon the children of Zion, even all.
>
> And they shall remain under this condemnation until they repent and remember the new covenant, even the Book of Mormon and the former commandments which I have given them, not only to say, but to do according to that which I have written. (D&C 84:54–57)

Writing this section has been intense, for I feel so deeply about this principle of feasting upon the word of God. I think of Mormon as he abridged the Book of Mormon. He often said that he was writing only a hundredth part of the proceedings of his people. Think about it. How much material did he have to summarize? The prophets always lamented the fact of how difficult it was to engrave upon the plates. Think of engraving and all the time it took to produce this magnificent record that will bring us closer to God than any other book. We follow "the Word," even Christ the Lord, and we hearken to His words, even the word of God. I am so full of gratitude for the word of God that I have difficulty expressing my innermost feelings. The Word is my Savior and Redeemer, and His words are the words of everlasting life, even the word of God.

15–16. I pray not that thou shouldest take them out of the world, but that thou shouldest keep them from the evil. They are not of the world, even as I am not of the world.

It is essential that we are tested here in mortality as the Lord has spoken: "And we will prove them herewith, to see if they will do all things whatsoever the Lord their God shall command them" (Abraham 3:25). It is imperative that we be tempted by the devil and enticed by the Holy Spirit so we can have the right to choose whether we will respond to the goodness or the evil we are presented with. "And it must needs be that the devil should tempt the children of men, or they could not be agents unto themselves; for if they never should have bitter they could not know the sweet" (D&C 29:39). And we are tempted constantly when choices are placed before us. I went through the teenage years without too many problems. Still, I recall the time when temptation came my way and my values and standards that my mother had taught were put to the test. Our high school football team, on which I played tight end, had just won a game, and we were having a party at a friend's house. Everything was great. We were having a great time. No one was doing anything wrong. A friend asked the host for a drink of water. He was directed to the kitchen cupboard for a glass. As he was getting a drink, he noticed a big dark bottle of sherry cooking wine. It was almost full. He suggested we should all have a sip of alcohol to prove ourselves. The players all came in for a little drink. Something in my heart and mind (my conscience) said, "Don't do it," and then I became bold and told them, "Don't do it." They said that one little drink wouldn't hurt. I told them no and if they did that I would leave the party. They said, "Go ahead. We don't like babies anyway."

So I left. As I walked out the door, a young deacon from our ward was standing there watching. I said to him that we didn't belong there, and so we left together. Can you imagine the thought of that young deacon looking up into my eyes at the sacrament table the following Sunday thinking about what I had just done? I am so thankful for resisting the temptation and making the right choice. It blessed my life, and it blessed the life of a young boy.

The phrase *keep them from the evil* was an appeal from the Lord, who knew full well the trials and vicissitudes of temptations from the devil himself. God our Father has taught us through His Beloved Son many truths dealing with temptation and having the power to overcome temptation and evil. The Lord emphasized the following

Prayer: The Lord has encouraged us, "Verily, verily, I say unto you, ye must watch and pray always lest ye enter into temptation; for Satan desireth to have you, that he may sift you as wheat" (3 Nephi 18:18). The Lord didn't just say to pray; He used the word *verily*. This means truthfully or truly. In Hebrew text, repetition is used to create emphasis. Thus our Savior was telling us how imperative it is to pray in order to avoid and overcome temptation. We must "ask with a firmness unshaken, that ye will yield to no temptation, but that ye will serve the true and living God" (Mormon 9:28).

Hold to the iron rod: Feast upon the word of God by searching the scriptures: "And I said unto them that it was the word of God; and whoso would hearken unto the word of God, and would hold fast unto it, they would never perish; neither could the temptations and the fiery darts of the adversary overpower them unto blindness, to lead them away to destruction" (1 Nephi 15:24). We truly must live by every word that proceeds forth from the mouth of God (see D&C 84:43–46). The word *hearken* is interesting because it means to listen and to do, not just to hear the word. Holding fast to the iron rod has many symbolic metaphors that flash through my mind. *To hold* connotes to accept, to bind, to possess, to cherish and appreciate, to retain, to keep, to defend, and to enfold. With all these synonyms going for us, we can imagine what Nephi was getting at when he said hold fast to the iron rod. *Fast* refers to being secure, firmly fixed, literally fastened to, immovable and impregnable, and to adhere to tenaciously. Now we have the picture of what Nephi was getting at when he said, "Whoso would hearken unto the word of God, and would hold fast unto it, they would never perish" (1 Nephi 15:24). This is an amazing promise with a tremendous amount of work entailed in receiving the promise. This is not a casual exercise. This is the ultimate effort requiring increased faith, diligence of the highest order, and an enormous amount of patience. These are the requirements Alma taught that were necessary to nourish the word of God (see Alma 32:41).

I shall not forget the day a young man came to my office, distraught and discouraged. He looked at me and said, "Bishop Ed, I need some real counsel. And don't give me those stock seminary answers of go pray and read your scriptures." I smiled, and we sat together for an hour, knee-to-knee so to speak, and discussed feasting on the word of God and crying unto the Father in mighty prayer. We would stop and discuss together the power of the word of God and how it can come into your soul, how to apply the word of God to your life, how the word of God has answers to your questions concerning daily life, and how we learn to live by every word that proceedeth forth from the mouth of God. It was an enlightening experience. His eyes began to see and his heart finally began to feel the power of the word of God and how we should learn from it. The problem was, he didn't want to pay the price to learn; he just wanted someone to give him the answers and then go merrily along his way. Such is not the case. We must each pay the price to understand and appreciate the word of God—and that takes continual effort. It requires faith, diligence, and patience. That is what Alma taught the humble Zoramites to do in order to nurture the word of God. As you nourish the word with an eye of faith, you can look forward to partake of the fruit of the tree of life (see Alma 32:27–42). He understood and made commitments to study and feast upon the word as a daily practice in his life.

When he began to delve into communing with our Heavenly Father, he was ready to learn. He knew what he must do. He taught me how he taught his investigators to pray, by asking with real intent. He spoke of how he taught them to pray with faith. We smiled, and he said, "Oh Bishop Ed, I can't believe how easy it is to get off track." We agreed and both realized how we could do better. We prayed together and embraced, and life was good.

Love God with all our hearts: Whenever we treasure the things of the world more than God, we become subject to the evil one.

This is exemplified in the children of Adam and Eve, who, after having been taught the plan of redemption, succumbed because their love of God was not deep enough: "And Satan came among them, saying: I am also a son of God; and he commanded them, saying: Believe it not; and they believed it not, and they loved Satan more than God. And men began from that time forth to be carnal, sensual, and devilish" (Moses 5:13). We did not become sinners because of mortality. We become sinners by choice. If we love God, we will keep His commandments (see John 14:15, 21). "The power of the Holy Spirit, which God bestows on those who love him, and purify themselves before him" (D&C 76:116). The Holy Spirit is a gift from God because we love Him. When the Holy Ghost is with us, we will be led to do good, and all good comes from God (see D&C 11:12). The Holy Ghost will show us all things that we should do (see 2 Nephi 32:5).

To love God with all our hearts, we should remember some key elements of this action. We act according to our feelings and affections. This literally creates within us our dedication and devotion to each other, to God, and to the principles we live by. Our affections are determined by the things or persons that we treasure and think about. Paul taught us well when he said, "I count all things but loss for the excellency of the knowledge of Christ Jesus my Lord: for whom I have suffered the loss of all things, and do count them but dung, that I may win Christ, and be found in him, not having mine own righteousness, which is of the law, but that which is through the faith of Christ, the righteousness which is of God by faith: that I may know him, and the power of his resurrection, and the fellowship of his sufferings, being made conformable unto his death" (Philippians 3:8–10). His treasure was in knowing Christ the Lord, being like Christ, and, through faith in Christ, becoming righteous. This becomes our quest in life too: "And this is life eternal, that they might know thee the only true God, and Jesus Christ, whom thou hast sent" (John 17:3). In knowing our Father and His Son, we will love Them, keep the commandments, and serve Them with all our heart, might, mind, and strength. And in this we will be free from evil!

The shield of faith: Faith in Jesus Christ gives us hope, causes us to act, and gives us the power to do all things: "Above all, taking the shield of faith, wherewith ye shall be able to quench all the fiery darts of the wicked" (Ephesians 6:16). Alma, giving counsel to his missionary son Helaman, reminded him to "teach them [the people] to withstand every temptation of the devil, with their faith on the Lord Jesus Christ" (Alma 37:33). Increase your faith with fasting and prayer, hearing the word of God in your soul, and having enough love so faith can operate (see Helaman 3:35; Romans 10:17; Galatians 5:6).

Shun evil with righteousness: When Amulek was debating with Zeezrom, he explained the power of righteousness: "Knowest thou that the righteous yieldeth to no such temptations?" (Alma 11:23). During the millennial reign, Satan will be bound (D&C 43:31) because of the righteousness of the people: "And in that day Satan shall not have power to tempt any man" (D&C 101:28). Righteousness is the principle of the powers of heaven, to which the priesthood is inseparably connected (see D&C 121:36). Righteousness is a principle of power, power to invoke the power of God. By the power of the priesthood and in the name of Jesus Christ you may cast out the devil.

We are free to choose. The perfect plan of God the Father requires that opposition, temptation, and agency are always functioning. These doctrines are eternal verities and are in continual operation. They do not turn off and on. Agency is supreme. We have the power to shun evil in the strength of the Lord.

17–19. Sanctify them through thy truth: thy word is truth. As thou hast sent me into the world, even so have I also sent them into the world. And for their sakes I sanctify myself, that they also might be sanctified through the truth.

We become sanctified through truth. The Lord is the way and the truth. Truth can and will make us free. The Holy Spirit testifies of all truth. The Spirit of truth testifies of Christ. We gird about our loins with truth. The word of God is truth and light. Truth is the knowledge, and the knowledge of God is what converts the souls to Christ. In all of this we are sanctified. Sanctification is the process whereby we are made clean, pure, and holy through the blood of our beloved Savior (see Moses 6:59–60). We then are "sanctified by the reception of the Holy Ghost" (3 Nephi 27:20) and "all those who love and serve God with all their mights, minds, and strength" (D&C 20:31). This process of sanctification is part of the process of becoming even as He is. This is why our Savior came, "to sanctify the world, and to cleanse it from all unrighteousness" (D&C 76:41). I love these scriptures and am filled with joy as I read them again and again. I have an overwhelming desire to be clean, pure, and holy—to be sanctified.

20–23. Neither pray I for these alone, but for them also which shall believe on me through their word; that they all may be one; as thou, Father, art in me, and I in thee, that they also may be one in us: that the world may believe that thou hast sent me. And the glory which thou gavest me I have given them; that they may be one, even as we are one: I in them, and thou in me, that they may be made perfect in one; and that the world may know that thou hast sent me, and hast loved them, as thou hast loved me.

Again the Lord prays for His disciples and for those who believe on their words. "And again, more blessed are they who shall believe in your words because that ye shall testify that ye have seen me, and that ye know that I am. Yea, blessed are they who shall believe in your words, and come down into the depths of humility and be baptized" (3 Nephi 12:2). It is important we understand that when they prophesy and speak for the Lord, we listen because they are speaking for Him. The Lord has condemned those who will not listen to His prophets: "And wo be unto him that will not hearken unto the words of Jesus, and also to them whom he hath chosen and sent among them; for whoso receiveth not the words of Jesus and the words of those whom he hath sent receiveth not him; and therefore he will not receive them at the last day; and it would be better for them if they had not been born. For do ye suppose that ye can get rid of the justice of an offended God, who hath been trampled under feet of men, that thereby salvation might come?" (3 Nephi 28:34–35). Those are strong words that teach the importance of listening to the prophets.

Again the doctrine of oneness is emphasized within the great intercessory prayer. All who believe in Christ are admonished to be one with the Father and the Son. "I am Jesus Christ, the Son of God, who was crucified for the sins of the world, even as many as will believe on my name, that they may become the sons of God, even one in me as I am one in the Father, as the Father is one in me, that we may be one" (D&C 35:2). And again, "Behold, thou art one in me, a son of God; and thus may all become my sons" (Moses 6:68). We are to be one even as They are one. Our perfection and completeness depend on our oneness. To the newly baptized Saints, Alma taught, "And he commanded them that there should be no contention one with another, but that they should look forward with one eye, having one faith and one baptism, having their hearts knit together in unity and in love one towards another" (Mosiah 18:21). Perfect unity brings the power of the Holy Spirit into our lives and we can do all that our Father has commanded us to do. "Endeavouring to keep the unity of the Spirit in the bond of peace" (Ephesians 4:3). What does this oneness entail?

Oneness is the unity of the faith and the knowledge of God and Christ (see Ephesians 4:13) and a cohesion and alignment in purpose, cause, and action. The temple teaches and demonstrates unity, equality, and oneness. We dress alike. We all receive the same covenants and ordinances. We can all qualify for the same blessings. This doctrine of oneness is emphasized in our covenants of the new and everlasting covenant of marriage. The Lord taught about the oneness and eternal union of a married couple: "But from the beginning of the creation God made them male and female. For this cause shall a man leave his father and mother, and cleave to his wife; and they twain shall be one flesh: so then they are no more twain, but one flesh. What therefore God hath joined together, let not man put asunder" (Mark 10:6–9). In Genesis we learn, "Therefore shall a man leave his father and his mother, and shall cleave unto his wife: and they shall be one flesh" (Genesis 2:24). This does not mean we lose our individuality, but rather this relationship is of the highest order with the greatest purpose of procreation and the rearing and nurturing the spirit children of God. There is nothing more holy or transcendently important to our relationship and purpose here on earth. We care for each other. We seek to fulfill the needs of each other. We seek selfless service for our companion's well-being and happiness. We are to cleave to one another. We literally cling faithfully to each other. We are glued together. And our purpose is to bring joy and happiness to each other and our families.

And all of this is a result of the love of God for His children. Our Father, ever concerned for our happiness, knows that there is no true happiness unless we are united and are one with the Father, the Son, and each other—partakers of the love of God. It is this love that drives contention from our hearts, and the heavenly gift of the Holy Spirit will reside in our souls (see 4 Nephi 1:1–18).

24–26. Father, I will that they also, whom thou hast given me, be with me where I am; that they may behold my glory, which thou hast given me: for thou lovedst me before the foundation of the world. O righteous Father, the world hath not known thee: but I have known thee, and these have known that thou hast sent me. And I have declared unto them thy name, and will declare it: that the love wherewith thou hast loved me may be in them, and I in them.

Our Savior, ever the Advocate, closes this imploring prayer for you and me, that we may be with Him and our Heavenly Father in the eternities. For we know that Christ was indeed sent from the Father that we might have eternal life and exaltation. And all of this because our Heavenly Father loves His Beloved Son and us (see John 3:16).

The Lord then teaches a profound truth that in all that He has done, He has sought that we might come to know the Father and to feel of His love, as He has felt His Father's love. When we love our Father, we will recognize and feel His love for us. It was the love of the Father that gave us His Beloved Son so that we might live again. It was the love of His Son, the Savior and Redeemer, that wrought the infinite and eternal Atonement. It was the love of the Father for His children that preceded the great plan of happiness, which was and is His work and His glory.

Surely the feelings of the Lord are expressed to our Father for us: "Listen to him who is the advocate with the Father, who is pleading your cause before him—saying: Father, behold the sufferings and death of him who did no sin, in whom thou wast well pleased; behold the blood of thy Son which was shed, the blood of him whom thou gavest that thyself might be glorified; wherefore, Father, spare these my brethren that believe on my name, that they may come unto me and have everlasting life" (D&C 45:3–5).

As I read the words of this great intercessory prayer, I pray that I grasp the significance of it. Do I appreciate the depth of concern our Savior has for me? Do I begin to understand our Savior's intent for my soul? I feel humbled and truly stand all amazed that our Savior went on to suffer for every living soul who ever came to this earth. His thoughts were about our "being one" with Him and our Father.

As we take time to ponder and understand the great intercessory prayer, we will have an overwhelming desire to show our love through obedience to the commandments of the Lord. It is indeed the covenant we have made at baptism and renewed each week with the sacrament. "And witness unto thee, O God, the Eternal Father, that they are willing to take upon them the name of thy Son, and always remember him and keep his commandments which he has given them" (D&C 20:77).

Chapter 4

GETHSEMANE

THE BEGINNING OF THE GREAT SUFFERING OF THE LORD

Following this great intercessory prayer, the Lord began His prodigious suffering in the Garden of Gethsemane, which was the expression of the love of God. My gratitude swells within my soul as I come to see the great love our Savior has for us. His life, His teachings, and His expressions of love through His service all testify of His goodness and perfection. And then the ultimate, His suffering and sacrifice, His death and resurrection, which brings about the completion of the Atonement, the At-one-ment, the bringing back together the children of God so as to be one with the Father and the Son. Our Savior "went forth with his disciples over the brook Cedron, where was a garden, into the which he entered" (John 18:1), "a place which was named Gethsemane: and he saith to his disciples, Sit ye here, while I shall pray" (Mark 14:32).

Gethsemane refers to "the place where olive oil is pressed" or "winepress of oils." Gethsemane was indeed the place of pressure and suffering to bring forth the oil of life, even the oil of our lamps, the oil of righteousness through Christ the Lord. Our hope is anchored in the suffering and sacrificing Christ. The Savior in Gethsemane suffered for us. He described it with a commandment to repent that we might not suffer the pain He did: "How sore you know not, how exquisite you know not, yea, how hard to bear you know not" (D&C 19:15; see also verses 16–19).

As I reread this verse, my heart shudders at the thought of pain so great we can't comprehend it, for "you know not." We have all had pain to one degree or another. Mothers understand the pain and suffering of childbirth. How can we gain greater empathy for the pain the Lord had to bear? There is physical pain, which not only can we sense but also sends tremors throughout our body and we sometimes cry out in anguish. This I can partially understand as it relates to my little finite mind. The physical pain of the suffering of our Lord was inestimable to His body and impossible for us to comprehend. King Benjamin reminds us, "Believe that man doth not comprehend all the things which the Lord can comprehend" (Mosiah 4:9). The pain of His suffering within His soul for all the sins of mankind was infinite. Alma gives us some insight: "I was tormented with the pains of hell" (Alma 36:13). "And now, for three days and for three nights was I racked, even with the pains of a damned soul" (Alma 36:16). This helps me begin to understand, and I emphasize *begin* to understand the suffering of our beloved Savior. Though we may not comprehend what our Savior endured, we can still be grateful. It is gratitude that draws us to our Savior. It is gratitude that causes a sense of indebtedness. It is gratitude for the goodness and mercy of our Savior that will cause us to change.

How can we begin to understand and appreciate all the suffering and sacrificing of Christ? We begin by knowing that Jesus, though born in mortality, was the Son of Almighty God. He had power and was perfect. He is the only one who could pay for our sins. Sometimes in our finite mortal minds we do not understand the ways of the Lord. Why was the suffering and sacrificing of God's Only Begotten Son the way to pay for our sins? Couldn't there be another way? We cannot possibly comprehend the ways of God. This is the way God our Father has ordained that His children might be redeemed from death and sin. Isaiah teaches us, "For my thoughts are not your thoughts, neither are your ways my ways, saith the Lord. For as the heavens are higher than the earth, so are my ways higher than your ways, and my thoughts than your thoughts" (Isaiah 55:8–9). Lest we forget the wisdom of God: "But behold, all things have been done in the wisdom of him who knoweth all things" (2 Nephi 2:24). The perfect plan of our Heavenly Father required payment for our sins; justice must have its way. Yet mercy will triumph: "And thus he shall bring salvation to all those who shall believe on his name; this being the intent of this last sacrifice, *to bring about the bowels of mercy, which overpowereth justice*, and bringeth about means unto men that they may have faith unto repentance" (Alma 34:15; emphasis added). Sins were paid for with the love of God through His Only Begotten Son. There was only one perfect, anointed Son of God, even Christ the Lord, who could make this payment through the infinite Atonement, which will *draw us to the Lord* (see 3 Nephi 27:14; emphasis added). Scripture after scripture the Lord speaks of paying for the sins of the world (see 2 Nephi 25:26; Mosiah 4:2–3; 16:13; Alma 4:14; 5:27, 48; 6:8; 22:14; 30:26; 34:8; 36:17; 39:15; 3 Nephi 6:20; 3 Nephi 7:16; Mormon 7:5; Moroni 10:33; D&C 19:15–19; 29:1; 35:2; 46:13; 138:7; 1 Corinthians 15:3; Ephesians 2:5; Hebrews 9:28; 1 Peter 3:18; Revelation 1:5). The sins of the entire world have been paid for by the grace of God the Father and our Savior Jesus Christ. As I read each one, I thought of the goodness and mercy of my Savior for being willing to pay the price so that we might live again and have everlasting life. There are countless scriptures that testify of His atoning sacrifice for us. Isn't it interesting that the Lord doesn't just say something once? It is repeated over and over again by His prophets, both in the scriptures and by those living today. This is how we learn. We will come to know and appreciate our Savior. Then we will testify of Christ. And He is the Christ because of the infinite Atonement. We invite people to come unto Christ and partake of His infinite Atonement to become free forever.

What would it take to get us mortals to appreciate the suffering and sacrifice of the Lord and pay attention to His Atonement? We need to recognize and feel the need for our Savior's ultimate gift. We must recognize our fallen state and our plight without the redeeming blood of our Savior. In our fallen state, we could not merit anything of ourselves (see Alma 22:14). We would be subject to the devil (see 2 Nephi 9:6–11), for we could have no hope without Christ the Lord. We were and are totally dependent upon Christ's Atonement. John explained why many do not feel this need for the Savior's love: "And this is the condemnation, that light is come into the world, *and men loved darkness rather than light, because their deeds were evil. For every one that doeth evil hateth the light, neither cometh to the light, lest his deeds should be reproved*" (John 3:19–20; emphasis added). And those who do not come to believe in Christ, "ye shall die in your sins" (John 8:24).

What would it take for us to begin listening to His words, that we would feast upon them, that we might begin to understand the doctrine of the Atonement? We can empirically prove His doctrine, "If any man will do his will, he shall know of the doctrine, whether it be of God, or whether I speak of myself" (John 7:17). Desire or the willingness to simply try can be the beginning of accepting the word of God.

> But behold, if ye will awake and arouse your faculties, even to an experiment upon my words, and exercise a particle of faith, yea, even if ye can no more than desire to believe, let this desire work in you, even until ye believe in a manner that ye can give place for a portion of my words.
>
> Now, we will compare the word unto a seed. Now, if ye give place, that a seed may be planted in your heart, behold, if it be a true seed, or a good seed, if ye do not cast it out by your unbelief, that ye will resist the Spirit of the Lord, behold, it will begin to swell within your breasts; and when you feel these swelling motions, ye will begin to say within yourselves—It must needs be that this is a good seed, or that the word is good, for it beginneth to enlarge my soul; yea, it beginneth to enlighten my understanding, yea, it beginneth to be delicious to me. (Alma 32:27–28)

When we are humbled, we are in a state of readiness. Those who are humble will believe in the word of God (see Alma 32:16). When we make room in our hearts for the word of God, we will come to recognize our need for our Savior Jesus Christ.

What will it take for us to be drawn to our Savior and seek to follow Him? Gratitude! When we are humbled to the point that we are willing to listen and try to understand and appreciate the goodness of God as expressed through the Atonement of His Beloved Son, we will begin to come unto Christ. Through this appreciation, our hearts will be consumed with gratitude, which literally opens our hearts to the love of God. The love of God is the source of all happiness and is centered in the infinite Atonement of His Son. Then we have an overwhelming desire to be good and to do good, that all mankind might come unto Christ.

THE SUFFERING CHRIST

In the midst of His great suffering, the Lord cried out in prayer, "O my Father, if it be possible, let this cup pass from me: nevertheless not as I will, but as thou wilt" (Matthew 26:39; see also Luke 22:42). And later He prayed, "O my Father, if this cup may not pass away from me, except I drink it, thy will be done" (Matthew 26:42). And yet a third time, He implored the Father, "saying the same words" (verse 44). In the Savior's pleading for relief, He always concluded with, "Nevertheless not as I will, but as Thou wilt" (verse 39). The Son was always submissive to the Father. In Gethsemane, our Savior came to that moment in His life where He had to face His ultimate challenge—His boundless suffering and sacrifice for our sins and His beginning the infinite Atonement. If we can begin to obtain an insight to the gravity of the Savior's situation, realizing that this was the moment He had to face the reality of the payment for the sins of the world, our gratitude should exude from our very beings. We would change. This was the most difficult task given to anyone who has ever lived upon the face of the earth. The suffering in Gethsemane and Golgotha was limitless, immeasurable, and infinite.

Blood came from every pore.

He anguished for the souls of mankind.

The pain was so excruciating it is impossible to comprehend.

He bore hunger, thirst, and fatigue more than a mortal can bear save it be unto death.

He was mocked, scourged, beat, and spit upon.

And then He endured the agony of the cross.

Mark records the Lord's request to His Father, "Take away this cup from me." In a tender moment, we are taught a transcending truth of the relationship of the Son to His Father. "And saith unto them, My soul is exceeding sorrowful unto death: tarry ye here, and watch. And he went forward a little, and fell on the ground, and prayed that, if it were possible, the hour might pass from him. And he said, Abba, Father, all things are possible unto thee; take away this cup from me: nevertheless not what I will, but what thou wilt" (Mark 14:34–36).

It is important to note that when Christ speaks to His Father, He uses the term *Abba*, which in Aramaic means "Papa" or "Daddy." In this affectionate and caring moment, we understand the true Father and Son relationship between God the Father and God the Son. And we as spirit children can have an intimate and close relationship with our Heavenly Father too as we come to know Him and do His will. We are the literal sons and daughters of God. The more our prayers are constant and, yes, even desperate, we will seek more intently to commune with our Heavenly Father. Many times we say our prayers and never ponder. We don't even give Heavenly Father time to respond to our needs. I confess the number of times I jump up from my prayers with no thought of an answer. Now that I am older, I ponder longer with a prayer in my heart, and I feel close to my Father. One day while worshipping in the temple, I was praying and pondering at length to my Heavenly Father. As I prayed, I began to hum in my mind the words "Heavenly Father, are you really there?" from the Primary song "A Child's Prayer." As I sat musing in the Lord's holy house, a voice came into my mind: "Ed, my son, I am always here." Yes, the glory and presence of the Lord is in His holy house, and we can feel it. I cannot thank my Father enough for those tender and priceless moments in my life. He is real. He is loving. He is our Father. My eyes well up with tears as I seek to share my innermost thoughts and feelings concerning my beloved Savior and my Heavenly Father. How much love does it take to offer a Son, even His Only Begotten Son in the flesh, as a ransom for His children? How much love does it take to see the Son of your flesh suffer in such agony so others might have everlasting life? Only a perfect and loving Father could make such an offering for His family. This intimate expression of love from our Heavenly Father is ever present. It is a blessing that is waiting to be received. When we receive the love of God, we receive Christ as our Redeemer.

To receive indicates acknowledgment and acceptance of knowledge, a gift, or a blessing from a giver. To receive the infinite Atonement with all the associated ordinances, covenants, and principles, we must accept them and act upon them, else we have not truly received. Receiving acknowledges that those things we have accepted are true. To *receive* the Atonement means taking it into our soul. This includes that the temple ordinances are received and faithfully honored. We start to receive the blessings of the Atonement as we begin to appreciate the suffering of our Savior—and gratitude is born.

Gratitude is crucial to the act of receiving. Both receiving and expressing gratitude are dependent on one another. If one is not grateful, one cannot truly receive, and if one does not truly receive, one cannot feel the gratitude of the blessing. Therefore the power to change (gratitude being the catalyst of change) will lie dormant because the blessings and gifts of God have not been accepted and received into our hearts. Remember the Nephites after the Savior visited them. They received the love of God into their hearts, evidenced by the happiness they enjoyed "because of the love of God which did dwell in the hearts of the people" (4 Nephi 1:15).

The sacrifice for our sins and the infinite Atonement by Christ was the expression of the love of God (see John 3:16). The sacrifice required the Lord to suffer infinitely and vicariously for all of our sins. As we seek forgiveness for sins in our own lives, we offer a sacrifice of a broken heart and contrite spirit, which is a form of godly sorrow. This sorrow, in a sense, is the suffering to a much lesser degree that we struggle with for the remission and forgiveness of our sins. We often want it to pass with no pain, grief, or emotional sorrow as we seek forgiveness. This is not the way. We seek healing immediately, and healing is commensurate with the nature of the sin. This is why many people, when they are in such deep pain and sorrow, seek relief—relief at any price and in any way. It is so sad to see people seek relief through sex, drugs, and alcohol to give them a time of reprieve. My heart aches because the false relief for a moment comes back with a greater vengeance on their soul with guilt and pain. There is no other way to come to the Lord except with a broken heart and contrite spirit. This is our sacrifice. This is what we offer on the altar of God. This sorrow, even godly sorrow, is a requirement for repentance that leads to forgiveness and freedom from guilt. We plead for forgiveness. We want freedom from pain and guilt. We seek peace for our souls. Enos struggled in the spirit as he began the process of being forgiven and having his guilt swept away (see Enos 1:1–8). And never forget the pain of Alma the Younger in his time of suffering.

The Lord knew He had much suffering to endure when He said to Peter, James, and John, "My soul is exceeding sorrowful, even unto death: tarry ye here, and watch with me" (Matthew 26:38; see also Mark 14:34). His soul was "sorrowful, even unto death." Luke describes His sorrow and suffering: "And there appeared an angel unto him from heaven, strengthening him. And being in an agony he prayed more earnestly: and his sweat was as it were great drops of blood falling down to the ground" (Luke 22:43–44). As His pain and sorrow increased, the greater was His petition to His Father. Likewise, in our greatest need do our pleadings increase.

Take a moment and think of your own pleading prayers. As I write, I remember those many moments of appealing to my Heavenly Father, pleading for a son. Pleading for my family. Pleading for strength. Pleading for protection. Pleading for relief from pain. Pleading to walk again. Pleading to breathe. The more desperate we are, the greater the pleadings.

One evening, we were sitting at the dinner table, eating my sweetheart's tacos—the most delicious tacos that were ever made. Unbeknownst to me, I had a little malady. My problem was that my little lower esophageal sphincter (the little valve that lets food into the stomach) wasn't working—it was closed. My food began to fill up my esophagus all the way up to my epiglottis. But I didn't know it, and I decided it was time for a drink of delicious cold milk. When I swallowed that milk, it covered up my epiglottis, and I could not breath. However I tried, I couldn't even make a sound. My sweetheart asked, "What's wrong? Honey, what can I do?" This went on for a few seconds, and my children cried, "Daddy, Daddy, what can we do?" They begin to cry.

I was struggling to breath, to no avail. Seconds went by, and thoughts flashed through my mind: *What should I do? What should*

I do? In my mind, I was pleading with my Heavenly Father, *I've tried to be a good boy, and I've been trying to do what's right. Help me. Help me.* And He did! I was inspired to initiate my gag reflex, and it dislodged the food. I could breathe! I testify to you, I am grateful to breathe. I am grateful to swallow. Every time I take a deep, deep breath, I can remember that breath of air when I thought life was over. Isn't it something that we never totally appreciate our blessings until they are taken away? I want you to know, I appreciate the capacity to swallow and to breathe. I am grateful. I am grateful for life and the goodness and tender mercies of God. I am grateful for the suffering and sacrificing of Christ, for in Him I can have eternal life.

The suffering, sacrificing Christ continued on in Gethsemane and on Golgotha's cross. "For, behold, the Lord your Redeemer suffered death in the flesh; wherefore he suffered the pain of all men, that all men might repent and come unto him" (D&C 18:11). The Savior, "surely he hath borne our griefs, and carried our sorrows" (Isaiah 53:4). King Benjamin describes our Savior's suffering: "And lo, he shall suffer temptations, and pain of body, hunger, thirst, and fatigue, even more than man can suffer, except it be unto death; for behold, blood cometh from every pore, so great shall be his anguish for the wickedness and the abominations of his people" (Mosiah 3:7). I read with gratitude these most instructive and empowering words of Elder James E. Talmage in *Jesus the Christ*:

> Christ's agony in the garden is unfathomable by the finite mind, both as to intensity and cause. The thought that He suffered through fear of death is untenable. Death to Him was preliminary to resurrection and triumphal return to the Father from whom He had come, and to a state of glory even beyond what He had before possessed; and, moreover, it was within His power to lay down His life voluntarily. He struggled and groaned under a burden such as no other being who has lived on earth might even conceive as possible. It was not physical pain, nor mental anguish alone, that caused Him to suffer such torture as to produce an extrusion of blood from every pore; but a spiritual agony of soul such as only God was capable of experiencing. No other man, however great his powers of physical or mental endurance, could have suffered

> so; for his human organism would have succumbed, and syncope would have produced unconsciousness and welcome oblivion. In that hour of anguish Christ met and overcame all the horrors that Satan, "the prince of this world" could inflict. The frightful struggle incident to the temptations immediately following the Lord's baptism was surpassed and overshadowed by this supreme contest with the powers of evil.
>
> In some manner, actual and terribly real though to man incomprehensible, the Savior took upon Himself the burden of the sins of mankind from Adam to the end of the world. Modern revelation assists us to a partial understanding of the awful experience. In March 1830, the glorified Lord, Jesus Christ, thus spake: "For behold, I, God, have suffered these things for all, that they might not suffer if they would repent, but if they would not repent, they must suffer even as I, which suffering caused myself, even God, the greatest of all, to tremble because of pain, and to bleed at every pore, and to suffer both body and spirit—and would that I might not drink the bitter cup and shrink—nevertheless, glory be to the Father, and I partook and finished my preparations unto the children of men" (D&C 19:16–19).
>
> From the terrible conflict in Gethsemane, Christ emerged a victor. Though in the dark tribulation of that fearful hour He had pleaded that the bitter cup be removed from His lips, the request, however oft repeated, was always conditional; the accomplishment of the Father's will was never lost sight of as the object of the Son's supreme desire. The further tragedy of the night, and the cruel inflictions that awaited Him on the morrow, to culminate in the frightful tortures of the cross, could not exceed the bitter anguish through which He had successfully passed. (James E. Talmage, *Jesus the Christ* [Salt Lake City: Deseret Book, 1915], 613–14.)

I have read and reread this passage from Elder Talmage. It helps me understand the suffering and anguish of the Lord. It gives me a greater appreciation for what He went through. My empathy for our Savior is increased. Though our comprehension is inadequate, our gratitude should be overflowing. If not, we may suffer from a most grievous sin of ingratitude for not acknowledging and appreciating the infinite suffering of our Lord and Savior Jesus Christ. President Ezra Taft Benson reminded us, "The Prophet Joseph is reported to have said at one time that one of the greatest sins for which the Latter-day Saints would be guilty would be the sin of ingratitude. I presume most of us have not thought of that as a serious sin. There is a great tendency for us in our prayers—in our pleadings with the Lord—to ask for additional blessings. Sometimes I feel we need to devote more of our prayers to expressions of gratitude and thanksgiving for blessings already received. Of course we need the daily blessings of the Lord. But if we sin in the matter of prayer, I think it is in our lack of the expressions of thanksgiving for daily blessings" (*The Teachings of Ezra Taft Benson* [Salt Lake City: Deseret Book, 1974], 363).

It follows that gratitude must be one of the cardinal virtues of life. Remember, if we fail to acknowledge God, we offend Him. Now we see why when people do not receive the Atonement, blessings are withheld and consequences follow; by contrast, when people receive and embrace the gift, they are blessed. The Lord explains to us, "For what doth it profit a man if a gift is bestowed upon him, and he receive not the gift? Behold, he rejoices not in that which is given unto him, neither rejoices in him who is the giver of the gift" (D&C 88:33). Christ suffered in order to fulfill the Atonement and provide for us an opportunity for life eternal. If we do not accept this supernal gift, we in effect refuse the Atonement and must suffer for our own sins (see D&C 19:15–19).

As a young man, I didn't even think about the Atonement, let alone realize the magnitude of the Lord and His power. I remember when I heard the word *Atonement* the first time (at least, the first time it registered in my brain). I was about seventeen. I can't remember much, but I simply recall the word. I had no idea of all the things the Atonement covered, as well as its relationship to our beloved Savior. I have come to understand that everything is a typifying of our Savior Jesus Christ, "and all things which have been given of God from the beginning of the world, unto man, are the typifying of him" (2 Nephi 11:4). This means that the Lord is exemplified, personified, and symbolized constantly within His creations, His prophets, the Church, and His priesthood, and there is nothing the Lord is not in, for He is in all things, as this scripture testifies: "He comprehendeth all things, and all things are before him, and all things are round about him;

and he is above all things, and in all things, and is through all things, and is round about all things; and all things are by him, and of him, even God, forever and ever" (D&C 88:41). The Lord is the way, the truth, and the light because of His enabling power of the Atonement.

UNDERSTANDING AND APPRECIATING GETHSEMANE

Gethsemane was crucial to the plan of redemption. Without the suffering and sacrificing of the Lord in Gethsemane, there could be no triumph over sin and the fallen state of mankind. The Atonement could not be completed and all would be lost. The Savior went on to say, "And behold, I am the light and the life of the world; and I have drunk out of that bitter cup which the Father hath given me, and have glorified the Father in taking upon me the sins of the world, in the which I have suffered the will of the Father in all things from the beginning" (3 Nephi 11:11). And again, "Which suffering caused myself, even God, the greatest of all, to tremble because of pain, and to bleed at every pore, and to suffer both body and spirit—and would that I might not drink the bitter cup, and shrink—nevertheless, glory be to the Father, and I partook and finished my preparations unto the children of men" (D&C 19:18–19).

There was no other way save it be through Christ the Lord, because He was the Anointed One, the Savior and Redeemer of the world. We must remember that Christ had power within Himself, "for as the Father hath life in himself; so hath he given to the Son to have life in himself" (John 5:26). We cannot separate Gethsemane, the suffering from Golgotha, and death from the Garden Tomb, the resurrection, and eternal life. All of this is part of the Atonement and enabling power of Christ. We are all made alive in Christ (see 1 Corinthians 15:22; 2 Nephi 25:25–26). Gethsemane began the greatest suffering, and as in all things, it would become the beginning of the greatest triumph.

We can think of the bitter cup, relating it to our lives. When things seem unfair, we can remember our beloved Savior, for He was the ultimate victim. We can, in the strength of the Lord and enabling Atonement, overcome every situation we face that might seem unfair. Christ did not sin in any degree, yet He paid the price for the sins of the world. Christ did no wrongs, yet He paid for all the wrongdoings here upon the earth. And He did this voluntarily. Our Savior and the prophets throughout the scriptures referred to His great suffering time and time again (see 1 Nephi 19:9; Mosiah 4:6, 11; Alma 5:6; 7:11–12; Moroni 9:25; D&C 19:15–19). Do we always remember His sacrifice? This transcending truth proves the complete and perfect love Christ has for us. Father Lehi made this clear when he said,

> Behold, he offereth himself a sacrifice for sin, to answer the ends of the law, unto all those who have a broken heart and a contrite spirit; and unto none else can the ends of the law be answered.
>
> Wherefore, how great the importance to make these things known unto the inhabitants of the earth, that they may know that there is no flesh that can dwell in the presence of God, save it be through the merits, and mercy, and grace of the Holy Messiah, who layeth down his life according to the flesh, and taketh it again by the power of the Spirit, that he may bring to pass the resurrection of the dead, being the first that should rise. (2 Nephi 2:7–8)

I would like to highlight an insightful truth taught in the suffering of Christ. In very fact, He took upon Himself all of our sins. So in effect, He suffers for us. He is vicariously acting for us. In this mighty act when He is suffering for us, we are becoming like Him, even perfected in Him. It is through the grace of the Lord, which includes all aspects of the Atonement, that we are perfected in Christ. This grace is sufficient only as we come unto Christ and are perfected in Him by denying ourselves of all ungodliness. Moroni explains,

> Yea, come unto Christ, and *be perfected in him*, and deny yourselves of all ungodliness; and if ye shall deny yourselves of all ungodliness, and love God with all your might, mind and strength, *then is his grace sufficient for you, that by his grace ye may be perfect in Christ; and if by the grace of God ye are perfect in Christ*, ye can in nowise deny the power of God.
>
> And again, if ye by the grace of God are perfect in Christ, and deny not his power, then are ye sanctified in Christ by the grace of God, through the shedding of the blood of Christ, which is in

> the covenant of the Father unto the remission of your sins, that ye become holy, without spot. (Moroni 10:32–33; emphasis added)

Christ is the power of our perfection, and He is the great Intercessor in our behalf. Again I testify that He pleads with the Father for us: "Listen to him who is the advocate with the Father, who is pleading your cause before him—saying: Father, behold the sufferings and death of him who did no sin, in whom thou wast well pleased; behold the blood of thy Son which was shed, the blood of him whom thou gavest that thyself might be glorified; wherefore, Father, spare these my brethren that believe on my name, that they may come unto me and have everlasting life" (D&C 45:3–5). This advocacy is a selfless demonstration of the Lord supporting us at every turn. He gave His all for us, and then He pleads for us with the Father, that we might return to His presence. The Savior literally campaigns for our eternal life. We must always remember that no one can come unto the Father save it be by His Beloved Son.

Let us seek to empathize and gain understanding of our Beloved Savior's situation as He suffers such agony in Gethsemane. The Savior spent hours of pleading prayers and suffering like no one has ever suffered physically, mentally, emotionally, or spiritually—for all of us. In the following sections, we will seek to answer the questions this great suffering of Christ brings to our minds.

HOW DO WE FEEL ABOUT CHRIST'S SUFFERING?

Because of what we have felt and come to understand and appreciate, our indebtedness for our Savior's infinite suffering and sacrifice should be immeasurable. We have compassion and sorrow in our hearts for being part of the cause of the Lord's suffering. As we have read all the scriptures related to the Atonement and our own transgressions, we will seek to make amends. In our prayers we will express our grief and have a desire to make things right through the process of repentance. We will make the mighty change. And we will live the words of Alma: "And now behold, I say unto you, my brethren, if ye have experienced a change of heart, and if ye have felt to sing the song of redeeming love, I would ask, can ye feel so now?" (Alma 5:26). We will seek to show our love to our Father and our Savior by keeping the commandments. We will have the desire to bring souls unto Christ. We will be member missionaries. We will become saviors on Mount Zion. We will become clean from the blood and sins of this generation through our faithfulness. We will please God and will seek any way possible to prove our love and gratitude to our Savior for all that He has done for us. We can do it in the strength of the Lord. I pray that each one of us will reexamine our feelings regarding the Savior's suffering and seek to make the changes needed in our attitudes and lives so that we might please our Heavenly Father by showing gratitude and love for His Beloved Son.

The last paragraph can become a pedagogy of change. When . . .

We understand and appreciate . . .

We become indebted to our Savior . . .

Our compassion increases . . .

Our gratitude enlarges . . .

We seek to make amends . . .

We express our grief and sorrow and are moved to repent . . .

We make the mighty change . . .

We sing the song of redeeming love . . .

We keep the commandments . . .

We desire to bring souls unto Christ . . .

We will be member missionaries . . .

We will be saviors on Mount Zion . . .

We become clean through our faithfulness . . .

We seek to please God and prove our love for Him and our Savior . . .

We can do it in the strength of the Lord.

And it all began as a feeling of gratitude for our suffering and sacrificing Christ.

I suppose to gain empathy, we would do as the old saying states: "You'll never understand a person until you walk a mile in their shoes." We can never fully understand someone else's heart, but let us still try our best. Here are some things that may be able to help us gain empathy for our Savior's suffering. As our relationship with Christ deepens, our understanding of all that He has done will become more meaningful to us, and thus our compassion for and identification with His suffering will become part of us as we become part of Him. Knowing that we are totally dependent upon Christ because He is the Savior can help us in the sense that we cannot do for ourselves what He is doing for us. This brings a reality of responsiveness to Christ because of our indebtedness and gratitude to Him. Our pains and afflictions are swallowed up in Christ, thus we are again not only identified with Christ but nurtured by Him in all of our suffering. Our empathy for Him and His goodness becomes immeasurable. Not only do we feel for Him, but we are also moved by Him to greater heights of goodness. And last, since we are totally dependent upon God for all things, surely He has the power through His abundant grace to give us an empathetic soul. We could be endowed with empathy and compassion as a gift. We can have empathy and compassion.

HOW DO OUR INTENTIONS CHANGE WITH UNDERSTANDING AND APPRECIATION?

I find it fascinating how our intents change according to the situation. For example, when things are going along without any problems or challenges, our prayers are often offered without much passion or desperation. However, as soon as we have a problem, our prayers are more intensified. We implore our Heavenly Father with all our hearts for intercession in our lives. The greater the need, the greater our passion in our prayers. We even go to the temple for additional help in solving our problems. Mormon counseled us in regard to our intentions, "Wherefore, my beloved brethren, *pray unto the Father with all the energy of heart*, that ye may be filled with this love, which he hath bestowed upon all who are true followers of his Son, Jesus Christ; that ye may become the sons of God; that when he shall appear we shall be like him, for we shall see him as he is; that we may have this hope; that we may be purified even as he is pure. Amen" (Moroni 7:48; emphasis added). I remember many times in my life when a crisis would occur with health, relationships, or anything that was high on my priority list, and I began to plead in earnest. I made promises. I fasted not just one day a month but many days a month. I increased my temple attendance, seeking answers and power to be blessed. When the need is great, change is dramatic. As mortals, we have a natural tendency to call upon the Lord when times are trying. It has been said, "Put an atheist at the brink of death, and God becomes his friend and last resort."

All things, including our prayers, are dependent upon our intent, as Mormon reminds us: "And likewise also is it counted evil unto a man, if he shall pray and not with *real intent of heart*; yea, and it profiteth him nothing, for God receiveth none such" (Moroni 7:9; emphasis added).

"For behold, God hath said a man being evil cannot do that which is good; for if he offereth a gift, or prayeth unto God, except he shall do it *with real intent* it profiteth him nothing" (Moroni 7:6; emphasis added).

Nephi makes this principle clear:

> My beloved brethren, I know that if ye shall follow the Son, with full purpose of heart, acting no hypocrisy and no deception before God, but *with real intent*, repenting of your sins . . . [are] are willing to take upon you the name of Christ, by baptism, then shall ye receive the Holy Ghost; and . . . speak with the tongue of angels, and shout praises unto the Holy One of Israel. . . .
>
> Thus came the voice of the Son unto me, saying: After ye have repented of your sins, and witnessed unto the Father that ye are willing to keep my commandments, by the baptism of water, and have received the baptism of fire and of the Holy Ghost, and can speak with a new tongue, yea, even with the tongue of angels, *and after this should deny me*, it would have been better for you that ye had not known me. . . .
>
> He that endureth to the end, the same shall be saved. (2 Nephi 31:13–15; emphasis added)

Intentions are not enough. We must endure to receive the blessings.

Note the intent of the Savior's sacrifice: "And thus he shall bring salvation to all those who shall believe on his name; *this being the intent of this last sacrifice*, to bring about the bowels of mercy, which overpowereth justice, and bringeth about means unto men that they may have faith unto repentance" (Alma 34:15; emphasis added). If the intent or desires of our hearts are good, we will "be restored unto that which is good" (Alma 41:3).

The intent makes all the difference.

> And if your eye be single to my glory, your whole bodies shall be filled with light, and there shall be no darkness in you; and that body which is filled with light comprehendeth all things.
>
> Therefore, sanctify yourselves that your minds become single to God, and the days will come that you shall see him; for he will unveil his face unto you, and it shall be in his own time, and in his own way, and according to his own will. (D&C 88:67–68)

Our eye single to the glory of God should be our intent in all we do, and the blessings will be immeasurable. We will be filled with light, and we will be able to comprehend all those things that will bring us closer to God.

Our intent and resolve to do better must be coupled with a determination and commitment to achieve our goals. It takes great effort to make a plan to understand the Atonement of our Savior so that it is efficacious in our lives. Our real intent is expressed through our works and the desires of our hearts, which is key in our judgment of the Lord: "For I, the Lord, will judge all men according to their works, according to the desire of their hearts" (D&C 137:9). So let us be of good cheer, "cheerfully do all things that lie in our power" (D&C 123:17).

Surely we are convinced that intent makes the difference in our actions. The question is, why do we wait to change until we are being crushed by problems and afflictions? It is because need is the mother of change. We teach and preach of another need—another fuel to cause change, another feeling that can motivate action. That feeling is gratitude. If gratitude is deep enough, then the love of God is great enough and we will choose to change. We will act positively in moments of peace and serenity. When things are going well, we will show greater gratitude, which will result in greater good. We will express our love and acts of service as a natural response to our feelings of gratitude. Feeling gratitude and thanksgiving creates a need through love and indebtedness that can move us to action. Thus our intentions are directly proportional to our feelings of gratitude as is our devotion, dedication, and commitment.

WHAT DO THESE FEELINGS OF GRATITUDE DO FOR OUR RELATIONSHIP WITH OUR SAVIOR?

In my heart, I cry out for my Savior's pain and suffering, expressing my distress and sadness. At the same time, I shout inside my soul with gratitude, knowing full well my plight without my Savior's Atonement. My being is tied to the Lord and His goodness. My relationship to my Savior is forged in the fiery furnace of His sacrifice of all things throughout His life, and especially in Garden of Gethsemane and on the cross on Golgotha's hill. I love, trust, respect, and reverence my Savior more each day. I come to know my Savior, and thus the Father, as I understand and appreciate better the perfect plan of our Father, which is centered in and on His Beloved Son. This plan of redemption is why the Lord was sent, and we see that our relationship deepens as we seek to do as He would do (see Acts 10:38), love as He loved (see John 13:34–35; 21:15–17), and live as He lived (see John 8:28--29). And thus we can take upon ourselves His divine nature and go about doing good (see 2 Peter 1:3–10). With gratitude, our relationship and oneness is increased as we seek to become even as He is (see 3 Nephi 27:27).

If our gratitude is pure, our actions will follow. If we truly love God, we will keep His commandments. I have found in my life that as the doctrines of the temple have distilled upon my soul, as my gratitude has increased to its greatest height, I find myself seeking to emulate my Savior. I want to be a good person. I want to keep all of His commandments. The Holy Ghost leads us to do good. One night after counseling with a couple, the Spirit was strong with me. I felt the desire to do good, to do justly. I was humbled and felt great joy. I really wanted to keep every commandment of God, and more if there were any. I went out on our deck, and with great feelings of gratitude, I looked up into the heavens and prayed to my Heavenly Father with the desire to keep all the commandments. In my naiveté, I asked for additional commandments to keep, and into my mind and heart came this request: "Ed, my son, have another child." The little boy within me said, "Father, will Thou tell my sweetheart?"

I began fasting and praying for Heavenly Father to tell my sweetheart. We had six children at the time, and pregnancy was extremely difficult for my wife. She'd had multiple problems. I fasted one day a week for several months. While we were visiting one night, my wife said, "Sweetheart, we have to have another child right now." I smiled, agreed, and thanked my Heavenly Father. Years later, I confessed my anxiousness in telling her about my revelation. It could have been hard for her to accept. Her pregnancy would not cause me any physical pain, just emotional concern and stress for my sweetheart. She is the one who would suffer and sacrifice for our baby so that mortality might come to a spirit child of God the Father.

CHRIST'S SUFFERING ALLOWS US TO REPENT AND BE FORGIVEN

There can be no repentance save there be an Atonement. We come unto Christ and apply the Atonement of Christ to our lives through faith unto repentance, baptism for the remission of sins, receiving the Holy Ghost, and receiving all the ordinances and covenants in the temple. Remember, Christ has paid for our sins through the Atonement, but if we do not repent, we must suffer for our sins ourselves (see D&C 19:15–18).

The Lord has made clear through His prophets our source of redemption: "In whom we have redemption through his blood, the forgiveness of sins, according to the riches of his grace" (Ephesians 1:7). "In whom we have redemption through his blood, even the forgiveness of sins" (Colosians 1:14). "And they had viewed themselves in their own carnal state, even less than the dust of the earth. And they all cried aloud with one voice, saying: O have mercy, and apply the atoning blood of Christ that we may receive forgiveness of our sins, and our hearts may be purified; for we believe in Jesus Christ, the Son of God, who created heaven and earth, and all things; who shall come down among the children of men" (Mosiah 4:2). "Therefore I say unto you, Go; and whosoever transgresseth against me, him shall ye judge according to the sins which he has committed; and if he confess his sins before thee and me, and repenteth in the sincerity of his heart, him shall ye forgive, and I will forgive him also" (Mosiah 26:29). We learn that the Atonement goes hand in hand with our faithfulness. We work out our salvation through our faithfulness, and we are healed by our faith in Christ: "Be of good comfort; thy faith hath made thee whole. And the woman was made whole from that hour" (Matthew 9:22; see also Mark 5:34; 10:52; Luke 7:50; 8:48; 17:19).

We are forgiven of our sins when we exercise our faith in Jesus Christ. "And, behold, they brought to him a man sick of the palsy, lying on a bed: and Jesus seeing their faith said unto the sick of the palsy; Son, be of good cheer; *thy sins be forgiven thee*" (Matthew 9:2; emphasis added; see also Mark 2:5; Luke 5:20; James 5:15). King Benjamin's people recognized the connection between forgiveness and our Savior's Atonement: "And they had viewed themselves in their own carnal state, even less than the dust of the earth. And they all cried aloud with one voice, saying: *O have mercy, and apply the atoning blood of Christ that we may receive forgiveness of our sins, and our hearts may be purified; for we believe in Jesus Christ, the Son of God*, who created heaven and earth, and all things; who shall come down among the children of men" (Mosiah 4:2; emphasis added). We must never forget that it is through the atoning blood of Christ that we may have forgiveness of sins, and it requires us to receive the Atonement and act upon it: "Behold, he who has repented of his sins, the same is forgiven, and I, the Lord, remember them no more. By this ye may know if a man repenteth of his sins—behold, he will confess them and forsake them" (D&C 58:42–43). Remember, it is the plan of redemption that through the suffering Christ and the Atonement we can be forgiven.

Chapter 5

The ATONEMENT

THE ATONEMENT

To atone means to suffer for another or to make amends for another's sins. It is restitution for us and reconciles us to God. It expiates or compensates for everything within our own lives that is not right with Heavenly Father. It removes the effects of the Fall and provides the way for us to repent of our sins, including having our guilt swept away through faith in Jesus Christ. Christ's love for us was expressed through His Atonement: "He doeth not anything save it be for the benefit of the world; for he loveth the world, even that he layeth down his own life that he may draw all men unto him. Wherefore, he commandeth none that they shall not partake of his salvation" (2 Nephi 26:24). Remember, "Jesus saith unto him, I am the way, the truth, and the life: no man cometh unto the Father, but by me" (John 14:6).

The word *atonement*—or at-one-ment—means "to return to the presence of" or "be at one with." *At*—the place or condition of. *One*—being united with. *Ment*—The act of. The Atonement is literally the act of being united to the place or condition that we were at previously—in the presence of our Heavenly Father. Bringing about this oneness with the Father and the Son is fulfilled as we come back into Their presence. Does not our Savior's great intercessory prayer take on greater significance when we understand that the Atonement is the enabling power that brings oneness about? Being one with the Father and the Son on earth is to be one in purpose, cause, and action, all according to the will of God. We seek to please God our Father and do His will even as Christ did His will. We can receive an endowment of power in the Lord's holy house, feel His presence and glory, and enjoy the fulness of the Holy Ghost, thus being given power to go about doing good.

The Atonement covers us. The Lord's Atonement covers everything. It is infinite and eternal. In fact, the Hebrew word for atonement, kaphar, means to cover, to embrace, or to forgive. These words capture well the essence of the atoning sacrifice. The Atonement literally "covers" us. We are covered with a coat of skins, the robes of righteousness, even the garment of the holy priesthood. It covers our fallen state, our guilt and shame, as expressed in our nakedness: "Wherefore, we shall have a perfect knowledge of all our guilt, and our uncleanness, and our nakedness; and the righteous shall have a perfect knowledge of their enjoyment, and their righteousness, being clothed with purity, yea, even with the robe of righteousness" (2 Nephi 9:14). Nephi pled with the Lord, "O Lord, wilt thou encircle me around in the robe of thy righteousness! O Lord, wilt thou make a way for mine escape before mine enemies" (2 Nephi 4:33). John reiterates these precious truths when he recorded, "I counsel thee to buy of me gold tried in the fire, that thou mayest be rich; and white raiment, that thou mayest be clothed, and that the shame of thy nakedness do not appear; and anoint thine eyes with eyesalve, that thou mayest see" (Revelation 3:18). It is this garment, even the robe of righteousness, that we "have washed . . . and made . . . white in the blood of the Lamb" (Revelation 7:14). For us to be empowered by our robes of righteousness, we must receive Christ and His Atonement into our souls. Then we will be prepared to return to our Father's presence and receive all that He has. "Why is it that ye receive not the preaching of him whom God hath sent? If ye receive not this in your hearts, ye receive not me; and if ye receive not me, ye receive not him of whom I am sent to bear record; and for your sins ye have no cloak" (JST Matt. 3:34). This scripture is borne out in the oath and covenant of the priesthood: "And he that receiveth me receiveth my Father; And he that receiveth my Father receiveth my Father's kingdom; therefore all that my

Father hath shall be given unto him. And this is according to the oath and covenant which belongeth to the priesthood" (D&C 84:37–39). We must come unto Christ and receive Him as our Savior and Redeemer. Thus, He will cover us, and we will be perfected and empowered by Him. This is the very thing the Prophet Joseph prayed for in the dedicatory prayer of the Kirtland temple, "That our garments may be pure, that we may be clothed upon with robes of righteousness, with palms in our hands, and crowns of glory upon our heads, and reap eternal joy for all our sufferings" (D&C 109:76). Our Savior Jesus Christ is the author and finisher of our faith.

The Atonement embraces us. The Father and our Savior embrace us in the arms of Their love. "Be faithful and diligent in keeping the commandments of God, and I will encircle thee in the arms of my love" (D&C 6:20). Lehi described this great embrace: "But behold, the Lord hath redeemed my soul from hell; I have beheld his glory, and I am encircled about eternally in the arms of his love" (2 Nephi 1:15). Repeatedly the Lord speaks of this intimate relationship of being within His arms (see Alma 5:33; 34:16; Mormon 5:11; 6:17). This great expression of love is captured in a most thrilling manifestation of the Lord to Elder Melvin J. Ballard:

> As I entered the door, I saw, seated on a raised platform, the most glorious Being my eyes have ever beheld or that I ever conceived existed in all the eternal worlds. As I approached to be introduced, he arose and stepped towards me with extended arms, and he smiled as he softly spoke my name. If I shall live to be a million years old, I shall never forget that smile. He took me into his arms and kissed me, pressed me to his bosom, and blessed me, until the marrow of my bones seemed to melt! When he had finished, I fell at his feet, and, as I bathed them with my tears and kisses, I saw the prints of the nails in the feet of the Redeemer of the world. The feeling that I had in the presence of him who hath all things in his hands, to have his love, his affection, and his blessing was such that if I ever can receive that of which I had but a foretaste, I would give all that I am, all that I ever hope to be, to feel what I then felt! (quoted in Bryant S. Hinckley, *Sermons and Missionary Services of Melvin J. Ballard* [Salt Lake City: Deseret Book, 1949], 156)

And that is just how personal the Atonement can be for each of us. We, through the love of our Savior, can and will be embraced by Him and our Father.

The Atonement makes reconciliation for us. Our lives depend upon the infinite Atonement of our Savior. The Lord's Atonement includes His suffering in the Garden of Gethsemane, the shedding of His blood, the sacrificing of His life on Golgotha's hill, and the subsequent Resurrection from the grave (see Isaiah 53:3–12; Mosiah 3:5–11; Alma 7:10–13). The Greek word for Atonement refers to "reconciliation." We are indeed reconciled to God through Christ the Lord. The scriptures testify that if Christ had not atoned for our sins, nothing could satisfy the demands of justice, and man could never regain God's presence (see 2 Nephi 2; 9). Yes, the Atonement makes possible the forgiveness of sins, and thus we can become reconciled to God, being clean, pure, and holy. We are justified and sanctified through the Atonement and by the power of the Holy Ghost (see 3 Nephi 27:20).

The Atonement is infinite. It is the enabling power of all things, including forgiveness of sins, the restoration of all things, and even the resurrection of every living soul ever born upon the face of this earth. The word *infinite*, which describes the Atonement, means to exceed all, greater than all and more, or so large that there can be no assigned value for it. It exceeds all limits, for it is unlimited in its coverage of all of mankind's trials, tribulations, inflictions, and sins, including our fallen state. And because the Lord completed the infinite Atonement, He is able to succor us in all of our trials, tribulations, temptations, and afflictions. Yes, the Atonement is infinite because it covers and empowers everything (see 2 Nephi 9:7; 25:16; Alma 34:12). Oh, if we have eyes to see and a heart to feel, we will recognize the infinite power of the Atonement in every aspect of our lives. And we will be drawn to our Savior with overwhelming gratitude. We will see the Atonement and Christ the Lord in all of His goodness and mercy. We will begin to recognize that everything is the personification of Christ. Christ is indeed the Light and Life of the world. He redeems our souls. He is the *Light*! He is the Light of truth; the Light of the sun and the power thereof; the Light of the moon, the stars, and the earth; the

Light that enlightens our eyes and quickens our understanding. And He is the Light that proceedeth forth from the presence of God, which is in all things and giveth life to all things (see D&C 88:1–17). Incredibly amazing!

The infinite Atonement includes the infinite suffering and sacrificing of Christ when He took upon Himself the sins of the world—not human suffering, but only the suffering that a God could endure for the sins of His brothers and sisters, the sins of His covenant children. Only the infinite and an eternal Son of God could suffer enough to pay the debt for the sins of all mankind. "He suffereth the pains of all men, yea, the pains of every living creature, both men, women, and children, who belong to the family of Adam" (2 Nephi 9:21). He vicariously stood in for us to pay the debt. We cannot pay for our sins! Only God the Son, as the Savior of the world, could pay for our sins. Should we choose not to repent, we must "suffer" for our sins, because He has paid for our sins with this ultimate sacrifice through His atoning blood—the blood of the sinless, perfect Son of Almighty God.

Why is it then that some sins are unpardonable and do not qualify for the Atonement? What sin could be so unforgiveable and inexcusable? The scriptures teach us what the unpardonable sin is and why it is unforgiveable.

Jacob records the words of Sherem the anti-Christ: "And he said: I fear lest I have committed the unpardonable sin, for *I have lied unto God; for I denied the Christ*, and said that I believed the scriptures; and they truly testify of him. And because I have thus lied unto God I greatly fear lest my case shall be awful; but I confess unto God" (Jacob 7:19; emphasis added).

"For behold, if ye *deny the Holy Ghost when it once has had place in you, and ye know that ye deny it*, behold, this is a sin which is unpardonable; yea, and whosoever murdereth against the light and knowledge of God, it is not easy for him to obtain forgiveness; yea, I say unto you, my son, that it is not easy for him to obtain a forgiveness" (Alma 39:6; emphasis added).

"For it is impossible for those who were once enlightened, and *have tasted of the heavenly gift*, and were made partakers of the Holy Ghost, and have tasted *the good word of God, and the powers of the world to come, if they shall fall away*, to renew them again unto repentance; seeing *they crucify to themselves the Son of God afresh*, and put him to an open shame" (Hebrews 6:4–6; emphasis added).

"But the blasphemy against the Holy Ghost shall not be forgiven unto men. And whosoever speaketh a word against the Son of man, it shall be forgiven him: but *whosoever speaketh against the Holy Ghost, it shall not be forgiven him*, neither in this world, neither in the world to come" (Matthew 12:31–32; emphasis added).

"For if we *sin wilfully* after that *we have received the knowledge of the truth*, there remaineth no more sacrifice for sins" (Hebrews 10:26).

"But whoso breaketh this covenant after he hath received it, and altogether turneth therefrom, shall not have forgiveness of sins in this world nor in the world to come" (D&C 84:41).

"Thus saith the Lord concerning all those who know my power, and have been made partakers thereof, and suffered themselves through the power of the devil to be overcome, and to deny the truth and defy my power—They are they who are the sons of perdition, of whom I say that it had been better for them never to have been born; For they are vessels of wrath, doomed to suffer the wrath of God, with the devil and his angels in eternity; Concerning whom I have said there is no forgiveness in this world nor in the world to come—Having denied the Holy Spirit after having received it, and having denied the Only Begotten Son of the Father, having crucified him unto themselves and put him to an open shame" (D&C 76:31–35).

Those who have committed the unpardonable sin have

- Lied to God.
- Denied the Christ.
- Denied the Holy Ghost.
- Broken the covenants after they have received them (see D&C 84:41), for they crucify the Lord and put Him to open shame.
- Willfully blasphemed and spoken against the Holy Ghost.

As we look at all these scriptures and their salient points, we come to understand why it is an unpardonable sin. They choose willfully to *not accept or receive* the infinite sacrifice of the Atonement of Christ after having actually received the knowledge that it is true from the Father by the power of the Holy Ghost. They openly deny Christ by refusing to receive His infinite Atonement. And this is exactly what Lucifer did. He did willfully rebel against the truth after having been taught it by the Father. And he was denied a body. The word of God speaks likewise to the sons of perdition: "Of whom I say that it had been better for them never to have been born" (D&C 76:32). Surely in sorrow we weep, "for the heavens wept over him—he was Lucifer, a son of the morning" (D&C 76:26). And we weep for all who deny our beloved Savior, who gave His all for the children of God. I pray every day for those who struggle, in hope that they will come to realize the gravity of denying the Holy Ghost and His witness of Christ.

The Atonement is incomprehensible. We may know the *why* and the *what* of it, and even the *where* and the *when* of it, but we do not know the *how* of it—just like the *how* of all things done by the power of God. We do not understand His ways; His knowledge and wisdom we are woefully lacking. We are finite mortals with limited knowledge and comprehension. We simply cannot comprehend all the things of God (see Mosiah 4:9; Mormon 9:16). This lack of comprehension does not impede us from appreciating the Atonement or feeling great gratitude for the grace and goodness of our Father and our Savior. It is through faith in Jesus Christ that we come unto Christ and partake of His infinite Atonement—and this is comprehensible. We can come unto Christ and be perfected and complete in and through Him. He is *the Way*—the pathway to exaltation. He is *the Truth*—the word of God by which we must live. He is *the Life*—even eternal life (see John 14:6).

The infinite Atonement covers all time and space. It is retroactive from premortality to infinity. As King Benjamin taught, "And the Lord God hath sent his holy prophets among all the children of men, to declare these things to every kindred, nation, and tongue, that thereby whosoever should believe that Christ should come, the same might receive remission of their sins, and rejoice with exceedingly great joy, even as though he had already come among them" (Mosiah 3:13). "I say, that this is the man who receiveth salvation, through the atonement which was prepared from the foundation of the world for all mankind, which ever were since the fall of Adam, or who are, or who ever shall be, even unto the end of the world" (Mosiah 4:7). We can see that since the time of Adam and before Christ should come, the Atonement covered everyone and everything—but what about in our premortal lives? Was there agency? Did we exercise it? Was there sin? Was there righteousness and faithfulness?

Speaking of premortality, we were

> called and prepared from the foundation of the world according to the foreknowledge of God, on account of their exceeding faith and good works; in the first place being left to choose good or evil; therefore they having chosen good, and exercising exceedingly great faith, are called with a holy calling, yea, with that holy calling which was prepared with, and according to, a preparatory redemption for such.
>
> And thus they have been called to this holy calling on account of their faith, while others would reject the Spirit of God on account of the hardness of their hearts and blindness of their minds, while, if it had not been for this they might have had as great privilege as their brethren.
>
> Or in fine, in the first place they were on the same standing with their brethren; thus this holy calling being prepared from the foundation of the world for such as would not harden their hearts, being in and through the atonement of the Only Begotten Son, who was prepared. (Alma 13:3–5)

In our premortal lives

- We had agency, and we exercised it.
- We chose our Father's plan.
- We chose good over evil.
- Others chose to disobey and followed Lucifer.
- There were varying degrees of righteousness as we exercised faith.

- The Atonement was prepared and operating from the foundation of the world.

Yes, there were varying degrees of sin and righteousness in the spirit world prior to coming to the earth, and the Atonement was operating there, for "every spirit of man was innocent in the beginning; and God having redeemed man from the fall, men became again, in their infant state, innocent before God" (D&C 93:38; see also Moses 6:54). The Atonement is always operating, even as are all the eternal truths of God. "All truth is independent in that sphere in which God has placed it, to act for itself, as all intelligence also; otherwise there is no existence" (D&C 93:30). Truth is truth. Laws are laws. God is God. Edward L. Hart, in the inspiring hymn "Our Savior's Love," has written, "We love thy law; we will obey" ("Our Savior's Love," *Hymns*, no. 113). Our love of God was from the beginning.

THE ATONEMENT AND SYMBOLISM IN ALL THINGS

Symbolism is inherent in the gospel of Jesus Christ. We must learn to recognize it and begin to understand and appreciate the mysteries of God. Our Beloved Savior taught with symbolism through His parables, and in all of His teachings we see symbolic language. We can see symbolism in all the ordinances of the gospel, and especially in the temple. Symbolism is everywhere. We should seek to understand the symbols so we can better appreciate the truths taught within the symbol. Sometimes we are told, "Oh, don't worry about those symbols." We needn't worry about symbols, but we should do something about them so that we can understand and appreciate their deeper meaning and be uplifted and edified. Alonzo Gaskill, the brilliant Biblical and symbolic scholar, has suggested several things that can help us understand symbolism (see *The Lost Language of Symbolism* [Salt Lake City: Deseret Book, 2003], 19–22)..

1. "Rightly determine which elements of the verse under consideration are meant to be interpreted as symbols."

Do the words or the object make common sense? If so, it can be taken literally and applied to life. If the meaning seems obscured or beyond our present knowledge, it could be highly symbolic, like the imagery in the book of Revelation. This requires diligent effort and study over time (see Revelation 12:1–4; 13:1–2). There can always be additional meanings or explanations from other scriptures (see John 2:19, 21).

2. "Look beyond the symbol."

Always look for the setting and context in which the words were used. This becomes apparent in seeking to understand the parables. Symbols have denotations—their literal meaning—and connotations—what our mind associates with a symbol and the meaning the symbol stirs within us. This is exemplified time and again in the temple ceremonies. If we are watchful, attentive, and prayerful, we can come to understand the doctrines of the temple.

3. "Consider what the scriptures or modern prophets teach regarding the symbol."

The symbol may be explained within the same verse or the verses that follow. For example, we read an account of Nephi's brothers, stating, "What meaneth the rod of iron which our father saw, that led to the tree? And I said unto them that it was the word of God; and whoso would hearken unto the word of God, and would hold fast unto it, they would never perish; neither could the temptations and the fiery darts of the adversary overpower them unto blindness, to lead them away to destruction" (1 Nephi 15:23–24). Likewise, when the Prophet Joseph inquired concerning several scriptures in the book of Revelation, the Lord revealed to him the symbolic meanings (see D&C 77).

4. "Let the nature of the symbol help clarify its meaning."

As noted earlier in this chapter, the temple garment covers our nakedness. We can discern more about the meaning of the symbolism involved in this act by considering the nature of the garment. How does it "cover" us? Just what does it represent? As we answer these questions, we come to realize that when we understand a doctrine, we can better understand the symbol it represents. For example, we understand that the degrees of glory are symbolized by the glories of the sun, the moon and the stars; the nature of each of these things, and the degree of light each emits, helps us understand more about each degree of glory.

5. "Watch for consistency in use of particular symbols."

There is usually a consistency in the use of words and symbols, yet they often represent quite different things. Words like *water*, *serpent*, and *lion* connote different meanings, both good and bad, depending on the context in which those words occur.

6. "Study the meaning and origin of the idioms employed."

Symbols not to be taken literally are called *idioms*. Exodus 3:8 refers to a land "flowing with milk and honey," which refers to the land being fertile. Ezekiel 3:7 speaks of a "hard forehead," which means being stubborn.

7. "Balance the interpretation of symbols with an overall knowledge of gospel teachings."

All interpretations should be in harmony with the doctrines of the gospel and the teachings of our prophets.

8. "Use the footnotes, chapter headings, dictionary, and other study aids provided in the standard works of the Church."

Throughout the scriptures, footnotes are used to help us understand the word or phrase used. See also "Explanation Concerning Abbreviations" on the page facing Genesis 1 of your Bible. Footnotes, cross-references, and abbreviations are study aids to searching the scriptures. Chapter headings provide a concise summary for a chapter. Section headings in the Doctrine and Covenants provide background information on the setting for each revelation.

9. "Be attentive to linguistics."

Our scriptures are translations from Hebrew, Greek, and, in the case of the Book of Mormon, reformed Egyptian. When we understand the root meaning of words, we may better understand the English translation. Many words in the Book of Mormon reflect meanings common in the early nineteenth century, when that book of scripture was translated; and many words and phrases also occur in our English translation of the Bible. Dictionaries and lexicons (the vocabulary for a language or branch of knowledge) are of great assistance. This is why I use *Webster's Revised Unabridged Dictionary* (1828) when studying the Restoration scriptures.

These suggestions can be of great personal assistance as we seek to understand and appreciate symbolism in the scriptures and the temple. The scriptures themselves are full of symbolic words and other figurative representations, and there is symbolism in all the ordinances of the gospel. For example, every Sabbath day, we partake of the sacrament, symbolic emblems of the Lord's broken flesh and spilt blood. When we are buried in the waters of baptism, we are symbolically buried in death; when we rise out of the water, we are symbolically resurrected. As the Apostle Paul taught, "Therefore we are buried with him by baptism into death: that like as Christ was raised up from the dead by the glory of the father, even so we should also walk in newness of life" (Romans 6:4). Baptism is symbolic of the Atonement.

Consider these additional meanings in the ordinance of baptism, which introduces us into the Lord's Church:

- In baptism, we symbolically put on Christ (Galatians 3:27).
- Through immersing us in water, baptism symbolizes the washing away and the remission of sins (Acts 22:16; D&C 19:31).
- Baptism symbolizes our willingness to take upon us the name of the Lord Jesus Christ through following His example in being baptized (D&C 20:37).
- Baptism symbolizes that we have become sons and daughters of Christ through taking His name upon us (Mosiah 5:7).

Jesus explained to His chosen disciples that He used *parables*, which are short symbolic stories, "because it is given unto you to know the mysteries of the kingdom of heaven, but to them [the multitudes] it is not given" (Matthew 13:11). In other words, the Savior often cloaked His meaning in such stories so that only a certain number of His followers, or even some of His enemies, would grasp the symbolic meaning in those stories. This is another reason symbolism is used in much of the Lord's teachings in the temple and in the scriptures we use today as well.

King Benjamin, in gathering his people and urging them to renew their covenants, used the key words of symbolism: "And many *signs*, and *wonders*, and types, and *shadows* showed he unto them [the Israelites], concerning his [the Lord's] coming" (Mosiah 3:15; emphasis added). From these scriptures, we learn that the essence of the law of Moses, and *all* things from the beginning, *typify* (that is, symbolize or foreshadow) and bear record of the advent of the Lord and Savior Jesus Christ. Not only was this the way the Lord would teach ancient Israel and the Nephites, but it is also the way He teaches us today, since the Book of Mormon was directed specifically at the modern house of Israel.

Indeed, as the Book of Mormon prophet Jacob taught, "All things which have been given of God from the beginning of the world, unto man, are the typifying of him" (2 Nephi 11:4), that is, all things *prefigure* or *represent* Jesus Christ and His atoning sacrifice.

The Atonement was symbolized constantly from Adam down to Christ through sacrificial offerings:

> And he gave unto them commandments, that they should worship the Lord their God, and should offer the firstlings of their flocks, for an offering unto the Lord. And Adam was obedient unto the commandments of the Lord.
>
> And after many days an angel of the Lord appeared unto Adam, saying: *Why dost thou offer sacrifices unto the Lord? And Adam said unto him: I know not, save the Lord commanded me.*
>
> *And then the angel spake, saying: This thing is a similitude of the sacrifice of the Only Begotten of the Father, which is full of grace and truth.* Wherefore, thou shalt do all that thou doest in the name of the Son, and thou shalt repent and call upon God in the name of the Son forevermore. (Moses 5:5–8; emphasis added)

The Passover prefigured and symbolized the Atonement of Christ. The Passover began as a symbol to represent the empowering and saving capacity of the Atonement. It was an ordinance to be kept in the law of Moses. Moses pronounced the plague of death upon Egypt. All Israelite families were commanded to take a lamb without blemish, a male of the first year. This lamb was slain in the evening without breaking any bones, and its blood was to mark the two door posts and the upper door post. The Lord promised to *pass over* the homes and the plague would not be upon them. They were literally saved by the blood of the lamb (see Exodus 12; 1 Nephi 12:11; Alma 13:11; Mormon 9:6; Ether 13:10–11). Blood is symbolic as the base and center of life, for it "maketh for the atonement for the soul" (Leviticus 17:11). It gives vitality and power to life; therefore, the Israelites were forbidden to partake of blood (see verses 10–14).

After the Atonement of the Lord, the law of sacrifice was fulfilled and there was no more shedding of blood required. "And ye shall offer up unto me no more the shedding of blood; yea, your sacrifices and your burnt offerings shall be done away, for I will accept none of your sacrifices and your burnt offerings" (3 Nephi 9:19; see also Hebrews 10:12). Now the Lord required a sacrifice of a broken heart and a contrite spirit: "And ye shall offer for a sacrifice unto me a broken heart and a contrite spirit. And whoso cometh unto me with a broken heart and a contrite spirit, him will I baptize with fire and with the Holy Ghost, even as the Lamanites, because of their faith in me at the time of their conversion, were baptized with fire and with the Holy Ghost, and they knew it not" (3 Nephi 9:20).

The Passover and baptism are symbolic of the Atonement. In the ordinance of the sacrament, we partake in remembrance of the body of Christ and of His blood, which was shed for us. Thus the sacrament reflects both the Atonement and baptism symbolically. Many parables symbolize the Atonement.

The list of symbolic language used in the gospel and in the temple could go on and on; my purpose here is only to show that the gospel, the infinite Atonement of Christ, is rich in symbolism. We need to embrace it rather than shy away from it, especially as it pertains to the teachings of Christ and the ordinances of the gospel, including worshipping in the holy temples. All things in the temple are symbolic to one degree or another of the Atonement.

I, like many of you, once viewed tentatively the symbolism of the gospel ceremonies; I did not study them as I should have. I lacked in knowledge and understanding of their significant meaning and potential power. Now in my later years, especially as a temple worker and student of the parables, I am finding great joy in the study of gospel symbolism and its application to my life.

The Atonement is in everything—every doctrine and principle, every ordinance and covenant. I've found that it's not a matter of simply asking and receiving a revelation of meaning; we are to follow the counsel of the Lord to Oliver Cowdery when He said, "Behold, you have not understood; you have supposed that I would give it unto you, when you took no thought save it was to ask me. But, behold, I say unto you, that you must study it out in your mind; then you must ask me if it be right, and if it is right I will cause that your bosom shall burn within you; therefore, you shall feel that it is right" (D&C 9:7–8). If we look, we can see the Atonement and our Savior Jesus in all things. We must study, ponder, pray, and allow the Spirit to teach us eternal truths, for He is the witness of the Son, sent from the Father for that very purpose. We can make many applications to our lives, but remember all things speak of Christ and His Atonement. Look for the message of our Savior within symbolic language and other types of symbols. Everything is an appendage to Christ and His infinite and eternal Atonement.

THE ATONEMENT IN THE PARABLES

With careful and intimate study of the parables, we can see the symbolic representation of the plan of redemption, the Atonement, and gospel truths often unfold before our eyes. The Lord in Matthew, Mark, and Luke taught over twenty parables to teach His children the mysteries of the kingdom. "And he said, Unto you it is given to know the mysteries of the kingdom of God: but to others in parables; that seeing they might not see, and hearing they might not understand" (Luke 8:10). John W. Welch has a great, insightful mind and is a scholar of the scriptures. He discovered chiasms in the Book of Mormon. He has paid the price with research and prayer and has pondered much to understand the parables as well. Note his insights to the parable of the good Samaritan.

The Parable of the Good Samaritan

Brother Welch sets the context for the parable:

> One of the most influential stories told by Jesus Christ is the parable of the good Samaritan. Jesus recounted this parable to a man who had asked, "Master, what shall I do to inherit eternal life?" Jesus responded by asking, "What is written in the law?"
>
> The man answered, referring to Deuteronomy 6:5 and Leviticus 19:18, "Thou shalt love the Lord thy God with all thy heart . . . and thy neighbour as thyself."
>
> When Jesus promised, "This do, and thou shalt live," the man challengingly replied, "And who is my neighbour?" In answer to this man's questions, Jesus told the parable of the good Samaritan. (John W. Welch, "The Good Samaritan: Forgotten Symbols" *Ensign*, February 2007)

The scriptures testify of Jesus the Christ, the plan of redemption, and the goodness of God. The parable of the good Samaritan is no different; it teaches of the plan of salvation, the love of God as expressed through His Beloved Son's Atonement, and our promised blessings of eternal life. The story has many sweet and tender applications, but as you shall see, there is a depth to this story that speaks symbolically of all of us coming down to earth and how we can be saved through the grace and goodness of God and our Savior. These connotations within the story become evident through the light of revelation as explained by Brother Welch. We read, a certain man (you and I) went down (planned a journey knowing the difficulty) from Jerusalem (heaven) to Jericho (earth), and he fell (our fallen state) among thieves (the devil and his minions) who stripped him of his raiment (stripped off our covering or garment) and wounded him (tribulations, trials, and sins of life) and departed, leaving him half dead (we suffered the first death, mortality and separation from God). By chance a Jewish priest and later a Levite priest both passed by (representing the law of Moses and possibly the Old Testament prophets, neither of which had the power to save). But a certain Samaritan (the representation of Christ, as He was "despised and rejected of men" like unto the Samaritans [see Isaiah 53:3]) as he journeyed (apparently He was prepared to help with all the material he had brought with him) saw him and had compassion (this word speaks of the pure love of Christ) on him and bound up his wounds (with love and

His word, which leads to righteousness) and pouring oil (to sooth his wounds and to anoint and heal the sick) and wine (to cleanse the wound; with the word of God and the blood of Christ, we can be healed) and set him on his own beast (bearing all of our trials and afflictions [see Alma 7:11–12]) and brought him to an inn (even the Church of Christ). And on the morrow, he departed (Christ having been raised from the dead, the disciples carried on) and gave what was necessary to the host to care for his needs (the leaders of the Church). And when the Lord comes again (the Second Coming of the Savior), he will repay him (all the costs will be paid), for the innkeeper was the servant of the Lord.

The applications are many, for we can identify with each character and the principles being taught by the Lord. The interpretation seems to teach, like so many of our symbols, the goodness of God and the power of the infinite Atonement of Christ. The lesson is clear: we need to be like Christ. "Then said Jesus unto him, Go, and do thou likewise" (Luke 10:37). Now go to LDS.org to the February 1997 *Ensign* and read "The Good Samaritan: Forgotten Symbols" by John W. Welch.

The Parable of the Prodigal Son—Luke 15:11-32

This is a parable of the gospel of Jesus Christ and the enabling power of His infinite Atonement. We are all lost and fallen and need to "find" our way back to Christ. This parable touches many aspects of the basic concepts of the gospel—temptation, agency, sin, repentance, and forgiveness. It has been said, after all is said and done, all we need to do is repent and forgive others. In the parable, the father represents our Heavenly Father, and the sons represent us as we struggle in life with different challenges. Often these challenges in our lives come from our poor decisions and making wrong choices when we respond to different situations. And we will learn again that agency is supreme!

As the parable begins, the younger son seeks his inheritance early, which would have been half of his elder brother's portion (see Deuteronomy 21:15–17). Seeking an early inheritance was not looked upon with much favor, and even worse, he went to a far country, away from his family and probably his God and "wasted" it with "riotous" living. He was indeed a profligate son who dishonored his father and mother with his life. When he had spent all, there was a famine in the land, and he stood in need of both physical and spiritual food. What could he do? How would he survive? What would we do to survive?

He took work from a Gentile to feed swine. He being an Israelite, this was not proper, as the swine was an unclean animal in the law of Moses (see Leviticus 11:7). Therefore, he became ceremonially unclean. In all of this, he was the lowest kind of servant, and hungry at that. He ate whatever he could get, which ended up being the pigs' food. This was not enough, and so being very hungry, he came to himself (he finally was humbled and realized where he was and where there was hope) and returned to his father. He turned around. He started the process of repentance.

Hope is in Christ the Lord, who is mighty to save through His infinite Atonement. Here the symbolism of a loving father and Heavenly Father is demonstrated in how only our Father loves. "But when he was yet a great way off, his father saw him, and had compassion, and ran, and fell on his neck, and kissed him" (Luke 15:20). His father—ever loving, praying, and watching for his son with compassion (the love of Christ)—runs to him. God the Father's love is expressed through His Beloved Son and is called the love of God. This expression of love was forgiveness and reconciliation. He "fell on his neck and kissed him." This is the expression of love and forgiveness Esau gave to Jacob (see Genesis 33:4). The prodigal confessed his sins and sought simply to be a servant: "Father, I have sinned against heaven, and before thee, and am no more worthy to be called thy son: make me as one of thy hired servants" (Luke 15:18–19). His father (and our Father) offered mercy. Though undeserved, we gratefully receive, as did the prodigal. The best robe, the robe of his father, was placed upon him. Symbolically, the robe has many connotations, for we are covered by the Atonement with the robe of righteousness. The son came home, and the power of the Atonement was placed upon him when he came again to Christ, who has the power through His Father to make him whole, clean, and pure. The robe also protected him from temptation and evil (see Isaiah 61:10; 2 Nephi

4:33; Revelation 3:18). A ring was put on his hand as a sign of his place within the family and the restoration of his authority. And being no longer a slave of a Gentile, he had shoes upon his feet. The fatted calf was slain, and they did eat and were merry, or rather they "rejoiced" in the return of the prodigal. Why? "For this my son was dead, and is alive again; he was lost, and is found" (Luke 15:24). And they did rejoice! The prodigal had separated himself from God and his family and was lost spiritually and physically, but now he was found. The joy of finding the lost is significant in the parables of the lost coin and the lost sheep. There is joy in finding and the returning of the "lost."

Now to a sad yet enlightening portion of the parable. The elder son, who was faithful and dependable in all things, did not feel the joy of the returning of his younger brother. He came upon the party not knowing what was going on. The servant made him aware of his younger brother's return and that a great feast was being given in his honor. The elder brother was hurt and angry and would not go into the gathering, so his loving father came out to entreat him. Oh, the plight of parenthood. The devoted son explains his pain and hurt feelings to his father. "Lo, these many years do I serve thee, neither transgressed I at any time thy commandment: and yet thou never gavest me a kid, that I might make merry with my friends" (Luke 15:29). In this claim of the elder son, we see character flaws we can all relate to. He was lacking in love. He was jealous. He was selfish, prideful, and demanding. He wanted more. He couldn't find joy in the joy of others. The universal sin of pride had raised its ugly head and the elder son had sinned. Oh, the sorrow of it all. The elder son continues in his tirade, questioning his father's wisdom and judgment in rewarding the younger son for misdeeds (no, for repentance). He becomes full of bitterness, resentment, and envy. Remember, the son had been faithful to his father, but he was still human, and he too was struggling with "becoming." Then his loving father said, "Son, thou art ever with me, and all that I have is thine. It was meet that we should make merry, and be glad: for this thy brother was dead, and is alive again; and was lost, and is found" (Luke

15:31–32). The father reminds him that all he has is his but to please find joy in his brother who was lost, for he is found.

This parable, like all parables, has an interpretation with many applications to life. There are hidden truths that can bring depth to our understanding and wisdom to our souls as we understand and appreciate these transcending truths. How do we relate to and interact with our father and Heavenly Father? And how do we deal with our brothers and sisters? How do we react when we take offense? Do we seek to understand before we judge? Many questions could be asked that can and will reveal doctrines and principles by which we should live.

Symbolically, we see the father as our Heavenly Father, ever the perfect, compassionate, loving Father, who cares for all of His children and seeks to express His love and mercy to all of His children all of the time. Remember in the parable of the laborers in the vineyard, the laborers were all given equal pay, regardless of the time spent working. Eternal life is the reward of the faithful, for which we should find joy. Do we not want all of Father's children to receive their Father's love? Surely we wouldn't be selfish being the only ones who would want to be saved. It would be quite lonely. For those who want more because they have been faithful, remember that the Lord has said, "And if a person gains more knowledge and intelligence in this life through his diligence and obedience than another, he will have so much the advantage in the world to come" (D&C 130:19). Father is always fair! We need to find joy in others like Alma did: "But I do not joy in my own success alone, but my joy is more full because of the success of my brethren, who have been up to the land of Nephi" (Alma 29:14). Isn't Alma wonderful and charitable with no envy or jealousy in his heart? Father always seeks to express love toward His children, and His work and His glory is in us. He cares about us. In the parable, He is never defensive or offended by our weaknesses. He always extends His love and gentle kindness and seeks for us to love one another. "Beloved, let us love one another: for love is of God; and every one that loveth is born of God, and knoweth God. He that loveth not knoweth not God; for God is love" (1 John 4:7–8). We are as Lehi described: "But behold, the Lord hath redeemed my soul from hell; I have beheld his glory, and I am encircled about eternally in the arms of his love" (2 Nephi 1:15). The Lord is always helping His children who are in a "lost and fallen state." This application of the parable we can all relate to, for are we not all prodigal? Have we not all sinned to one degree or another? Do we not all need the grace of God, which we do not merit or deserve? We all need the loving kindness and tender mercy of our Father and His Beloved Son, for we are to one degree or another like the younger and elder brothers who were weak and needed help from a loving Heavenly Father. We need the grace of God and the Son at all times and in all ways so that we can be empowered to go about doing good.

As we seek to understand and appreciate the parables of our Savior, the Bible Dictionary gives us some great counsel. Here are some sound principles to better understand and appreciate the parables:

> Interpretation of parables. It is important to distinguish between the interpretation of a parable and the application of a parable. The only true interpretation is the meaning the parable conveyed, or was meant to convey, when first spoken. The application of a parable may vary in every age and circumstance. But if the original meaning is to be grasped, it is important to consider its context and setting. The thought to which it is linked, the connection in which it is placed, the persons to whom it is addressed, all give the clue to the right interpretation. Other rules of interpretation are: (a) Do not force a meaning on subordinate incidents. (b) Do not regard as parallel parables that are connected by superficial likeness of imagery. (c) Bear in mind that the same illustration does not always have the same significance - leaven, e.g., signifies a principle of good as well as a principle of evil. (d) Remember that the comparison in a parable is not complete, does not touch at every point. Thus, the characters of the unjust judge or the unjust steward or the nobleman who went into a far country—possibly referring to the infamous Archelaus—do not concern the interpretation of the parable. The parable draws a picture of life as it is, not as it ought to be, and compares certain points in this picture with heavenly doctrine. (e) Observe the proper proportions of a parable, and do not make the episode more prominent than the main line of teaching. (Bible Dictionary, "Parables")

THE ATONEMENT, THE GRACE OF GOD, AND GOOD WORKS

Grace is a demonstration of the love of God and His divine gifts or blessings He has given to His children. It is a display of His power and goodness. We see and feel this grace through the gift of His Son's infinite Atonement. The grace of God and the Atonement cannot be separated. The grace of God is exemplified by His expressions of loving kindness, benevolence, tender mercies, and everything He has bestowed upon us. We, though unworthy, are totally dependent upon the grace of God, because He gave His Only Begotten Son to atone for our sins. This act of grace, when we receive it and act upon it, becomes the empowerment and the fruit of our lives. We cannot, I repeat, cannot qualify for the blessings of God without the Atonement of His Beloved Son. We are saved by grace: "But we believe that through the grace of the Lord Jesus Christ we shall be saved, even as they" (Acts 15:11). The grace of God is sufficient for us when we receive His grace in coming unto Christ. "Yea, come unto Christ, and be perfected in him, and deny yourselves of all ungodliness; and if ye shall deny yourselves of all ungodliness, and love God with all your might, mind and strength, then is his grace sufficient for you, that by his grace ye may be perfect in Christ; and if by the grace of God ye are perfect in Christ, ye can in nowise deny the power of God" (Moroni 10:32). It is through this grace that we are enabled and empowered by the Atonement to take upon ourselves His nature, even the divine nature of Christ. We become like Him. We do the things He would do. You see, we are blessed, exalted, and become not of ourselves because in His grace, our natures are changed. Good works is a fruit of the empowerment of Christ and being endowed with power and the Holy Ghost. As Alma taught, "And see that ye have faith, hope, and charity, and then ye will always abound in good works" (Alma 7:24). As we repent and apply the Atonement of Christ to our lives we will "be brought unto repentance and good works, that they [we] might be restored unto grace for grace, according to their [our] works" (Helaman 12:24). To take full advantage of this transcending gift, we must receive the gift into our souls. "For what doth it profit a man if a gift is bestowed upon him, and he receive not the gift? Behold, he rejoices not in that which is given unto him, neither rejoices in him who is the giver of the gift" (D&C 88:33). Receiving is actually obtaining the gift. It in this case becomes part of you.

Remember, we do not earn grace. We do not merit it. The fruits of us receiving the grace of God through Christ's atoning sacrifice are expressed in our righteousness. We become, and thus we are what we are through Christ the Lord. "For by grace are ye saved through faith; *and that not of yourselves: it is the gift of God*: not of works, lest any man should boast. *For we are his workmanship, created in Christ Jesus unto good works, which God hath before ordained that we should walk in them*" (Ephesians 2:8–10; emphasis added). These quintessential verses describe perfectly how grace operates and how our works follow when we receive grace into our lives. Sometimes we feel like we work out our own salvation; note how Paul helps us understand how God works within us: "Wherefore, my beloved, as ye have always obeyed, not as in my presence only, but now much more in my absence, work out your own salvation with fear and trembling. *For it is God which worketh in you both to will and to do of his good pleasure*" (Philippians 2:12–13; emphasis added). This was exemplified through Christ when He was anointed by His Father. Note how He went about doing good: "How God anointed Jesus of Nazareth with the Holy Ghost and with power: who went about doing good, and healing all that were oppressed of the devil; *for God was with him*" (Acts 10:38; emphasis added). God was with Him. God is with us by the power of the Holy Ghost. The good comes from God (see Omni 1:25; Moroni 7:12–13). These scriptures surely demonstrate that our works follow our faith and conversion to Christ and that the good we do comes from God and the power He puts into us.

The Lord has said, "But he that believeth these things which I have spoken, him will I visit with the manifestations of my Spirit, and he shall know and bear record. For because of my Spirit he shall know that these things are true; for it persuadeth men to do good" (Ether 4:11). The Spirit beareth witness to things that are true, and you will have a desire to do good. Therefore we need to "trust in that Spirit which leadeth to do good" (D&C 11:12).

Moroni records, "And whatsoever thing is good is just and true; wherefore, nothing that is good denieth the Christ, but acknowledgeth that he is" (Moroni 10:6). All good comes from God. All truth persuades us to come unto Christ and go about doing good.

As we contemplate the grace of God, we must act upon it. It is a gift of God that is freely given to all, and the resurrection will come upon all as a gift of God. To receive His grace through the Atonement of Christ totally, we must act. We must receive the gift through our sacrifice and faith unto repentance, and then the fulness of the Atonement and its exalting powers will exalt us. This mercy and grace as given from the Lord is totally efficacious in our lives when we accept our Savior and His infinite Atonement, repent, and come unto Him. "He is merciful unto the children of men, and that he has all power to save every man that believeth on his name and bringeth forth fruit meet for repentance" (Alma 12:15). We are never righteous enough to merit the gift, but we can accept it as we act upon it in faith, and then all the facets and blessings associated with the Atonement can be ours. Then we will be judged according to our works and the desires of our hearts. Remember that our works are empowered by the Atonement of God, for all good comes from God, and the desires of our hearts in righteousness are fueled by the love of God (the atoning sacrifice, the fruit of the tree) and the pure love of Christ. You see, we are forever indebted to our Savior and our Father, for we were and are Their workmanship to become like Them.

To work out our salvation does not mean that *we work it out* or earn it, but rather it means we come to the Lord with all our hearts (we accept His infinite Atonement), and then we are empowered to work it out through our faithfulness (see Mormon 9:27). We are saved by the grace of God, and we are judged by our works and the desires of our hearts (see Alma 41:3; D&C 137:9). We are motivated by our love of and for God and by gratitude, for His goodness becomes our motivation. The commandments are not a check-off list of things to do, but rather they become the joy of our expression for the love of God and the empowerment of the Atonement and grace of God in our lives. It simply is the *right* and *natural* thing to do. Not only have we obtained a hope in Christ, but Christ is also in and through us, empowering us to do good as all good comes from God. He becomes our strength, "for in his strength I can do all things" (Alma 26:12). He is our strength and our power.

Amulek in Alma 34 taught the struggling Saints about the coming of Christ, that the word is in Christ unto salvation, that redemption cometh through the Son of God, that He would atone for our sins, and that if no Atonement had been made, we being fallen must perish. He continued teaching that it was expedient for a great and last sacrifice to be made, and thus the law of Moses would be fulfilled. He then teaches how those who receive the Atonement exercise faith unto repentance, and those who do not receive the grace of God through the Atonement are exposed to the whole law and the demands of justice. That is how we accept the great gift of the Atonement—we exercise faith unto repentance and begin to call upon God, that He would have mercy upon us. Then Amulek exhorts them to pray, repent, and prepare to meet God. He reminds them, "And now, *my beloved brethren, I desire that ye should remember these things* [all the things mentioned above in this paragraph], and that ye should work out your salvation with fear before God, and that ye should no more deny the coming of Christ" (Alma 34:37). When we remember all that Amulek taught, including the plan of redemption and the Atonement, we can in the strength of the Lord faithfully receive and accept the Atonement. We are empowered by the Lord to act, as we will work out our salvation through Christ the Lord. The Lord knows it is by grace we are saved and there are no exceptions. We cannot do enough to merit all our blessings, but we *must* receive His grace so it can empower us to do good. Saved by grace—judged by our works.

THE ATONEMENT IS THE ONLY WAY TO OUR REDEMPTION

Redemption is the act of purchasing our souls from a lost and fallen state and from our sins. We are procured from the grasp of that awful monster death and hell. The ransom has paid for all our debts and wrongdoings. The plan of redemption is where the Lord, "having ascended into heaven, having the bowels of mercy; being filled with compassion towards the children of men; standing betwixt them and justice; having broken the bands of death, [has] taken upon himself their iniquity and their transgressions, having redeemed them, and satisfied the demands of justice" (Mosiah 15:9). And the mercy of the Lord is displayed, and our acceptance of the Atonement is made evident through our faith unto repentance. "And thus mercy can satisfy the demands of justice, and encircles them in the arms of safety, while he that exercises no faith unto repentance is exposed to the whole law of the demands of justice; therefore only unto him that has faith unto repentance is brought about the great and eternal plan of redemption" (Alma 34:16).

The Lord has admonished us to live by every word that proceedeth forth from the mouth of God. Why? Because this is where the eternal truths are found that should direct our lives. Our bodies live on proteins, carbohydrates, and fats. When we go out to eat, sometimes it is simply to get full, and other times we go out to not only eat but also enjoy the ambiance of the restaurant and have an enjoyable evening. We savor every bite. Tonight while I write, I am thinking differently because I have read countless numbers of scriptures about our beloved Savior. These I call the spiritually enticing food for the soul. Consider each one and ponder upon the goodness of the Lord, His infinite Atonement, and how it affects your redemption.

Paul has stated, "For all have sinned, and come short of the glory of God; being justified freely by his grace through the redemption that is in Christ Jesus" (Romans 3:23–24). It is interesting that in the following verses we learn our propitiation, the conciliation and appeasement for our sins, is made possible though our faith in the atoning blood of Christ. We are justified through our faith. The just shall live by faith. Faith is necessary to please God and is the act by which we accept and receive the gift of the Atonement. The receiver of the gift must take this gift into His soul, for the gift is concerning His soul and cannot be accepted unless acted upon. We come unto Christ and partake of the goodness of God, the Atonement of His Beloved Son.

Again Paul reminds us, "In whom we have redemption through his blood, even the forgiveness of sins" (Colossians 1:14; see also Ephesians 1:7). In the verses prior to verse 14, they were praying that we would be filled with knowledge, wisdom, and spiritual understanding, and that they would walk worthy of the Lord, pleasing and being fruitful in good works and increasing in the knowledge of God. We can be strengthened according to His power and give thanks to the Father, for we can be partakers of the inheritance of the Saints being delivered from the power of darkness into the kingdom of our Savior *and then we have redemption through His blood.*

The writer of Hebrews has taught, "Neither by the blood of goats and calves, but by his own blood he entered in once into the holy place, having obtained eternal redemption for us" (Hebrews 9:12). In the Mosaic law, the high priest would enter the Holy of Holies yearly on the day of Atonement to offer a sacrifice symbolic of the Atonement of Christ and the redemption of all mankind. This was no longer the case. The Lord entered once into the press of Gethsemane and at the cross on Golgotha's hill and came forth from the Garden Tomb as He completed the Atonement and fulfilled the plan of redemption. Our Savior had rent the veil: "Jesus, when he had cried again with a loud voice, yielded up the ghost. And, behold, the veil of the temple was rent in twain from the top to the bottom; and the earth did quake, and the rocks rent; and the graves were opened; and many bodies of the saints which slept arose" (Matthew 27:50–52).

Lehi, when he taught and blessed his sons, explained, "Wherefore, redemption cometh in and through the Holy Messiah; for he is full of grace and truth. Behold, he offereth himself a sacrifice for sin, to answer the ends of the law, *unto all those who have a broken heart and a contrite spirit; and unto none else can the ends of the law be answered*" (2 Nephi 2:6–7; emphasis added). When we sacrifice with a broken heart and contrite spirit, we show our acceptance of the infinite Atonement. "And thus mercy can satisfy the demands of justice, and encircles them in the arms of safety, *while he that exercises no faith unto repentance is exposed to the whole law of the demands of justice; therefore only unto him that has faith unto repentance is brought about the great and eternal plan of redemption*" (Alma 34:16; emphasis added).

Abinadi sought to teach the rebellious King Noah and his priests: "And now, did they understand law? I say unto you, Nay, they did not all understand the law; and this because of the hardness of their hearts; for they understood not that there could not any man be saved except it were through the redemption of God" (Mosiah 13:32). To live the law, we must know of the law, understand and appreciate the law, and take the law into our hearts because we love His law, and then we will live the law. Live to learn, and learn to love, and then we will love to live the laws of God.

Abinadi continues to plead: "For were it not for the redemption which he hath made for his people, which was prepared from the foundation of the world, I say unto you, were it not for this, all mankind must have perished" (Mosiah 15:19; see also Alma 12:25). Abinadi was doing everything he could to bring wicked King Noah and his nefarious priests to repentance. He painted the picture of their need to be redeemed and that they would perish without the redemption of the Lord from chapter 14 to 16. They had ripened in iniquity, the Holy Spirit had no place in them, and thus they refused Christ's Atonement and would perish.

Alma taught that "God did call on men, in the name of his Son, (this being the plan of redemption which was laid) saying: If ye will repent, and harden not your hearts, then will I have mercy upon you, through mine Only Begotten Son" (Alma 12:33; see also Alma 18:39).

Aaron sought to teach the Amalekites: "There could be no redemption for mankind save it were through the death and sufferings of Christ, and the atonement of his blood" (Alma 21:9; see also 34:7, 16, 31; 42:11, 13, 26; 3 Nephi 9:17, 21; Mormon 9:12–13). The mercy of God is given through His Son's Atonement to those who repent. Repent, repent, repent—the most preached of all doctrines of the kingdom of God. Repent and come unto Christ that "your sins may be blotted out, when the times of refreshing shall come from the presence of the Lord" (Acts 3:19). The Lord really wants us to change, and we can as we choose to change through faith unto repentance.

The transcending truths taught in these scriptures teach us concerning the redemption of all mankind. There is no other way by which we can be redeemed, for this is the plan of God the Father. God our Father has decreed that redemption through Christ the Lord was the plan from the beginning. Mormon has recorded, "For he [Ammon] expounded unto them [King Lamoni] the plan of redemption, which was prepared from the foundation of the world; and he also made known unto them concerning the coming of Christ, and all the works of the Lord did he make known unto them" (Alma 18:39). Redemption is only through His Beloved Son, who suffered, sacrificed, and died so that we might live. We can appreciate this great blessing and be filled with gratitude, although we may have difficulty comprehending the nature of this law and the intimate workings of it. We are totally indebted to Christ and His Atonement. There is no hope without it. We perish without Christ.

When we discuss these sobering doctrines, sometimes we don't feel or realize the magnitude of the situation. This surely pleases the devil and the wicked who would say, "Eat, drink, and be merry; nevertheless, fear God—he will justify in committing a little sin; yea, lie a little, take the advantage of one because of his words, dig a pit for thy neighbor; there is no harm in this; and do all these things, for tomorrow we die; and if it so be that we are guilty, God will beat us with a few stripes, and at last we shall be saved in the kingdom of God" (2 Nephi 28:8). When we read and feast upon the scriptures with intensity, we are more likely to be moved by the doctrines being taught. The doctrine shall distill upon our souls: "My doctrine shall drop as the rain, my speech shall distil as the dew, as the small rain upon the tender herb, and as the showers upon the grass" (Deuteronomy 32:2). Because the people are "full of charity towards all men, and to the household of faith, and let virtue garnish thy thoughts unceasingly; then shall thy confidence wax strong in the presence of God; and the doctrine of the priesthood shall distil upon thy soul as the dews from heaven" (D&C 121:45). And if not, we will simply read them and move on, having missed the tender moment of the empowering word of God. I have witnessed both scenarios in my own life—being touched to tears and simply reading on. Feasting upon the words of eternal life is feasting upon the love of God—the plan of redemption. And gratitude and thanksgiving will fill our souls with the love of God.

THE ATONEMENT AND THE TEMPLE

The Atonement is inseparably connected to all the ordinances and covenants of the gospel and is especially evident in the temple. The Atonement and the full endowment are uniquely related in that the Atonement, as mentioned earlier, is the act of bringing us back into the presence of the Father, while the endowment ceremony is the symbolic and ritual presentation that brings us back into the presence of the Father through the ordinances and covenants administered by the greater priesthood. The prophet Brigham Young made this abundantly clear when he defined the endowment: "Your *endowment* is, to receive all those ordinances in the house of the Lord, which are necessary for you, after you have departed this life, *to enable you to walk back to the presence of the Father*" (quoted in John A. Widstoe, *Discourses of Brigham Young* [Salt Lake City: Deseret Book, 1941], 416; emphasis added). The Atonement is the enabling power of the greater priesthood: "And this greater priesthood administereth the gospel and holdeth the key of the mysteries of the kingdom, even the key of the knowledge of God. Therefore, in the ordinances thereof, the power of godliness is manifest. And without the ordinances thereof, and the authority of the priesthood, the power of godliness is not manifest unto men in the flesh; For without this no man can see the face of God, even the Father, and live" (D&C 84:19–22). This scripture describes receiving all of the ordinances and covenants associated with endowment and sealing ordinances in the temple that qualify us to return to the presence of our Father. Then the Father can give us all that He has.

The endowment is a gift from God. It clothes us, empowers us, and provides a multiplicity of gifts when we receive the ordinances and covenants associated with it. Through the keys of this greater priesthood, we can come to the knowledge of the mysteries of the kingdom, the knowledge of God, and have the power of godliness manifested unto us. We become endowed with power and the Holy Ghost, even like unto our Savior Jesus Christ. For us to be able to do all things and withstand all the fiery darts of the adversary, we need to be endowed with this power. The risen Lord gave explicit instructions to His disciples concerning their temple blessings: "And, behold, I send the promise of my Father upon you: but tarry ye in the city of Jerusalem, until ye be endued with power from on high" (Luke 24:49). The results of this were immediate as they were "continually in the temple, praising and blessing God" (Luke 24:53). These same instructions were given to the disciples in this dispensation: "Yea, verily I say unto you, I gave unto you a commandment that you should build a house, in the which house I design to endow those whom I have chosen with power from on high; for this is the promise of the Father unto you; therefore I command you to tarry, even as mine apostles at Jerusalem" (D&C 95:8–9). The Lord continues, "For behold, I have prepared a great endowment and blessing to be poured out upon them, inasmuch as they are faithful and continue in humility before me. Therefore it is expedient in me that mine elders should wait for a little season, for the redemption of Zion" (D&C 105:12–13). And even today, the Lord's anointed servants are endowed with power as they go forth preaching the gospel to every nation, kindred, tongue, and people. Without the enabling power of the Lord through His infinite Atonement and receiving the empowerment through the greater priesthood, we would not be able to do all that is required of us to serve the Lord.

THE ATONEMENT AND THE LAWS OF OPPOSITION, TEMPTATION, AND AGENCY

The three great pillars of the perfect plan of God are the Creation, the Fall, and the infinite Atonement. They are all intimately connected with each other and the plan of exaltation. There are three doctrines in mortality we need to come to understand and appreciate in regard to our making choices—opposition, temptation, and agency. They too are intimately connected with each other and are part of the plan of exaltation. Always remember that of the three, agency is supreme—you have the power to choose your destiny. You are responsible and accountable.

As we discuss each one individually, ponder on how the Atonement affects each one and how the Lord can help and strengthen us through the Atonement. Alma has expressed how the Lord through His suffering and sacrificing would know how to help us in all of our opposition, adversity, and temptations and how to strengthen us to use our agency in righteousness.

The law of opposition requires that there be polarizing forces at play in our world. It is ordained of God and is part of the perfect plan. Father Lehi has made it clear that opposition is necessary for all aspects of life: "For it must needs be, that there is an opposition in all things. If not so, my firstborn in the wilderness, righteousness could not be brought to pass, neither wickedness, neither holiness nor misery, neither good nor bad. Wherefore, all things must needs be a compound in one; wherefore, if it should be one body it must needs remain as dead, having no life neither death, nor corruption nor incorruption, happiness nor misery, neither sense nor insensibility" (2 Nephi 2:11). As we shall see, the Lord will help us in all the opposition we face, our adversities, our trials, and our tribulations.

> And he shall go forth, suffering pains and afflictions and temptations of every kind; and this that the word might be fulfilled which saith he will take upon him the pains and the sicknesses of his people. And he will take upon him death, that he may loose the bands of death which bind his people; and he will take upon him their infirmities, that his bowels may be filled with mercy, according to the flesh, that he may know according to the flesh how to succor his people according to their infirmities. (Alma 7:11–12)

The Lord will helps us in every form of adversity: "All intelligent beings who are crowned with crowns of glory, immortality, and eternal lives must pass through every ordeal appointed for intelligent beings to pass through, to gain their glory and exaltation. Every calamity that can come upon mortal beings will be suffered . . . to prepare them to enjoy the presence of the Lord. . . .

Every trial and experience you have passed through is necessary for your salvation" (*Teachings of Presidents of the Church: Brigham Young* [Salt Lake City: The Church of Jesus Christ of Latter-day Saints, 1997], 261–62). Not only is it necessary for our salvation as a reward, it is necessary for us to grow line upon line and precept by precept. Each trial we face comes with a blessings of accomplishment.

Temptation is always present in varying degrees in our lives. We must be enticed by the good and the bad. "And it must needs be that the devil should tempt the children of men, or they could not be agents unto themselves; for if they never should have bitter they could not know the sweet" (D&C 29:39). The question is, will we yield to temptation? What can we do to overcome temptation? We can pray. We pray not to yield to temptation (see 3 Nephi 18:18). And this is in the name of Jesus Christ. The enabling power of the Atonement will help us not to yield to temptation.

We can and should put on the armor of God (see Ephesians 6:11–18; D&C 27:15–18). The armor will cover the most vulnerable parts of our body, which are susceptible to the powers of darkness and evil.

Our loins girded with truth, thus covering our virtue—Christ is the way, the truth, and the life. Truth is the word. We are sanctified by truth. The truth can make us free.

The breastplate of righteousness covering the heart—It is from the heart that flows all of our affection, decisions, conduct, and actions. In righteousness, we will not yield to temptation (see Alma 11:23). We choose righteousness by the power of the Holy Ghost, which our Father has given us because we believe in Christ.

Our feet shod with the preparation of the gospel of peace—We are founded and rooted to the knowledge of the gospel, the knowledge of which will provide for us a sure foundation: "My sons, remember, remember that it is upon the rock of our Redeemer, who is Christ, the Son of God, that ye must build your foundation; that when the devil shall send forth his mighty winds, yea, his shafts in the whirlwind, yea, when all his hail and his mighty storm shall beat upon you, it shall have no power over you to drag you down to the gulf of misery and endless wo, because of the rock upon which ye are built, which is a sure foundation, a foundation whereon if men build they cannot fall" (Helaman 5:12). We will stand firm and tall on the foundation of Christ.

The shield of faith—Faith in Jesus Christ is our power. We can do all things that are expedient in the Lord by faith (see Moroni 10:23).

The helmet of salvation—We are covered by Christ, for He is the power of our salvation (see Alma 15:6).

The sword of the Spirit, which is the word of God—The Spirit will show you all things to do, and the word will tell you all things to do. This is our weapon against the adversary. We can live by the word of God. As we hold to the iron rod, feasting upon the word and hearkening to it, the temptations of the devil can never overpower us (see 1 Nephi 15:24; 2 Nephi 32:3). Christ is the Word of God.

Praying always—We call upon our Father in the name of Jesus Christ, and we can call down the powers of heaven.

Putting on the whole armor of God literally means that we put on Christ and thus we are protected through His atoning sacrifice.

Elder Carlos E. Asay has stated, "Endowed members of the Church wear the garment as a reminder of the sacred covenants they have made with the Lord and also as a protection against temptation and evil. How it is worn is an outward expression of an inward commitment to follow the Savior" (Carlos E. Asay, "The Temple Garment: 'An Outward Expression of an Inward Commitment,'" *Ensign*, August 1997).

Elder J. Richard Clarke has stated concerning the garment as a protection from Satan, "As you receive your endowments in the temple, you receive the privilege of wearing the sacred temple clothing and the garments of the holy priesthood. The garments are a tangible reminder of your covenants with God. . . . The temple garment reminds us that virtue sets us apart from the world and, in a special way, makes us one with God" (J. Richard Clarke, "The Temple—What It Means to You," *New Era*, April 1993). No one is immune from temptation. That is part of the trial and test of mortality. To one degree or another, some type of temptation is working on all of us all of the time. The Atonement will assist us in every temptation we face.

A third critical part of the plan is agency, the ability to act for oneself. There must be the opposition of two forces—good and bad—that are enticing for agency to operate. "Wherefore, the Lord God gave unto man that he should act for himself. Wherefore, man could not act for himself save it should be that he was enticed by the one or the other" (2 Nephi 2:16). For agency to be operative, it requires laws, opposition (good and bad), knowledge of good and evil, temptation or enticement for one or the other, and the freedom to choose. We cannot be agents unto ourselves without temptation.

The Lord will also help us choose wisely. "For the natural man is an enemy to God, and has been from the fall of Adam, and will be, forever and ever, unless he yields to the enticings of the Holy Spirit, and putteth off the natural man and becometh a saint through the atonement of Christ the Lord, and becometh as a child, submissive, meek, humble, patient, full of love, willing to submit to all things which the Lord seeth fit to inflict upon him, even as a child doth submit to his father" (Mosiah 3:19). We can yield to the enticings of the Holy Ghost and become a saint through the Atonement, and then we will be Spirit directed in our lives and make good choices. Through the greater priesthood, in the holy temple, we have been endowed with power and the fulness of the Holy Ghost. Father gave us the Holy Ghost because we believed in His Son (see 3 Nephi 19:22). And with all this enabling power from God, we are able to do good, for God is in us and all good comes from God. We are motivated, inspired, and empowered to do good. Remember, as to ourselves, we are nothing save it be in the strength of the Lord (see Alma 26:11–12), and the Holy Ghost will "leadeth to do good—yea, to do justly, to walk humbly, to judge righteously . . . which shall enlighten your mind, which shall fill your soul with joy" (D&C 11:12–13).

Oh, the joy of agency! The goodness and mercy of God is that we might be free so as to choose and thus be worthy of everlasting life in the presence of the Father and the Son. In making choices, we either follow the devil or we follow our beloved Savior Jesus

Christ by the power of the Holy Spirit. Remember that when we accept the grace of God and apply the Atonement to our lives, we will be empowered to live a righteous life. We will go about doing good, the fruits of the Atonement in our lives. The Holy Ghost, which is a gift from the Father because we believe in Christ, will assist us in making every choice we make by the enabling power of the Atonement.

THE ATONEMENT COVERS OUR FALLEN STATE

The Fall, one of the pillars of the plan of exaltation, brought many truths to Adam and Eve. Adam spoke of their transgression and how his "eyes are opened, and in this life I shall have joy, and again in the flesh I shall see God" (Moses 5:10). Eve taught us, "Were it not for our transgression we never should have had seed, and never should have known good and evil, and the joy of our redemption, and the eternal life which God giveth unto all the obedient" (Moses 5:11). Adam and Eve made the plan of redemption and all things known unto their children.

When we come to understand and appreciate our fallen state, we will come to realize our need for our Savior's redemption. The phrase is often stated as our "lost and fallen state." We are fallen and lost without hope without the Atonement! "For it is expedient that an atonement should be made; for according to the great plan of the Eternal God there must be an atonement made, or else all mankind must unavoidably perish; yea, all are hardened; yea, all are fallen and are lost, and must perish except it be through the atonement which it is expedient should be made" (Alma 34:9; see also 1 Nephi 10:6; 2 Nephi 25:17; Mosiah 16:4). Jacob reminds us of our plight without the Atonement:

> For as death hath passed upon all men, to fulfil the merciful plan of the great Creator, there must needs be a power of resurrection, and the resurrection must needs come unto man by reason of the fall; and the fall came by reason of transgression; and because man became fallen they were cut off from the presence of the Lord.
>
> Wherefore, it must needs be an infinite atonement—save it should be an infinite atonement this corruption could not put on incorruption. Wherefore, the first judgment which came upon

> man must needs have remained to an endless duration. And if so, this flesh must have laid down to rot and to crumble to its mother earth, to rise no more.
>
> O the wisdom of God, his mercy and grace! For behold, if the flesh should rise no more our spirits must become subject to that angel who fell from before the presence of the Eternal God, and became the devil, to rise no more.
>
> And our spirits must have become like unto him, and we become devils, angels to a devil, to be shut out from the presence of our God, and to remain with the father of lies, in misery, like unto himself; yea, to that being who beguiled our first parents, who transformeth himself nigh unto an angel of light, and stirreth up the children of men unto secret combinations of murder and all manner of secret works of darkness.
>
> O how great the goodness of our God, who prepareth a way for our escape from the grasp of this awful monster; yea, that monster, death and hell, which I call the death of the body, and also the death of the spirit. (2 Nephi 9:6–10)

Jacob in this empowering chapter teaches us the consequence of our fallen state if there had been no Atonement. I would have my Book of Mormon students read this chapter for thirty consecutive days. The responses were varied at the beginning. Why so many days in a row? Why not just thirty times over a month? I implored them to be obedient and they would see the blessings. Finally they began to see. The words of Christ had sunk deep into their souls. They understood and appreciated the goodness of God and their beloved Savior Jesus Christ, because with out the Atonement, we were lost forever! I have done this exercise, and it fills my soul with gratitude.

Remember this fallen state does not make us sinners, for we are born innocent (see D&C 93:38). We choose to be carnal, sensual, and devilish, as we learn from Moses 5:13: "And Satan came among them, saying: I am also a son of God; and he commanded them, saying: Believe it not [the things Adam and Eve had been teaching them]; and they believed it not, *and they loved Satan more than God. And men began from that time forth to be carnal, sensual, and devilish*" (Moses 5:13; emphasis added). The children of God, in our fallen state, can become saints through the Atonement when we yield to the enticings of the Holy Spirit.

Aaron taught King Lamoni's father about the Creation, the Fall, and plan of redemption:

"And since man had fallen he could not merit anything of himself; but the sufferings and death of Christ atone for their sins, through faith and repentance, and so forth; and that he breaketh the bands of death, that the grave shall have no victory, and that the sting of death should be swallowed up in the hopes of glory; and Aaron did expound all these things unto the king" (Alma 22:14).

Dependency upon our Savior draws us to Him. We cannot make it by ourselves. As Nephi said, "For we know that it is by grace that we are saved, after all we can do" (2 Nephi 25:23). No matter how much we do, we are saved by grace, yet we are judged by our works. And we are to have faith unto repentance, thus accepting the Atonement into our lives.

Moroni teaches us the connection between the Fall and the need for Christ to redeem us.

"Behold, he created Adam, and by Adam came the fall of man. And because of the fall of man came Jesus Christ, even the Father and the Son; and because of Jesus Christ came the redemption of man" (Moroni 9:12).

This was all part of the plan. There had to be a Fall. There had to be an Atonement, which provided a way back to the presence of our Father. Some ask why it's this way. Because it was ordained of God. Our Father's plan was and is perfect for us to follow. It is the way. "Now have we not reason to rejoice? Yea, I say unto you, there never were men that had so great reason to rejoice as we, since the world began; yea, and my joy is carried away, even unto boasting in my God; for he has all power, all wisdom, and all understanding; he comprehendeth all things, and he is a merciful Being, even unto salvation, to those who will repent and believe on his name" (Alma 26:35). King Benjamin reminds us too. "Believe in God; believe that he is, and that he created all things, both in heaven and in earth; believe that he has all wisdom, and all power, both in heaven and in earth; believe that man doth not comprehend all the things which the Lord can comprehend" (Mosiah 4:9). Our finite minds are not capable of comprehending all things, but we are capable of being grateful and exercising faith in Jesus Christ. This is why, in our infant state of eternity, the Lord said through the Apostle Paul, "But without faith it is impossible to please him [God]" (Hebrews 11:6). Faith is the foundation of all righteousness, and all things are done by faith, for it is the power of God.

Mormon explains that all good comes from God, else we would remain as fallen. "And God also declared unto prophets, by his own mouth, that Christ should come. And behold, there were divers ways that he did manifest things unto the children of men, which were good; and all things which are good cometh of Christ; otherwise men were fallen, and there could no good thing come unto them" (Moroni 7:23–24). The knowledge of the Fall helps us understand the need of the plan of redemption, which is centered in the infinite Atonement. When we realize we are in a fallen state, we can appreciate our dependence upon Christ. This understanding and appreciation draws us to our Savior. If we don't understand the Fall, we can't understand the need for the infinite Atonement. And thus we see that we would be lost and fallen forever without it. This is why the Lord through His prophets teaches us the plan of redemption. "And Aaron did expound unto him the scriptures from the creation of Adam, laying the fall of man before him, and their carnal state and also the plan of redemption, which was prepared from the foundation of the world, through Christ, for all whosoever would believe on his name" (Alma 22:13). When we understand and appreciate the plan of redemption, we will be filled with gratitude. With that gratitude, the love of God descends into our souls, and we have an overwhelming desire to do good. As we remember the infinite Atonement, knowing that our fallen state is covered and the seed of gratitude is embedded in our souls, we will live with hope through Christ the Lord. "And what is it that ye shall hope for? Behold I say unto you that ye shall have hope through the atonement of Christ and the power of his resurrection, to be raised unto life eternal, and this because of your faith in him according to the promise" (Moroni 7:41). We will be redeemed from our fallen state through the Atonement of Christ. And the Lord will cover our fallen state.

THE ATONEMENT COVERS OUR SINS

As stated earlier, the word *atonement* in Hebrew is *kaphar*, which means to cover, to embrace, and to forgive—the very meanings that capture the essence of the atoning sacrifice. The infinite, endless, perpetual, and everlasting Atonement covers everything. This section, like the previous section, covers a certain aspect of the Atonement, and in this case it is covering our sins. The pain and guilt of our sins cause us to suffer. They separate us from God. We lose the Holy Spirit. Being separated from God not only is hard to bear but also causes such emotional strife that life sometimes becomes unbearable. We sometimes withdraw into despair. Enos received relief from his guilt. Alma received relief from his pain. I have witnessed the relief of all of the above symptoms caused by sin as I have visited with countless numbers of wonderful Saints who sought relief from their sins through repentance and the enabling power of the Atonement. I would say, as a bishop I had a dynamic experience with the Atonement every week, as the infinite Atonement would strengthen them and cover their sins. Their guilt, which covers a multitude of feelings, would be taken away by their faith and the healing power of the Atonement. I would caution them that sometimes their memory, which helps them not return to sin, would be triggered and a moment of pain and sorrow can return. But in the strength of the Lord, they too will eventually fade away. Sometimes I would have to explain that the healing process takes time and everything they were experiencing would not be swept away instantly by confession alone.

I witnessed this healing process. I saw how people in the depth of sin encircled about by despair and hopelessness sought forgiveness. While we would visit, they would say something like, "Is there any hope for me?" There is hope in the Lord and His Atonement. The Savior performed this infinite Atonement just for them. Godly sorrow was evident. Tears were shed. The desire to do good and repent was expressed. Prayers were offered. The Atonement came into their lives. Light returned to their souls.

They were healed in time according to their faith and the desires of their hearts. Yes, it took time. Sometimes people would start the process and want immediate blessings and privileges restored. I would have to explain that their souls needed time, just like a broken bone takes time and you cannot hurry the process of healing. Each situation is different according to the individual, but the great Healer, even Christ the Lord, is always there, waiting to heal and bless His children and enable them to return to their Father.

Sometimes people would seem to report their sins instead of having a broken heart and a contrite spirit with godly sorrow for their sins. There is a big difference. King Benjamin's people sought the mercy of the Lord, like Alma: "O have mercy, and apply the atoning blood of Christ that we may receive forgiveness of our sins, and our hearts may be purified; for we believe in Jesus Christ" (Mosiah 4:2). The intent of our hearts must be full of sorrow as we go through the repentance process, and we will be forgiven (see Moroni 6:8). The Lord has promised us, "Behold, he who has repented of his sins, the same is forgiven, and I, the Lord, remember them no more. By this ye may know if a man repenteth of his sins—behold, he will confess them and forsake them" (D&C 58:42–43).

The Savior taught that He came to give His life for a ransom for all (see Matthew 20:28). He went on to say, while He was administering His sacrament, "This is my blood of the new testament, which is shed for many for the remission of sins" (Matthew 26:28). And in John we learn, "The good shepherd giveth his life for the sheep" (John 10:11). The Lord makes clear through His scriptures that He came to pay for the remission of our sins, and they can be covered through His infinite Atonement.

Paul explains to the Corinthians, "For I delivered unto you first of all that which I also received, how that Christ died for our sins according to the scriptures" (1 Corinthians 15:3). The great purpose of the Atonement was to make us "at one" with the Father and the Son. To do this, we must be free from our sins and be clean, pure, and holy. This can only be done through and by the blood of the Lamb—the infinite and eternal Atonement of Christ the Lord.

Nephi, in his vision of the tree of life, saw the Savior suffering for our sins: "I looked and beheld the Lamb of God, that he was taken by the people; yea, the Son of the everlasting God was judged of the world; and I saw and bear record. And I, Nephi, saw that he was lifted up upon the cross and slain for the sins of the world" (1 Nephi 11:32–33). Our Father, who knoweth all things and has ways that are not our ways, was pleased to offer His Beloved Son as a propitiation for our sins. "And he is the propitiation for our sins: and not for ours only, but also for the sins of the whole world" (1 John 2:2). This was the method of payment. This was the requirement of justice. Only by the Anointed One, through His blood, could we become clean. "There can be no man be saved except his garments are washed white; yea, his garments must be purified until they are cleansed from all stain, through the blood of him of whom it has been spoken by our fathers, who should come to redeem his people from their sins" (Alma 5:21).

Nephi who taught us the doctrine of Christ in 2 Nephi 31 also made sure to instruct us where we look for the remission of our sins. "And we talk of Christ, we rejoice in Christ, we preach of Christ, we prophesy of Christ, and we write according to our prophecies, that our children may know to what source they may look for a remission of their sins" (2 Nephi 25:26). We look to Christ in all things, for He is the Savior and Redeemer, who paid for our sins so that we might be forgiven as we exercise faith unto repentance.

The New Testament is emphatic about Christ forgiving us from our sins and making us clean. John has stated clearly, "The blood of Jesus Christ his Son cleanseth us from all sin" (1 John 1:7). "Unto him that loved us, and washed us from our sins in his own blood" (Revelation 1:5).

Paul, in his Epistles, states, "Grace be to you and peace from God the Father, and from our Lord Jesus Christ, who gave himself for our sins" (Galatians 1:3–4). "In whom [Jesus Christ] we have redemption through his blood, the forgiveness of sins, according to the riches of his grace" (Ephesians 1:7). Yes, it is Christ who can and will forgive us of our sins when we show forth meet unto repentance (see Matthew 9:6; Mark 2:10; Luke 5:20; Ephesians 4:32; Colossians 2:13).

King Benjamin, at the conclusion of his sermon, saw the effect when the people sought forgiveness of sins. "And they had viewed themselves in their own carnal state, even less than the dust of the earth. And they all cried aloud with one voice, saying: O have mercy, and apply the atoning blood of Christ that we may receive forgiveness of our sins, and our hearts may be purified; for we believe in Jesus Christ, the Son of God, who created heaven and earth, and all things; who shall come down among the children of men" (Mosiah 4:2). The people knew where to look for forgiveness of sins. They knew where to turn. The message of King Benjamin had shown them the way. They made the mighty change and had "no more disposition to do evil, but to do good continually" (Mosiah 5:2). They became the sons and daughters of Christ. Surely they would be forgiven, as their fruits plainly displayed.

The Lord indeed did heal them like He did the people here on the American continent when He visited them following His Resurrection. "O all ye that are spared because ye were more righteous than they, will ye not now return unto me, and repent of your sins, and be converted, that I may heal you?" (3 Nephi 9:13; see also 3 Nephi 18:32; D&C 112:13).

Each of these statements by prophets and the Lord Himself makes clear the doctrine that the Atonement covers our sins if we but repent—and if not, we must suffer for them. The Lord has paid for all sins. When we face opposition and temptation here upon the earth, we often make bad choices or neglect opportunities to do good, which leads to sin. In this vein, John counsels us, "But if we walk in the light, as he is in the light, we have fellowship one with another, and the blood of Jesus Christ his Son cleanseth us from all sin. If we say that we have no sin, we deceive ourselves, and the truth is not in us. If we confess our sins, he is faithful and just to forgive us our sins, and to cleanse us from all unrighteousness. If we say that we have not sinned, we make him a liar, and his word is not in us" (1 John 1:7–10). The scriptures have clearly taught us that all have or will sin, and the Atonement can cover our sins; it is the source of our remission of sins if we repent. Forgiveness of sins and being free from guilt can only come through the enabling power of the Atonement when we apply it to our lives through faith unto repentance. We are sanctified through Christ's Atonement and the power of the Holy Ghost. We are justified (acceptable before the Lord) through the redemption of the Lord (see Romans 3:24). We become clean through the blood of the Lamb. We can become clean, pure, and holy, even clean without spot. The Lord can heal the repentant sinner.

As we read the Book of Mormon, we witness the conversion and healing of Alma the Younger (see Alma 36:6–25). The pain of his sins was also taken away when the Atonement came into his life. We also witness the conversion and healing of Zeezrom: "Alma said unto him, taking him by the hand: Believest thou in the power of Christ unto salvation? And he answered and said: Yea, I believe all the words that thou hast taught. And Alma said: If *thou believest in the redemption of Christ thou canst be healed*. And he said: Yea, I believe according to thy words. And then Alma cried unto the Lord, saying: O Lord our God, have mercy on this man, and heal him according to his faith which is in Christ. And when Alma had said these words, Zeezrom leaped upon his feet, and began to walk" (Alma 15:6–11; emphasis added).

The Atonement makes possible the remission of all sins. We do not have the power to make payment for our sins. When we repent of our sins, we can be perfected in Christ and qualify for eternal life through Christ. Through our indebtedness and gratitude for the Atonement, we should seek to follow Him through faith unto repentance.

The plan required a payment for the sins of the world, and Christ made that payment. I remember a tender story that teaches this principle, one retold by President Hinckley:

> "Years ago there was a little one-room schoolhouse in the mountains of Virginia where the boys were so rough that no teacher had been able to handle them.
>
> "A young, inexperienced teacher applied, and the old director scanned him and asked: 'Young fellow, do you know that you are

asking for an awful beating? Every teacher that we have had here for years has had to take one.'

"'I will risk it,' he replied.

"The first day of school came, and the teacher appeared for duty. One big fellow named Tom whispered: 'I won't need any help with this one. I can lick him myself.'

"The teacher said, 'Good morning, boys, we have come to conduct school.' They yelled and made fun at the top of their voices. 'Now, I want a good school, but I confess that I do not know how unless you help me. Suppose we have a few rules. You tell me, and I will write them on the blackboard.'

"One fellow yelled, 'No stealing!' Another yelled, 'On time.' Finally, ten rules appeared on the blackboard.

"'Now,' said the teacher, 'a law is not good unless there is a penalty attached. What shall we do with one who breaks the rules?'

"'Beat him across the back ten times without his coat on,' came the response from the class.

"'That is pretty severe, boys. Are you sure that you are ready to stand by it?' Another yelled, 'I second the motion,' and the teacher said, 'All right, we will live by them! Class, come to order!'

"In a day or so, 'Big Tom' found that his lunch had been stolen. The thief was located—a little hungry fellow, about ten years old. 'We have found the thief and he must be punished according to your rule—ten stripes across the back. Jim, come up here!' the teacher said.

"The little fellow, trembling, came up slowly with a big coat fastened up to his neck and pleaded, 'Teacher, you can lick me as hard as you like, but please, don't take my coat off!'

"'Take your coat off,' the teacher said. 'You helped make the rules!'

"'Oh, teacher, don't make me!' He began to unbutton, and what did the teacher see? The boy had no shirt on, and revealed a bony little crippled body.

"'How can I whip this child?' he thought. 'But I must, I must do something if I am to keep this school.' Everything was quiet as death.

"'How come you aren't wearing a shirt, Jim?'

"He replied, 'My father died and my mother is very poor. I have only one shirt and she is washing it today, and I wore my brother's big coat to keep me warm.'

> "The teacher, with rod in hand, hesitated. Just then 'Big Tom' jumped to his feet and said, 'Teacher, if you don't object, I will take Jim's licking for him.'
>
> "'Very well, there is a certain law that one can become a substitute for another. Are you all agreed?'
>
> "Off came Tom's coat, and after five strokes the rod broke! The teacher bowed his head in his hands and thought, 'How can I finish this awful task?' Then he heard the class sobbing, and what did he see? Little Jim had reached up and caught Tom with both arms around his neck. 'Tom, I'm sorry that I stole your lunch, but I was awful hungry. Tom, I will love you till I die for taking my licking for me! Yes, I will love you forever!'" (Gordon B. Hinckley, "The Wondrous and True Story of Christmas," *Ensign*, December 2000)

How can we not fall in love with Jesus, who took our punishment for sin? His blood was poured out to cleanse us of our sins.

THE ATONEMENT NOURISHES IN OUR WEAKNESS

When we speak of "in the strength of the Lord," it is the enabling power of the Atonement. This is how we receive His strength in our lives. Ammon expressed this in a manner that we can all relate to: "But Ammon said unto him: I do not boast in my own strength, nor in my own wisdom; but behold, my joy is full, yea, my heart is brim with joy, and I will rejoice in my God. Yea, I know that I am nothing; as to my strength I am weak; therefore I will not boast of myself, but I will boast of my God, for in his strength I can do all things; yea, behold, many mighty miracles we have wrought in this land, for which we will praise his name forever" (Alma 26:11–12). This is not a passive scripture. This is the empowerment of being strong in your humility (depending upon the Lord). This is relying on the Lord in all things. This is receiving the Atonement and making it efficacious in our lives. It is like the Lord commanded when He said, "Therefore, whatsoever ye shall do, ye shall do it in my name" (3 Nephi 27:7). The Lord repeatedly commanded us to always call upon the Father in His name. All blessings and powers of the priesthood are always done in and through the name of the Lord Jesus Christ. When we understand and appreciate these great truths, we can be strengthened in the Lord.

This great truth was demonstrated in a tender moment while I was presiding at the Provo MTC. A young missionary was struggling in every way possible. He was frustrated, overwhelmed, and anxious to go home. It was evident that he was not ready or prepared to serve as a missionary. The branch president explained that the young man was upset at everybody, his companion was distraught, the district was upset, and everyone was concerned with the young missionary and his behavior. I invited the young missionary in. He expressed distaste for the mission and the missionary training center and explained why he really didn't want to come on a mission in the first place. We visited at length, and I hoped I could assess his needs and his real concerns. He continually expressed his desire to go home and get out of this trying and troubling situation. Since we had several hours before he would be able to leave simply because of packing and transportation concerns, I suggested that we visit. I asked him questions like, "How do you feel about your Heavenly Father?" Indeed, he loved his Heavenly Father. "How do you feel about life?" He mentioned he was so distraught, discouraged, and overwhelmed. He didn't like life. He didn't understand life. He was beside himself.

Then the Spirit taught me what to teach of Christ and preach of Christ—all things of Christ. The Spirit told me to teach of the magnificent and eternal atoning sacrifice and how it can heal us through its enabling power, for it is through Christ that we are nurtured and blessed in our weaknesses. And so at great length we talked of the Lord Jesus Christ and His atoning sacrifice. His heart began to soften and feel, his mind began to understand, and his eyes lightened. His countenance changed. The Holy Spirit had enlightened him. After this tender moment, I then again asked the question, "How do you feel?" And with tears streaming down his face, he said, "Oh, President Pinegar, I want to serve a mission. I love my Heavenly Father and my Savior. I need help. I understand better the goodness and mercy of my Heavenly Father and my Savior in my life. I am just so mixed up, I wanted to get out of here, but not anymore. I want to do it. I want to be a missionary."

A blessing was given. His heart was softened and reassured at the same time. He understood. He stayed and served his mission. He understood and appreciated the Atonement and its power to heal. He had a mighty change as he was empowered by the Atonement and the power of the Holy Ghost. The story doesn't end. I saw him in the temple twenty-four years later, and he reminded me of this life-changing moment. He is a mighty man of God. He radiates the love of God. He has the image of Christ in his countenance. With his beautiful wife beside him, he told me how he has been a seminary teacher for many years and loving it. We embraced. Gratitude for the goodness of God filled our souls as we departed. My heart swelled with eternal joy for the tender mercies of God our Father and our beloved Savior Jesus Christ. And life was good, for this young missionary felt the love of God as he came to understand and appreciate the infinite and eternal Atonement of our Savior Jesus Christ.

Our weaknesses can be as varied as our sins, which so easily beset us.

We can be weak in our faith.

We can be weak in our ability to repent.

We can be weak in our character.

We can be weak in keeping our covenants.

We can be weak in living by the Holy Spirit.

We can be weak in doing our duty.

We can be weak in expressing our love.

And on and on and on.

What we learn by this is that we are weak. "And if men come unto me I will show unto them their weakness. I give unto men weakness that they may be humble; and my grace is sufficient for all men that humble themselves before me; for if they humble themselves before me, and have faith in me, then will I make weak things become strong unto them" (Ether 12:27). This verse is empowering! The Lord will show us our weaknesses if we humble ourselves before Him and exercise faith in Him—"I make weak things become strong unto them." We become strong in all of our weaknesses as we exercise faith in Jesus Christ. This is what we do to apply the Atonement to our lives. This is how the Lord can nurture us in our weakness. We receive and accept the Atonement as we exercise faith in our Savior Jesus Christ.

This is how we become strong in the Lord. This is what Ammon was teaching us: his strength is in the Lord, whereby he can do all things. This is the miracle of the Atonement.

THE ATONEMENT NOURISHES US IN OUR PAINS AND AFFLICTIONS

The nourishing blessing of the Atonement is something we haven't always talked about. We just discovered how we are strengthened in our weaknesses. This nurturing part of the Atonement is ongoing in our lives. It is constant, continuous, and endless. It was this aspect of the Atonement that healed my heart after the loss of our son. It is this part of the Atonement that frees us from emotional trauma. It is this part of the infinite Atonement that is gloriously empowering so as it is with us every day, in every trial that lurks at every twist and turn of life. The Lord is ever there, helping us deal with our pains, afflictions, and tribulations. He is our strength.

Alma reminds us, "And he shall go forth, *suffering pains and afflictions* and temptations of every kind; and this that the word might be fulfilled which saith he will take upon him the pains and the sicknesses of his people" (Alma 7:11; emphasis added). Jacob instructs us, "And he cometh into the world that he may save all men if they will hearken unto his voice; for behold, he suffereth the pains of all men, yea, the pains of every living creature, both men, women, and children, who belong to the family of Adam" (2 Nephi 9:21).

Alma, having remembered the words of his father concerning the Atonement, now applied it to his life: "Now, as my mind caught hold upon this thought, I cried within my heart: O Jesus, thou Son of God, have mercy on me, who am in the gall of bitterness, and am encircled about by the everlasting chains of death. And now, behold, when I thought this, I could remember my pains no more; yea, I was harrowed up by the memory of my sins no more" (Alma 36:18–19). His pains could be remembered no more. Paul, always thanking his Savior, speaks of his deliverance:

"Persecutions, afflictions, which came unto me at Antioch, at Iconium, at Lystra; what persecutions I endured: but out of them all the Lord delivered me" (2 Timothy 3:11).

Christ suffered so He would know "according to the flesh" how to nurture and bless His children. Sometimes people say to one another, "You don't understand." This does not apply to our Savior. He suffered so He would understand and know how to help us as mortals. It is in our pain and afflictions that we are drawn back to our Savior and our Heavenly Father. Our prayers become more intent, more desperate, and more pleading. Through pain and afflictions, we are reminded of our weaknesses and dependence upon God. And the Lord will nurture us.

Alma, Nephi, and Paul have stated that the Lord knows exactly what to do and how to help us. First of all, these experiences are for our good, and we need them in order to grow. When anything draws us to Christ, it is a blessing, though it is often hard to believe when we are in severe pain and seemingly endless afflictions. This is why we need to accept our trials, knowing full well that we have the help and assistance of our beloved Savior to endure the situation and grow from the opportunity. I am full of joy as I write for what I have learned recently about the opposition and trial of pain. Pain is a real teacher. One of the most excruciating pains I have ever felt was when I developed a condition known as ankylosing spondylitis, in addition to having a growth on my spine. The pain was, at times, unbearable. It felt like electric shocks. I couldn't stand, sit, or sleep—it's an understatement to say I was in pain. It was in the midst of this trial that I began to study more intently the principle of opposition, listen more carefully to the covenants I made in the temple, and pray more earnestly. I began to see, because of the increased length of time and the tremendous amount of pain, that this was a great blessing in my life. I began to understand more clearly the foundational doctrine to the perfect plan of our Heavenly Father: *there must be opposition in all things.* My prayers at first became more pleading, that the trial be taken from me. Remember, desperation often brings more intensity to our prayers. Then, amazingly, as I held to my faith, I became grateful. I was exhilarated with joy even as I winced in pain. As I sit typing, I await the next shock—yet I am filled with hope. It's all part of the plan. If a solution becomes apparent, and if I act with faith in my Savior, the plan will be carried out; if it is not, that is okay, for that will help me understand more deeply the doctrine and my experience in mortality. Months later, following the operation, I can report that the pain has lessened. I stand more erect and I can move about with great gratitude for the healing power of God in my life. Yet the pain often returns and lingers for a time, reminding me to be thankful when there is no pain—and I am full of gratitude.

Let us take a moment to stop and consider the blessings of pain in our lives. Through the Savior's example, we learn that while pain is not enjoyable, it can be a teacher and a blessing in our lives. Pain can fulfill the following roles in our lives:

- It is a warning sign of a possible problem with our body or our soul, depending on whether the pain is physical or emotional.
- With the capacity to feel pain, we are protected from greater harm and injury, whether it be physical or spiritual.
- It causes us to act. The greater the pain, the quicker the action.
- Having pain gives us the power to empathize with those who suffer.
- We seek relief from pain, and thus in humility we call upon God. The pain—whether it is physical, emotional, or spiritual—will draw us closer to God, for we are in need of His help.

Pain is a blessing, though it is often the least recognized as such. Lest we forget, it is through the pain and suffering of the Lord that the infinite Atonement was fulfilled. Because of the pain of the suffering and sacrificing Christ, we are not only healed but drawn to Him. Without experiencing pain, we can never feel the joy of being free from pain. Remember, opposition is necessary and vital for life so that we may come unto the knowledge of the goodness and mercies of God. In overcoming adversity, we are grateful to God.

The emotional and spiritual pain of sin is excruciating for the unrepentant, for "the demands of divine justice do awaken his immortal soul to a lively sense of his own guilt, which doth cause him to shrink from the presence of the Lord, and doth fill his breast with guilt, and pain, and anguish, which is like an unquenchable fire, whose flame ascendeth up forever and ever" (Mosiah 2:38). Pain helps us repent.

It was this emotional and spiritual pain that brought Alma to repentance:

> And now, for three days and for three nights was I racked, even with the pains of a damned soul.
>
> And it came to pass that as I was thus racked with torment, while I was harrowed up by the memory of my many sins, behold, I remembered also to have heard my father prophesy unto the people concerning the coming of one Jesus Christ, a Son of God, to atone for the sins of the world.
>
> Now, as my mind caught hold upon this thought, I cried within my heart: O Jesus, thou Son of God, have mercy on me, who am in the gall of bitterness, and am encircled about by the everlasting chains of death.
>
> And now, behold, when I thought this, I could remember my pains no more; yea, I was harrowed up by the memory of my sins no more.
>
> And oh, what joy, and what marvelous light I did behold; yea, my soul was filled with joy as exceeding as was my pain! (Alma 36:16–20)

We cannot know the sweet without the bitter, "for if they never should have bitter they could not know the sweet" (D&C 29:39). This then brings a question: Do you always have to experience the bitter of everything to know the good? We know of the bitter and sweet. We can learn vicariously from the scriptures. We do not need to taste every bitter thing to appreciate the sweet. There is enough to go around without looking for opposition and adversity. We joy in righteousness. We joy in bringing souls to Christ. We joy in doing good. We joy in partaking of the love of God to the point that we are happy, the design of our existence. The Lord helps us grow through a multiplicity of things. We are blessed with wonderful principles and powers—from faith to charity. We are blessed with the power of the greater priesthood and all the ordinances and covenants administered and received from it.

It is through pain that some of the greatest blessings are made possible from God. Pain gets our attention. Pain opens our eyes to a greater sense of clarity regarding our purpose, compassion for others, and personal growth. How does a new mother who has experienced this extreme pain, sorrow, and sacrifice to bring a child of God into mortality feel? She is full of joy. I have witnessed this eight times with my dear, beloved sweetheart. We start to see that in suffering comes the greatest growth and the greatest good as exemplified by our Lord and Savior Jesus Christ. The pain of Gethsemane and Golgotha made possible the infinite sacrifice and Atonement, which is the enabling power of all things, so that we may be perfected through Christ. The greater burden, especially associated with pain, will bring about the greatest growth. Adam fell that man might be and also have joy. Surely the words echo from the scriptures: "That all these things shall give thee experience, and shall be for thy good" (D&C 122:7).

This does not mean that we should be in a "state" of pain and suffering—quite the contrary. It is just that pain is part of life. We don't seek it. It will come to all of God's children. We don't seek to be martyrs and aggrandize our pain and suffering. We look at pain to be relieved of it through Christ the Lord. For some of us, there is constant pain due to medical issues. We do our best to overcome pain. We seek relief. Each has crosses to bear, and we can never judge another, for we know not their hearts or their crosses that they bear. We love and are supportive to all with the pure love of Christ. We seek to be relievers of pain and suffering, even as Christ the Lord. The fact remains that pain is part of everyone's life. There is no escape from it; therefore we seek to learn from it.

I have become mindful of others who have faced physical, emotional, and spiritual pain. I have witnessed the sorrow and pain for victims of the sin of abuse who are sometimes so devastated that they suffer deep depression. Some are filled with anger and cry out in their hearts, "Where was my God?" There was no one there. "I looked on my right hand, and beheld, but there was no man that would know me: refuge failed me; no man cared for my soul" (Psalm 142:4). Where were the caring adults? "Is there no balm in Gilead" (Jeremiah 8:22). Some cling so long for vengeance that their souls become consumed with hatred. Years, even decades, pass by, and the price of being sinned against has cost them precious freedom from the past. The memory of the past often becomes the destroyer of the present, for without warning, something will "trigger" events of the past, and pain comes crushing down upon their souls. These moments are hard moments. We can call upon Heavenly Father for help and eventually regain peace through Christ the Lord and His nurturing Atonement. Everyone must be patient and understanding with all who are involved with this kind of experience. They cry out for love and understanding.

I have witnessed emotional pain of others, especially victims, in tender moments as a bishop, stake president, and mission president. I remember the first time I faced the challenge of addressing this situation as a priesthood leader. A sister was struggling, and although we did not know why, her emotional pain was at the limit. Her roommates mentioned how she would remain in the apartment and cry. Other friends sought to assist but knew not what to do. The matter finally came to my attention, and I sought a time to interview her. As I sat down with her to begin the visit, she began to cry. I tried to console her, to no avail. I thought she might need a little time to be alone, so I stood to excuse myself. When I stood, I raised my hand to the side of my head, and she cowered in her chair. Devastated, I discerned immediately the situation and expressed my sympathy and love. She seemed quieted, and we began to talk. As we visited, it came out that in fact her father had physically and sexually abused her. I wept, and we wept together. We talked of life and her future. We talked of her desire to be happy once again. I asked her, "Do you want to be happy?" Of course, her response was positive. Then I asked her if she would do what I had been prompted to ask her to do so that she might be happy. She willingly said yes. The Lord and the Holy Spirit direct and guide encounters like these, and I was truly led by the Spirit, not knowing beforehand the things I should say or do. Oh, the goodness of God. I said, "Call your father, frankly forgive him, and encourage him to see the bishop immediately, so he might begin the process of repentance." She agreed that she would. We had prayer and planned our next visit. This was the beginning of many visits and nurturing moments. The Savior and His infinite Atonement came into her life. The healing began. Time was our ally. And the Lord was her strength. This was the answer the Lord gave me for this situation. The Lord might have another solution for a similar case. We simply follow the Holy Spirit. She had turned her burden over to the Lord. Her prayers were strong and fervent. And her soul was renewed with the love of God.

Over time this young woman's roommate mentioned that good things were happening. The distressed sister became more positive and upbeat. The enabling power of the Atonement was taking effect. She was being healed. She became enthusiastic, friendly, and outgoing. It was a miracle. She later returned home and married a wonderful young man in the temple, and she now has several children. Her life is good. Yes, there is a way, and it is in and through our Savior Jesus Christ and His infinite and empowering Atonement. He is always there. We must call upon God so that the nurturing and succoring power of our Savior's sacrifice and Atonement become efficacious in our lives.

To those who have been sinned against or suffered pain at the hands of others, forgiveness is the watchword to live by. Abuse is not to be tolerated or embraced; it must be addressed, and help should be sought. Sometimes it may take time, and sometimes healing will come bit by bit. But it will come. Remember that the victim has not sinned! Those who suffer such pain can, through the Savior's love, be healed. It is one of the great miracles of the Atonement that Christ can cure and heal such pain. We must look to the Lord for strength, knowing full well that the Lord Himself has suffered through opposition and temptation of the highest order and magnitude, and He was the ultimate victim, having never sinned. Yet even in great pain and agony, the Lord sought to forgive them, for they knew not what they were doing.

Repentance on the part of the abusers through Christ the Lord is the only way for those who have sinned to be forgiven.

May we never forget the suffering of physical, emotional, and spiritual pain of our beloved Savior Jesus Christ for all of us. Life is hard, yet in every distressful situation we can, if we choose, be drawn toward God, or we can yield to the enticing of the adversary with comments like, "Why me?" "This isn't fair," or "Where is Heavenly Father when I need Him most?" The law of opposition, temptation, and agency *always* remains in place. We must rely on the Lord and His infinite and eternal Atonement to strengthen us, else disappointment, discouragement, and even depression may be our lot. The Lord understands, and He will nurture us. As we do so, we come to understand why the Lord faced such opposition so He could nurture us. In pain, we can and will be nurtured and blessed by our beloved Savior Jesus Christ.

Challenges can turn into blessings, for they bring us back to the feet of the Lord. Need, the mother of change, causes us to act and again brings us to Christ. Humility is born through trials, adversity, pain, and affliction. Humility is the virtue that starts the process of change. We are dependent upon God for relief of pain as well as healing. Let us remember our Heavenly Father and our Savior in all things, and at all times we will acknowledge Their goodness with prayers of thanksgiving. Let our prayers of gratitude constantly ascend to heaven at all times.

May we never forget throughout our mortal life that solutions to relief from pain and afflictions *do not always happen instantly.* Often the answer to our pleadings to the Lord is no. This becomes a stumbling block for some. Why not, we ask. Why not this once? If God should intervene in all things, then opposition, temptation, and agency would have no consequences. Remember, when the people were being burned at the stake and Amulek pleaded with Alma to save them, he replied, "The Spirit constraineth me that I must not stretch forth mine hand; for behold the Lord receiveth them up unto himself, in glory; and he doth suffer that they may do this thing, or that the people may do this thing unto them, according to the hardness of their hearts, that the judgments which he shall exercise upon them in his wrath may be just; and the blood of the innocent shall stand as a witness against them, yea, and cry mightily against them at the last day" (Alma 14:11). Our Father knows the beginning from the end, which our minds cannot comprehend, so we trust in the Lord and lean not to our own understanding (see Proverbs 3:5–6). We must learn patience, especially in our interaction with loved ones as both they and we face threats and pains of an eternal nature. Our loved ones are likewise children of God the Father, and He and our Savior love them too—even with an eternal and perfect love. We will come to see that in every situation the Lord blesses us, there will be interplay with opposition, temptation, and agency. For these are the things Christ understood and suffered for in Gethsemane.

The suffering was not only difficult but also unbearable to the limits of what any mortal could imagine. The question was, just how much opposition could Christ endure? He was tempted in all things previously and again in the Garden. Pain and afflictions were at record heights like no man had ever thought to be able to endure, and in it all, it came down to this supernal and submissive statement as the Lord made His decision: "O my Father, if this cup may not pass away from me, except I drink it, thy will be done" (Matthew 26:42). Yes, the Lord in Gethsemane suffered pain, which brought agony to His soul, and He chose to accept all the suffering for the sins of the world and a multitude of other things that all mortals must face so He would know how to nurture and succor His children.

THE ATONEMENT STRENGTHENS US IN OUR INFIRMITIES

Our infirmities, our lack of strength, our weakness, our illness and sickness, our defects— including our disabilities, maladies, frailness—and even our character flaws are examples of one degree or another of our infirmities. We all have them. Some are more observable than others. All of us have infirmities, for it is part of mortality. The key is to be aware of them so we can do something about them. Our agency should be used to work through many of these problems while we gain strength from the Lord. Even in this state of being, the Lord comes to our rescue.

He is ever helping and nurturing us along the way. He will help us endure these and all types of hardships if necessary.

Alma ever reminds us of the healing nature of the Atonement: "And he will take upon him their infirmities, that his bowels may be filled with mercy, according to the flesh, that he may know according to the flesh how to succor his people according to their infirmities" (Alma 7:12). Matthew records the prophetic words of Esaias (Isaiah) regarding this aspect of the Atonement: "That it might be fulfilled which was spoken by Esaias the prophet, saying, Himself took our infirmities, and bare our sicknesses" (Matthew 8:17). Luke records that prior to the Savior's suffering, He was still going about healing people: "And in that same hour he cured many of their infirmities and plagues, and of evil spirits; and unto many that were blind he gave sight" (Luke 7:21).

As we learn from these scriptures, the Lord is all about doing good, for this is what He was empowered to do. For He "shall go forth amongst men, working mighty miracles, such as healing the sick, raising the dead, causing the lame to walk, the blind to receive their sight, and the deaf to hear, and curing all manner of diseases" (Mosiah 3:5). The Lord stands waiting to nurture and bless us. It is important with our infirmity that we do all that is within our power to overcome them. Sometimes we fail to see the hand of God and the power of the Atonement in the process of being made whole. We go to the doctor with a broken leg, and he puts it in a cast and tells us in a few weeks we will be just fine. We have taken care of recognizing the problem by getting the assistance of the doctor to set the leg so it can heal properly. Who is the healer? We have done all that we can do, but it is the power of God and Christ the Lord that all things are healed here upon the earth. Our bodies have within them special powers. The autonomic nervous system (the visceral nervous system or involuntary nervous system) is the part of the peripheral nervous system that controls our involuntary functions, including heart rate, respiration, digestion, and many more. We don't have to think about them; they work automatically. We were born with all of these powers and blessings. They are gifts of God. In addition, our bodies have the power within us to heal wounds, to fight infections, to rebuild bones, and again the list goes on. We are the miracles of God. Thus, King Benjamin taught, "I say unto you that if ye should serve him who has created you from the beginning, and is preserving you from day to day, by lending you breath, that ye may live and move and do according to your own will, and even supporting you from one moment to another—I say, if ye should serve him with all your whole souls yet ye would be unprofitable servants" (Mosiah 2:21). With gratitude, we will thank our Heavenly Father and our Savior for all our blessings we have been given even without asking. Should we not serve God unceasingly to keep His commandments? We will live by faith in all things.

He having done all, we exercise our faith in the Lord, and He brings us back to full health and says, "Thy faith hath made thee whole." Will we have the courage and faith to let the Lord into our lives? Remember too that these things sometimes become our cross to bear throughout our lives. It is hard to know and understand how some are healed and preserved while others bear the burden throughout mortality? And yet to many, the burden becomes a blessing.

Consider the *Portraits in Overcoming Adversity*:

> Cripple him, and you have a Sir Walter Scott. Lock him in a prison cell, and you have a John Bunyan. Bury him in the snows of Valley Forge, and you have a George Washington. Land him in poverty, and you have an Abraham Lincoln. Subject him to bitter religious strife, and you have a Disraeli. Strike him with infantile paralysis, and you have a Franklin D. Roosevelt, the only president of the United States to be elected to four terms of office. Burn him so severely in a schoolhouse fire that the doctors say he will never walk, and you have a Glenn Cunningham, who set a world record in 1934 for running the mile in 4 minutes, 6.7 seconds. Deafen a genius composer who continues to compose some of the world's most beautiful music, and you have a Beethoven. Drag him more dead than alive out of a rice paddy in Vietnam, and you have a Rocky Blaier, that beautiful running back for the Pittsburgh Steelers. Have him or her born black in a society filled with racial discrimination, and you have a Booker T. Washington, Harriet Tubman, or Martin Luther King Jr. Have him born of

> parents who survived a Nazi concentration camp, paralyze him from the waist down at the age of four, and you have an Itzhak Perlman, the incomparable violinist. Call him "retarded" and write him off as "uneducatable," and you have an Albert Einstein.
>
> After losing both his legs in an airplane crash, let an RAF fighter pilot fly, and you have World War II ace Douglas Bader, who was captured by the Germans three times and escaped three times on two artificial limbs. Label him too stupid to learn, and you have a Thomas Edison. Label him a hopeless alcoholic, and you have a Bill Wilson, the founder of Alcoholics Anonymous. Tell her she is too old to start painting at 80, and you have a Grandma Moses. Blind him at age 44, and you have a John Milton, who 10 years later, wrote *Paradise Lost.* Call him dull and hopeless and flunk him in the 6th grade, and you have a Winston Churchill.
>
> Tell a young boy who loved to draw and sketch that he had no talent, and you have a Walt Disney. Rate him mediocre in chemistry, and you have a Louis Pasteur. Take a crippled child whose only home was an orphanage, and you have a Louis E. West, the first chief executive of the Boy Scouts of America. Spit on him, humiliate him, betray his trust, say one thing and do another. Mistrust those whom he loves. Mock him. Make him carry a heavy wooden cross, and then crucify him—and he forgives you and calls you a friend. (Ted Engstrom)

Amazing. In our adversity, the Lord makes us equal to the task. President Ezra Taft Benson taught us this transcending truth, "Men and women who turn their lives over to God will discover that He can make a lot more out of their lives than they can. He will deepen their joys, expand their vision, quicken their minds, strengthen their muscles, lift their spirits, multiply their blessings, increase their opportunities, comfort their souls, raise up friends, and pour out peace. Whoever will lose his life in the service of God will find eternal life" (Ezra Taft Benson, *Ezra Taft Benson Remembers the Joys of Christmas* [Salt Lake City: Deseret Book, 1988], 11). We must also remember that the Lord has said, "Behold, I stand at the door, and knock: if any man hear my voice, and open the door, I will come in to him, and will sup with him, and he with me. To him that overcometh will I grant to sit with me in my throne, even as I also overcame, and am set down with my Father in his throne" (Revelation 3:20–21).

Just as Christ the Lord was submissive to the Father, so likewise we learn from His experience that we must be willing to open our souls and bear our burdens, weaknesses, and infirmities with the Lord, else He cannot heal us. Then in our suffering and bearing our burdens with the Lord, we will be nurtured and succored by Him.

THE ATONEMENT CAN PROTECT US IN OUR TEMPTATIONS

Alma prompts us in regard the infinite power of the Atonement: "And he shall go forth, suffering pains and afflictions and *temptations of every kind*; and this that the word might be fulfilled which saith he will take upon him the pains and the sicknesses of his people" (Alma 7:11; emphasis added).

There is a great insight given us by C. S. Lewis in regard to the temptations, which Christ suffered

> No man knows how bad he is till he has tried very hard to be good. A silly idea is current that good people do not know what temptation means. This is an obvious lie. Only those who try to resist temptation know how strong it is; after all, you find out the strength of the army by fighting against it, not by giving in. You find out the strength of a wind by trying to walk against it, not by lying down. A man who gives into temptation after five minutes simply does not know what it would have been like an hour later.
>
> That is why bad people in one sense know very little about badness. They've always lived a sheltered life by always giving in. We never find out the strength of the evil impulse inside us until we try to fight it: and Christ, because he was the only man who never yielded to temptation, is also the only man who knows to the full what temptation means—the only complete realist. (C. S. Lewis, *Mere Christianity* [New York: HarperCollins, 1952], 126)

This warning against the power of temptation was on the Lord's mind as He reminded us and pled with us to overcome and not yield to temptation. The Lord has given us many resources to protect ourselves against temptation. As discussed earlier, to overcome temptation, we should pray, put on the armor of God, rely on the power of the word of God, exercise our faith, seek righteousness and the Holy Spirit, and remember our temple blessings. All these things working together can help us overcome temptation in our lives.Temptation from the devil and yielding to the enticings of the Holy Spirit become the choices of life. Who will we listen to? There is a crystal-clear answer, "And now, verily, verily, I say unto thee, put your trust in that Spirit which leadeth to do good—yea, to do justly, to walk humbly, to judge righteously; and this is my Spirit. Verily, verily, I say unto you, I will impart unto you of my Spirit, which shall enlighten your mind, which shall fill your soul with joy" (D&C 11:12–13). When we allow the Spirit to direct our lives, life will be sweet. Just as the Lord yielded to the will of God through the Atonement, so likewise may we yield to the will of God, "[yield] to the enticings of the Holy Spirit, and putteth off the natural man and becometh a saint through the atonement of Christ the Lord" (Mosiah 3:19). And as Helaman declared, doing so will lead "even to the purifying and the sanctification of their hearts, which sanctification cometh because of their yielding their hearts unto God" (Helaman 3:35).

We need to realize of the necessity of temptation in our lives, for it is part of the plan in order to prove ourselves. There is a devil, he is real, and there is a war going on for the souls of all mankind. The plan was presented in premortality, where we, having exercised our moral agency, chose to accept the plan (see Job 38:7). War ensued (see Revelation 12:7). Lucifer was cast out with a third part of the hosts of heaven (see D&C 29:36–37; Revelation 12:9), and thus he became Satan, even the devil (see Moses 4:4). And the war rages on today for the souls of all humankind. The reality of the devil is taught throughout the scriptures (see D&C 76:25–27; Moses 4:1–4; Abraham 3:22–28; Revelation 12:7–8). He is the enemy of all righteousness (see Alma 34:23; Acts 13:10; Mosiah 2:37; Moroni 9:6). His purpose is to drag us down to hell (see Alma 30:60), so that we might be miserable like unto himself (see 2 Nephi 2:27). The devil seeks to destroy our agency (see Moses 4:3), to the extent that he would have us believe he does not exist (see 2 Nephi 28:22); yet he is the author of all sin and the source of all temptation (see Helaman 6:30).

Thus several important truths become clear:

- We are at war with Lucifer, the father of all lies, for the souls of all mankind. He tempts us.
- The devil is real, and his angels seek to destroy us. He tempts us.
- We are continually being enticed by good and evil. He tempts us.
- We are free to choose our destiny. Agency is supreme, and we can overcome our temptations.

We must yield our hearts to God and not to Satan (see Moses 5:13; Helaman 3:35), and thus not be led into temptation. In Hebrew, the word for *heart* refers to our affections, the desires of our minds and souls. In choosing to do good, we give our will to God. When we yield our hearts to God, we come to understand that we love our fellowmen. Our affection for the Lord and His work becomes evident. Our will is His will. Our desires are His desires. We want to do His will because we have yielded to Him our heart. This explains the problem that the children of Adam and Eve faced when Satan came to them: "And Satan came among them, saying: I am also a son of God; and he commanded them, saying: Believe it not; and they believed it not, and they loved Satan more than God. And men began from that time forth to be carnal, sensual, and devilish" (Moses 5:13).

It is evident that in yielding to the enticing of the devil, a person becomes unrepentant, an enemy to God, a "natural man," as we learn from King Benjamin (see Mosiah 3:19). Every moment is a time to overcome temptation, "choose the right," "listen to the Holy Spirit," and not succumb to the desires of the flesh and hearken to the enticing, beguiling cunningness of the devil. The devil rages in the hearts of the children of men, and this means war. When we forget that principle, we lose battles within our own lives because we cease to believe that the devil is really at war with us. What is he doing this moment to tempt us? It is explained carefully in 2 Nephi 28:20–30.

The devil rages in our hearts to stir us up to anger against that which is good. The tactics and subtleties the devil uses are easy to see when we step back and realize that there is war, but often we are so eager for some smooth sailing in life, with no ups and downs, that we ignore the warning signs. So the devil pacifies us with ease of living and the feeling that all is well. Thus the devil cheats our souls, and we think everything is okay. Materialism has ever been a temptation of the devil. Things of the world can get in the way of the things that matter most and can lead down the pathway of sin. Temptation is ever present. Yielding to temptation is the issue, but we will never be tempted beyond what we can bear (see 1 Corinthians 10:13).

We can be tempted by pride, so the Lord helps us with humility.

We can be tempted with selfishness, greed, and avarice, and the Lord helps us with charity. We can be tempted with lust, and Heavenly Father gives us the Holy Ghost. We are tempted by apathy, by jealousy, by envy, to covet, and even to gossip, and the Lord gives us His love.

We are tempted by the precepts of men, and the Lord gives us His word, even the iron rod.

We are tempted by the fear of men, and the Lord gives us prayer, knowledge, faith, love, and experience that will strengthen us.

We are tempted by anger, and through the power of prayer and gaining temperance, we gain self-control and self-mastery.

We are tempted by hypocrisy, and the Lord teaches us of our divine nature.

We are tempted by vanity and unbelief, and the Lord will help us become easily entreated with a softened heart.

We can overcome all temptations when we come unto Christ and allow His strength to empower our lives and the power of the Holy Ghost to show us all things to do (see 2 Nephi 32:5).

THE ATONEMENT IS THE ENABLING POWER OF OUR RESURRECTION

In continuing this discussion of the blessings of the Atonement, Alma said, "And he will take upon him death, that he may loose the bands of death which bind his people" (Alma 7:12). The resurrection is part of the Atonement. The resurrection is the last step to literally bring us back into the presence of our Father. I continually ponder the state of our being without the power of the resurrection. The prophets have made it abundantly clear as to our state of corruption without the Atonement. I am filled with gratitude and joy to know that I have overcome death and hell because of the love of God. As Lehi said, "But behold, the Lord hath redeemed my soul from hell; I have beheld his glory, and I am encircled about eternally in the arms of his love" (2 Nephi 1:15). We are literally encircled by the Lord in the robe of His righteousness (see 2 Nephi 4:33). The Lord is the power of the resurrection, and all of the children of God are blessed because of it.

Lehi's farewell blessings to his sons teach us precious truths related to the resurrection and the Atonement. "Wherefore, how great the importance to make these things known unto the inhabitants of the earth, that they may know that there is no flesh that can dwell in the presence of God, save it be through the merits, and mercy, and grace of the Holy Messiah, who layeth down his life according to the flesh, and taketh it again by the power of the Spirit, that he may bring to pass the resurrection of the dead, being the first that should rise" (2 Nephi 2:8). As we teach these things to our children, they too will begin to feel gratitude for our Savior Jesus Christ. There is so much to learn in the setting of the scripture as well as the context. The last thing Lehi did was bless and teach his children.

Jacob's address on the power of the Atonement likewise fills my heart with gratitude. As the words distill upon my soul, I feel the goodness and power of the Lord in my life. "And this death of which I have spoken, which is the spiritual death, shall deliver up its dead; which spiritual death is hell; wherefore, death and hell must deliver up their dead, and hell must deliver up its captive spirits, and the grave must deliver up its captive bodies, and *the bodies and the spirits of men will be restored one to the other; and it is by the power of the resurrection of the Holy One of Israel*" (2 Nephi 9:12; emphasis added). It is hard to comprehend something we have not experienced yet. This is the purpose of many scriptures, so that we begin to learn these transcending truths that can help our gratitude for the goodness of God increase.

Abinadi also taught powerful truths that Alma heard and acted upon, and so should we. "But behold, the bands of death shall be broken, and the Son reigneth, and hath power over the dead; therefore, he bringeth to pass the resurrection of the dead" (Mosiah 15:20). The Prophet Joseph did this very thing. Joseph acted upon the words of James: "If any of you lack wisdom, let him ask of God, that giveth to all men liberally, and upbraideth not; and it shall be given him" (James 1:5). "Never did any passage of scripture come with more power to the heart of man than this did at this time to mine. It seemed to enter with great force into every feeling of my heart. I reflected on it again and again, knowing that if any person needed wisdom from God, I did; for how to act I did not know, and unless I could get more wisdom than I then had, I would never know; for the teachers of religion of the different sects understood the same passages of scripture so differently as to destroy all confidence in settling the question by an appeal to the Bible" (Joseph Smith—History 1:12). Joseph acted upon this scripture, went to the Sacred Grove in humble prayer, and received the vision of the Father and the Son and answers to his questions.

Alma reminds us of the great plan of redemption that we agreed to in premortal earth life: "Now, if it had not been for the plan of redemption, which was laid from the foundation of the world, there could have been no resurrection of the dead; *but there was a plan of redemption laid, which shall bring to pass the resurrection of the dead*, of which has been spoken" (Alma 12:25; emphasis added). We agreed to the great plan of redemption. When we read and begin to understand these scriptures, we can see why we chose to follow the plan of our Heavenly Father.

There are hundreds more scriptures speaking of the resurrection. It is clear that the Lord is the power of the resurrection: "Jesus said unto her, I am the resurrection, and the life: he that believeth in me, though he were dead, yet shall he live" (John 11:25). The power of the resurrection is intimately connected to the enabling power of the Atonement. "Now Aaron began to open the scriptures unto them concerning the coming of Christ, and also concerning the resurrection of the dead, and that there could be no redemption for mankind save it were through the death and sufferings of Christ, and the atonement of his blood" (Alma 21:9). The prophet Alma continues in showing the connection when he said, "But God ceaseth not to be God, and mercy claimeth the penitent, and mercy cometh because of the atonement; and the atonement bringeth to pass the resurrection of the dead; and the resurrection of the dead bringeth back men into the presence of God; and thus they are restored into his presence, to be judged according to their works, according to the law and justice" (Alma 42:23).

The prophets Nephi, Jacob, Moroni, and Mormon have given us additional insights to the resurrection. As I feast upon these verses, I am filled with gratitude, for that is the purpose for which I write this book—that our gratitude might increase and draw us ever closer to God our Father and our Savior Jesus Christ.

Nephi shows us the goodness of God and our promised blessings. "Wherefore, may God raise you from death by the power of the resurrection, and also from everlasting death by the power of the atonement, that ye may be received into the eternal kingdom of God, that ye may praise him through grace divine" (2 Nephi 10:25). The last phrase is significant: "that ye may praise him through grace divine." What do we do when we praise God? Through our praise, we show we are thankful continually, thus pleasing God and strengthening our relationship. In the act of praising God, we are in a state of humility, which empowers our ability to grow through the goodness of God. We become strong in our humility. As we praise God, we in effect confess of the greatness and goodness of God our Father and Jesus the Christ—the very thing Moroni was attempting to teach us in our pondering (see Moroni 10:3). We praise God as we see His hand in all things. We sing hymns of praise. We pray with praise. It is in this state that our minds are on the things of God and His goodness, thus as we think of Him we will become like Him. We speak of the goodness and mercy of God as we praise Him in our communications with others. This will help others come to know of His goodness and mercy in all things. Praising God brings miracles in our own lives.

Jacob seeks to help us understand our role in being reconciled to God through faith in Jesus Christ. "Wherefore, beloved brethren, be reconciled unto him through the atonement of Christ, his Only Begotten Son, and ye may obtain a resurrection, according to the power of the resurrection which is in Christ, and be presented as the first-fruits of Christ unto God, having faith, and obtained a good hope of glory in him before he manifesteth himself in the flesh" (Jacob 4:11). We are restored from our separation from God and all things are made right through the reconciliation of Christ the Lord. As Jacob recorded these truths he had to exercise his faith before Christ had even come to the earth. Jacob knew of Christ and had beheld of His glory. Surely Jacob stands as an example of one who has exercised his faith in the Lord Jesus Christ. This fact is exemplified as we read his words in 2 Nephi 9, which teaches great depth to the doctrine of the Atonement.

Jacob, ever the pleading prophet, is trying to help us understand some things we need to do, and if we don't, we stand in shame before the bar of God. "Wherefore, my beloved brethren, I beseech of you in words of soberness that ye would repent, and come with full purpose of heart, and cleave unto God as he cleaveth unto you . . . ye have been nourished by the good word of God all the day long. . . . Will ye reject the words of the prophets . . . and deny the good word of Christ, and the power of God, and the gift of the Holy Ghost . . . and make a mock of the great plan of redemption" (Jacob 6:5–8). Now if we do these things we put to shame our Savior, and then we will stand before Him in guilt and shame at the judgment bar. "Know ye not that if ye will do these things, that the power of the redemption and the resurrection, which is in Christ, will bring you to stand with shame and awful guilt before the bar of God?" (Jacob 6:9). This is what prophets do. They seek to help us understand the gravity of disobedience and the blessings of obedience.

Moroni makes clear that the resurrection is power over temporal death. "And because of the redemption of man, which came by Jesus Christ, they are brought back into the presence of the Lord; yea, this is wherein all men are redeemed, because the death of Christ bringeth to pass the resurrection, which bringeth to pass a redemption from an endless sleep, from which sleep all men shall be awakened by the power of God when the trump shall sound; and they shall come forth, both small and great, and all shall stand before his bar, being redeemed and loosed from this eternal band of death, which death is a temporal death" (Mormon 9:13). The universality of the resurrection is our immortality. We are saved from the temporal death. Then we stand to be judged according to our works and the desires of our hearts before the Lord. Then we are restored good for good and evil for evil. Our degree of righteousness determines our degree of glory.

Mormon in his great sermon on faith, hope, and charity taught their power in our lives. "And what is it that ye shall hope for? Behold I say unto you that ye shall have hope through the atonement of Christ and the power of his resurrection, to be raised unto life eternal, and this because of your faith in him according to the promise" (Moroni 7:41). Moroni, ever the dutiful son, recorded his Father's words in Moroni 7. The doctrine of faith, hope, and charity are expounded on. Sometimes we fail to see the power of hope. Without hope, we are miserable at best. We cannot look forward to a state of happiness. Hope is the anchor to our souls. Our hope is founded in Christ, His infinite Atonement, and the power of His Resurrection because of our faith in Him. Faith is our hope, the moving cause of action and our power to do all things. Thus, we please God through our faith in Christ the Lord (see Hebrews 11:6).

We are indebted to God the Father and the Lord Jesus Christ for our resurrection unto the newness of life through the infinite and eternal Atonement. Our Savior's suffering and sacrificing was the price He paid so that we might live again and at the same time be nurtured and blessed in our sojourn here upon the earth. We cannot separate the suffering and sacrificing from the death and Resurrection, for they are all part of Jesus becoming the Christ, the Savior and Redeemer of the world. As we grow through our adversities and pain, we are refining ourselves. Through the infinite Atonement and the power of the Holy Ghost, we are being sanctified (see 3 Nephi 27:20). This earth life was not to be a blissful, carefree experience. It was and is to be a trying and most difficult task. It requires sacrifice. Were it not so, how could we be exalted? Exaltation requires us to sacrifice. The Prophet Joseph taught,

> Let us here observe, that a religion that does not require the sacrifice of all things never has power sufficient to produce the faith necessary unto life and salvation; . . . it is through the medium of the sacrifice of all earthly things that men do actually know that they are doing the things that are well pleasing in the sight of God. When a man has offered in sacrifice all that he has for the truth's sake, not even withholding his life, and believing before God that he has been called to make this sacrifice because he seeks to do his will, he does know, most assuredly, that God does and will accept his sacrifice and offering, and that he has not, nor will not seek his face in vain. Under these circumstances, then, he can obtain the faith necessary for him to lay hold on eternal life. (Joseph Smith, *Lectures on Faith* [Salt Lake City: Deseret Book, 1835], 69)

Sacrifice brings forth the blessings of God.

Chapter 6

APPLYING ALL ASPECTS *of the* ATONEMENT *to* OUR LIVES

APPLYING THE ATONEMENT TO OUR MINDS AND HEARTS

When the Holy Ghost touches our hearts and minds, truth is revealed to our soul. We come to understand eternal verities. As King Benjamin taught his people of the suffering of our Savior and His infinite Atonement, they came to this knowledge and said,

> Yea, we believe all the words which thou hast spoken unto us; and also, we know of their surety and truth, because of the Spirit of the Lord Omnipotent, which has wrought a mighty change in us, or in our hearts, that we have no more disposition to do evil, but to do good continually.
>
> And we, ourselves, also, through the infinite goodness of God, and the manifestations of his Spirit, have great views of that which is to come; and were it expedient, we could prophesy of all things.
>
> And it is the faith which we have had on the things which our king has spoken unto us that has brought us to this great knowledge, whereby we do rejoice with such exceedingly great joy.
>
> And we are willing to enter into a covenant with our God to do his will, and to be obedient to his commandments in all things that he shall command us, all the remainder of our days, that we may not bring upon ourselves a never-ending torment, as has been spoken by the angel, that we may not drink out of the cup of the wrath of God.

> And now, these are the words which king Benjamin desired of them; and therefore he said unto them: Ye have spoken the words that I desired; and the covenant which ye have made is a righteous covenant.
>
> And now, because of the covenant which ye have made *ye shall be called the children of Christ, his sons, and his daughters; for behold, this day he hath spiritually begotten you; for ye say that your hearts are changed through faith on his name; therefore, ye are born of him and have become his sons and his daughters.*
>
> *And under this head ye are made free, and there is no other head whereby ye can be made free. There is no other name given whereby salvation cometh*; therefore, I would that ye should take upon you the name of Christ, all you that have entered into the covenant with God that ye should be obedient unto the end of your lives. (Mosiah 5:2–8; emphasis added)

As the Atonement touched their minds and hearts, they changed. They were drawn to the Lord. Feelings of gratitude draw us to the Lord: "He doeth not anything save it be for the benefit of the world; for he loveth the world, even that he layeth down his own life that he may draw all men unto him. Wherefore, he commandeth none that they shall not partake of his salvation" (2 Nephi 26:24). The Lord explained this as a power of the Atonement when He said, "And my Father sent me that I might be lifted up upon the cross; and after that I had been lifted up upon the cross, that I might draw all men unto me" (3 Nephi 27:14). "And I, if I be lifted up from the earth, will draw all men unto me" (John 12:32). We literally come unto Christ when we partake of His Atonement through the ordinances and covenants of the gospel of Jesus Christ.

Applying the Atonement to our lives is the essence of life. The design of our existence is to be happy. The love of God is the source of all happiness. The love of God is expressed through His Beloved Son through all things and is centered in His atoning sacrifice. When we partake of all the life-saving ordinances and covenants of the gospel of Jesus Christ, we take the infinite Atonement into our lives. We understand and appreciate the Atonement to the point that gratitude consumes our hearts and the love of God consumes our souls. We are different. We are not only born of God but also perfected in Christ. We are made complete. We can come to understand this profound truth as we worship in His holy house. We can ponder in the celestial room. We can search the scriptures and feast upon the word, which is a personification of our Savior in all things, for they are His words of eternal life. And because of these things, we can come closer to our God, having gained the knowledge of our Father and our Savior. Not only is the Atonement the saving action that makes all things possible, but it is also the enabling power of our lives, which brings us to a state of never-ending happiness.

We are privileged to partake of the ordinances and covenants of the gospel of Jesus Christ. We begin to understand and appreciate the doctrine of Christ. "Now this is the commandment: Repent, all ye ends of the earth, and come unto me and be baptized in my name, that ye may be sanctified by the reception of the Holy Ghost, that ye may stand spotless before me at the last day. Verily, verily, I say unto you, this is my gospel; and ye know the things that ye must do in my church; for the works which ye have seen me do that shall ye also do; for that which ye have seen me do even that shall ye do; therefore, if ye do these things blessed are ye, for ye shall be lifted up at the last day" (3 Nephi 27:20–22). We are familiar in a general sense with the first four principles and ordinances of the gospel. The real question in life is, where do we stand on the matter of understanding and appreciating the Atonement of our Savior Jesus Christ? Have we truly received it into our souls? What do we need to do about it? Let us consider the following:

First: Let us evaluate our lives as we read Alma 5 carefully and decide what we need to do. My sweetheart has shared with me a record she made in her journal about reevaluating her life and the things that matter most.

> When our children were young and many—we had eight children—at times I felt overwhelmed with all I had to do. And yes, at times I felt a little discouraged. We lived in our dream home; Ed was doing wonderfully well teaching and practicing dentistry.
>
> I remember tidying up the family room and kitchen area before he came home in the evening so there would be some sense

of order. On this particular afternoon, I was vacuuming up the graham cracker crumbs and other debris on the carpet, and Ed walked in, much earlier than I expected. He came over to me, I turned off the vacuum, and he gave me a wonderful hug. He whispered in my ear that he loved me, and then he said something that gave me cause to think and take action. He said, "I know what you're going to be doing in the eternities." I, of course, eagerly asked, "What?" He replied, "You are going to be the chief vacuumer."

That statement is funny now, but then it was devastating. That is not what I wanted to be doing in the eternities. Being a woman of action, that evening I got on the phone and called a babysitter to come the next day, for the entire day. I was able to use a little cabin in the mountains.

The next day, I remember it as a beautiful fall day, I drove up to the backside of Mount Timpanogos with stacks of paper, pens, my scriptures, and a calendar and in the attitude of fasting. I began my experience with prayer, asking for help and guidance. Then I started to write. I made lists of everything I needed to do in regards to everything: cleaning our home, teaching our children, preparing to live with my sweetheart forever.

I remember writing things such as clean out the refrigerator with the moldy vegetables in the drawer, mend the children's clothes before they grow out of them, clean out the bathroom drawers where the toothpaste is mixed in with the combs and yucky hair. I wrote them in no special order, including things of an eternal nature as they came to my mind, such as read the scriptures more regularly, live in the eternities as a forever family, go to the temple more regularly, have better family home evenings, tell my children I love them more often.

I worked on my list all morning; I had pages. Then I stopped, went for a lovely walk and enjoyed the beautiful colored leaves, and thought, what did I really want?

I returned to the cabin. I knew what I wanted. I knew what was most important. I wanted to live my life so I would be worthy to live with Ed in the eternities and have a forever family. It was interesting because I knew that before, but that little exercise of writing down all the things that were distracting me was enlightening.

> I went back to my lists and put a number one by what was most important, and a number two, and on down my list. I never did put a number by that yucky bathroom drawer.
>
> I went to my scriptures and read a few of my favorites. "Trust in the Lord with all thine heart; and lean not unto thine own understanding. In all thy ways acknowledge him, and he shall direct thy paths" (Proverbs 3:5–6).
>
> My next step was to draw up a calendar with the hours of the day. I began to put onto my calendar the things I needed to do and when. I scheduled a temple day, when I was going to read my scriptures, plans for family home evening, and so on. I felt so at peace.
>
> I drove home that fall afternoon with such gratitude to my Heavenly Father for the direction I had been given. I felt such peace. When I got home and had a chance to visit with Ed about my experience and share with him how wonderful it was, I asked him if he felt it was something we would want to do together. He readily agreed, and that became the beginning of our weekly, monthly, and yearly planning session. We were making plans to follow the perfect plan of our Heavenly Father. We were making plans to know God and Jesus Christ, whom He had sent so that we might enjoy eternal life. We were making plans to partake of the infinite Atonement and to more fully understand the doctrines, ordinances, and covenants made in the temple.
>
> Those planning times drew us closer together than we had ever been. We attended the temple weekly and later had lunch together in the cafeteria and did our planning. We talked about our individual goals and how we were doing. We talked about each of our children, what their current needs were, and what we could do to encourage them and bless their lives. We talked about future goals and plans, family plans and outings. We talked about current conference talks and the direction we had received and planned how to implement that direction. We would change.
>
> Yearly, Ed and I would go on a little overnighter and make a plan for the entire year. What a blessing in our lives. What a wonderful way to stay on track and work together toward what mattered most in both our lives.

This was a magnificent moment in our lives. We became a better husband and wife. We became a better father and mother. We changed. We improved. It brought joy to our lives, and never again did we think, "We are just fine the way we are." This has been a blessing to our lives.

Just as our Father made a perfect plan, even the plan of happiness enabled by His Beloved Son's Atonement, so should we make plans to fulfill the measure of our creation by having a Christ-centered home where the fruits of the Atonement are enjoyed.

Second: Let us feast upon the scriptures, general conference talks, and other Church publications, for in them we are reminded of Christ. They all stand as a testament of Christ, reminding us to become like Him and to repent, improve, and change. We should feast upon the words of the Book of Mormon, for it is another witness of Christ, another witness of the Anointed One, another witness of His infinite Atonement. In the 6,607 verses of the Book of Mormon, there are over 3,925 references to our beloved Savior, with hundreds of different names and descriptions. These descriptions bring a depth of understanding to our beloved Savior and help us understand His many roles within our lives. Whenever I have a question about life and living, it seems the answer is in this precious book. This book draws us to Christ. We come unto Christ through faith unto repentance. Remember that of all the doctrines preached and recorded, repentance is the most often spoken of. We need to change, and that means improvement and repentance.

The Book of Mormon has literally saved my life. This book of books was saved for our dispensation. It was the way the Lord chose to reestablish His gospel and His word here upon the earth in the fulness of times. It is not only another witness of Jesus Christ; it is the perfect witness of Christ. As a priesthood leader, when I asked a question, the Spirit would often say, "The Lord has said," and then a scripture from The Book of Mormon would come to mind that would give the answer or inspire one to move forward having hope and faith in our Savior. Five pages a day, and you can read the Book of Mormon three times a year. Remember that the scriptures testify of Christ, which means they bear witness of the Atonement of Christ.

Third: Let us choose to partake of the infinite Atonement through faith unto repentance and make the mighty change to become even as He is. Change is the essence of becoming and growing. We choose to receive liberty and eternal life though Christ the Lord. We choose to change our values, attitudes, thoughts, and the way we live our lives—we live after the manner of happiness. We choose to change our hearts and souls and turn back to Christ the Lord and our Heavenly Father. This always includes temple worship, where we will come closer to God and the knowledge of Him, gaining insights to the mysteries of the kingdom and the power of godliness, all of which will empower us to do good—to change and to become.

Sometimes we mistakenly think that repentance is an event rather than a process. The Lord will heal us as we repent and are converted; however, that process may take a short time or quite a long time: "Will ye not now return unto me, and repent of your sins, and be converted, that I may heal you? Yea, verily I say unto you, if ye will come unto me ye shall have eternal life. Behold, mine arm of mercy is extended towards you, and whosoever will come, him will I receive; and blessed are those who come unto me" (3 Nephi 9:13–14). The Lord in His ever-loving way seeks out the lost and weary: "I, the Lord, will feel after them, and if they harden not their hearts, and stiffen not their necks against me, they shall be converted, and I will heal them" (D&C 112:13). Because our Savior truly loves us, He has commanded us to repent so that we may receive the blessings of forgiveness and eternal life. We change in order to become.

Let us always remember that the Lord in His infinite goodness has suffered all things so He would be able to nurture us in all things. We need to receive the enabling power of the Atonement to help us in our moments of trials, tribulations, pain, afflictions, and temptation. "Behold, I stand at the door, and knock: if any man hear my voice, and open the door, I will come in to him, and will sup with him, and he with me" (Revelation 3:20). Ask with faith and real intent, and the hand of Lord will bless us and strengthen us in all things. His nurturing us is part of His Atonement, the enabling power of all things.

Chapter 7

GOLGOTHA

PRIOR TO THE CROSS

This chapter is a chronology from the betrayal to the cross to help us understand and appreciate all that our beloved Savior went through prior to the suffering on the cross. He was ever the victim of cruel men who sought His life.

The infinite Atonement has been effective in the lives of mankind from the time of Adam. The actual suffering and sacrificing began in Gethsemane and continued on Golgotha's cross, and concluded in the glorious Resurrection from the Garden Tomb.

After the Lord's suffering in Gethsemane, the great Redeemer is betrayed: "And while he yet spake, lo, Judas, one of the twelve, came, and with him a great multitude with swords and staves, from the chief priests and elders of the people. Now he that betrayed him gave them a sign, saying, Whomsoever I shall kiss, that same is he: hold him fast. And forthwith he came to Jesus, and said, Hail, master; and kissed him. And Jesus said unto him, Friend, wherefore art thou come? Then came they, and laid hands on Jesus, and took him. And, behold, one of them which were with Jesus stretched out his hand, and drew his sword, and struck a servant of the high priest's, and smote off his ear" (Matthew 26:47–51). This betrayal by one in whom He had placed trust and responsibility was yet another bitter moment.

The Savior was taken first to Annas and then to the high priest Caiaphas. The Jews accused Him on the charge of blasphemy. From Caiaphas, the Lord was brought before Pontius

Pilate. Then the Savior was sent from Pilate to Herod and back to Pilate. Pontius Pilate, after his conversation with Christ and having washed his hands before the multitude, said, "I am innocent of the blood of this just person: see ye to it" (Matthew 27:24). Pilate released Christ to the will of the Jewish leaders to be crucified. The Lord was then stripped of His clothing, given a scarlet robe, and had a crown of thorns put on His head and a reed in His right hand. All this was done, and many illegalities were brought to bear in the so-called trial of Jesus. They mocked Him. They spit upon Him. They smote Him on the head with the reed. They scourged Him. Yet there were many who bewailed and lamented the fate of their Savior. The Savior was soon to be on His way to the cross on Golgotha's hill. Jesus "bearing his cross went forth into a place called the place of a skull, which is called in the Hebrew Golgotha" (John 19:17).

This illegal prosecution, persecution, mocking, scourging, and all manner of ill-doing from His tormentors within the so-called trial is simply to remind us that Christ, ever so mistreated and unappreciated, carried on to fulfill His sacred assignment from the Father. He was meek in His triumph and ever full of love. His dignity and reverence for staying the course will be forever an example to us. And our gratitude will be deepened for His goodness and mercy toward us.

PROPHECIES OF HIS CRUCIFIXION

There were many prophecies of the coming of the Lord, His foreordination, His divine Sonship of His redeeming roles, His anointed purpose being the Messiah and the Lamb of God, the infinite Atonement, His authority, His betrayal and death, His condescension unto the children of men, His Crucifixion and death, His Resurrection, and His Second Coming.

In the prophecies of the Crucifixion, David described some of the events of the Crucifixion and words of our Savior in Psalm 22. He records Jesus's pleading words to His Father: "My God, my God, why hast thou forsaken me?" (Psalm 22:1); the mocking of His enemies: "But I am a worm, and no man; a reproach of men, and despised of the people. All they that see me laugh me to scorn:

they shoot out the lip, they shake the head, saying, He trusted on the Lord that he would deliver him: let him deliver him, seeing he delighted in him" (Psalm 22:6–8); the piercing of His hands and feet: "They pierced my hands and my feet" (Psalm 22:16). They cast lots for His garments: "They part my garments among them, and cast lots upon my vesture" (Psalm 22:18).

Isaiah spoke messianically of the Savior as well in many instances, such as, "Therefore will I divide him a portion with the great, and he shall divide the spoil with the strong; because he hath poured out his soul unto death: and he was numbered with the transgressors; and he bare the sin of many, and made intercession for the transgressors" (Isaiah 53:12).

Zechariah foretold the feelings of those witnessing His Crucifixion: "And I will pour upon the house of David, and upon the inhabitants of Jerusalem, the spirit of grace and of supplications: and they shall look upon me whom they have pierced, and they shall mourn for him, as one mourneth for his only son, and shall be in bitterness for him, as one that is in bitterness for his firstborn" (Zechariah 12:10). And later he records, "And one shall say unto him, What are these wounds in thine hands? Then he shall answer, Those with which I was wounded in the house of my friends" (Zechariah 13:6).

Surely reading such words we better understand the statement of the Savior when He said, "Search the scriptures; for in them ye think ye have eternal life: and they are they which testify of me" (John 5:39). The scriptures are testaments or witnesses of Christ. All scriptures testify and bear witness that Jesus is the Christ, the Savior and Redeemer of the world, the Almighty and Beloved Son of God.

DEATH BY CRUCIFIXION

Christ was crucified on the cross on Golgotha's hill. Crucifixion was one of the most punishing forms of death ever created by man. The pain and agony were intense, to say the least, brutal beyond description. Man cannot comprehend the extent of the agony that Christ suffered. Just as Gethsemane was beyond our power to comprehend, so likewise was the suffering of Christ on the cross.

Though many others had been crucified, the Lord was carrying the weight of all the sins of the world that added punishment and sorrow to His soul. Pilate had inscribed on the cross to add insult to His unfathomable injuries, "King of the Jews." Prior to being taken to the cross on Golgotha's hill, the Lord was scourged. It has been said that the victims of crucifixion were scourged thirty-nine times. The persecutors would use a rod about a foot long with nine leather straps. At the end of each strap were pieces of broken bones or sharp rocks. The purpose of the scourging was to break the skin and remove as much of the outer layer of skin as possible, thus intensifying the pain and agony of the victims as they were crucified. Then the Lord was required to carry the top part of the cross to Golgotha. It is estimated that this could have weighed 80–120 pounds—a tremendous amount following His scourging. The Savior started out bearing His cross, but due to His weakened state, He was unable to continue the approximately third of a mile to Golgotha. He had suffered in Gethsemane to the extent of sweating blood from every pore. He had been beaten and scourged almost to death.

Simon, a man of Cyrene, was compelled to carry the cross. We do not have detailed information concerning Simon, but why would he be compelled to carry the cross if he were not associated with Christ in some manner? It has been conjectured that he was a believer from North Africa who was there at the time and showed compassion for our Savior, so likely he loved and cared for our Savior. His sons Alexander and Rufus were mentioned by Mark, and Paul indicates that he knew Rufus's mother, who would have been Simon's wife (see Mark 15:21; Romans 16:13). Surely there is evidence that Simon cared for His Savior, and thus with him showing this compassion, the Romans insisted on him carrying a portion of the cross to Golgotha. Blessed be Simon, a man of Cyrene.

The crucifixion form of execution was purported to have been invented by the Persians in approximately 300 BC, however there are records indicating the usage of crucifixion for executions as early as the sixth century BC and the Romans perfected the process. Constantine, the Roman Emperor, later abolished crucifixion as a form of execution in the Roman Empire in AD 337 out of respect for the Savior. The pain inflicted upon the victim was excruciating, and that is where the word *excruciating* originated (Latin *excruciatus*, or "out of the cross"). It is a slow and agonizingly painful death. The body is nailed to the cross, and in case of the Savior, there were nails in the palms of His hands, in His wrists, and in His feet. These nails, according to archeological data, were tapered iron spikes 5–7 inches in length. The nails through the Savior's wrists were near to or pierced the median nerve, which would be stimulated with any movement, and then horrific shocks would send tremors throughout His body. The nails in the Lord's feet would have been placed through both feet as they were placed on top of one another and pierced through the metatarsal space. At the base of the cross, Mary witnessed the death of her beloved Son, with her sister, Mary the wife of Cleophas, Mary Magdalene, and John the beloved.

As Christ hung on the cross, surely His scourging was bleeding and the loss of blood only exacerbated His pain and weakness. When He could no longer bear His weight by pushing up from His feet, surely His shoulder joints became separated due to the weight of his body. On the cross, the Savior's breathing was severely hampered, and the muscle cramping continuously prevented the full respiration cycle. The mere act of breathing evoked pain either in His chest or in His body to raise up high enough to get a full breath of air. The feeling of suffocation and the inability to get enough air often led to asphyxia, which is one of the many factors leading to death by crucifixion. Dehydration, cardiovascular problems—especially heart arrhythmia and congestive heart failure—and plural effusions or discharges all can contribute to death. It is a slow form of dying, often lasting several hours (some scholars state that it could be up to two or three days), all of which is not only agonizing and excruciating but also physiologically impossible to bear. With all the precursors of death weighing upon the Lord's body, it seems that eventually His heart gave out—only fitting for the Lord dying of a broken heart. I can hardly type as my heart is so heavy and my eyes so moist for my suffering Savior. As I have studied the way my beloved Savior died on the cross—with so much pain and agony, fighting for every breath He took—and knowing that He is the Giver of every breath we breathe, my heart is broken and I am totally submissive to my Savior and my Father's will. And then He died. The spear pierced His side, and blood and water came forth. Our beloved Savior had finished His work on Golgotha's hill.

Don and Jay Parry in their epic work on the Atonement of Christ have written,

> Why did the Romans use a cross for their executions? It is likely that it was the most horrible form of suffering they were able to devise. In the classic *Life of Christ*, Frederic Farrar wrote,
>
> "A death by crucifixion seems to include all that pain and death can have of the horrible and ghastly—dizziness, cramp, thirst, starvation, sleeplessness, traumatic fever, tetanus, publicity of shame, long continuance of torment, horror of anticipation, mortification of untended wounds, all intensified just up to the point at which they can be endured at all, but all stopping just short of the point which would give to the sufferer the relief of unconsciousness. The unnatural position made every movement painful; the lacerated veins and crushed tendons throbbed with incessant anguish; the wounds, inflamed by exposure, gradually gangrened; the arteries, especially of the head and stomach, became swollen and oppressed with surcharged blood; and, while each variety of misery went on gradually increasing, there was added to them the intolerable pang of a burning and raging thirst. Such was the death to which Christ was doomed." (Frederic Farrar, *Life of Christ* [Minneapolis, MN: Cumorah Foundation, 2008], 505)
>
> "No word can be found adequate to describe so monstrous a proceeding," the Roman statesman Cicero wrote, as a man who likely had opportunity to see that monstrous proceeding firsthand (Cicero died in 43 BC). It is noteworthy that the words *excruciating* and *crucifixion* derive from the same Latin root (*crucis*).
>
> If the Romans used crucifixion because it was so dreadful a way to die, why did the Father require the Son to die in such a manner? The following are some possibilities:
>
> First, it was required that the Son descend below all things. The descent brought together a combination of the intense suffering in the Garden of Gethsemane, the sleepless night, the deep pain of betrayal, the sadistic treatment of the Romans and Jews, the brutality of the cross, the spiritual death of a sinless being, and

> more—all combined in an emotionally heightened state that has sometimes, with meaning, been called "the passion."
>
> Second, death by crucifixion represented a curse on the victim. Paul wrote, "Christ hath redeemed us from the curse of the law, being made a curse for us: for it is written, Cursed is every one that hangeth on a tree" (Galations 3:13). Thus, in submitting Himself to crucifixion, Jesus Christ was "made a curse for us," in keeping with the pronouncement in the law of Moses: "And if a man have committed a sin worthy of death, and he be to be put to death, and thou hang him on a tree: His body shall not remain all night upon the tree, but thou shalt in any wise bury him that day; (for he that is hanged is accursed of God)" (Deuteronomy 21:22–23).
>
> Third, the symbolism of crucifixion is instructive. The arms are reached out as in surrender. The crucified individual was forced into that position and held there by the cruelest of means—but Christ willingly drank of this portion of the bitter cup, that the will of the Father might be done in every detail. (Donald W. Parry and Jay A. Parry, *Symbols and Shadows: Unlocking a Deeper Understanding of the Atonement* [Salt Lake City, Desert Book, 2009], 234–5)

Understanding and appreciating what literally happens in death by crucifixion can increase our empathy for our beloved Savior. As we conclude this section, I can hardly write. Every moment of the Atonement brought agony to our beloved Savior. My mind and heart are in overload trying to comprehend and feel enough appreciation for all my Savior went through for me and you. Our minds are not able to comprehend all things, so we need to grow through faith, hope, and charity with an eye single to the glory of God and love our Father and our Savior with all our heart, might, mind, and strength. If we ponder just a little, we will readily see what Moses came to understand: "For this cause I know that man is nothing, which thing I never had supposed" (Moses 1:10). This is what Paul was trying to teach the Galatians: "For if a man think himself to be something, when he is nothing, he deceiveth himself" (Galatians 6:3). Moses and Paul were not teaching that we as the divine children of God are nothing; quite the contrary. They were teaching that man—in our fallen state—is really lost, fallen, and mortal, totally and completely dependent upon the grace of God. This is true! This is why Ammon said, "Yea, I know that I am nothing; as to my strength I am weak; therefore I will not boast of myself, but I will boast of my God, for in his strength I can do all things" (Alma 26:12).

In this state of mortality, we have to live by faith. Our power comes as we exercise faith in the Lord Jesus Christ. When we use the priesthood, it is by faith and in the name of Jesus Christ, through which all things can be done. Our dependence on God our Father and our Savior Jesus Christ was and is part of the plan. This too draws us to God and Christ because we know, like Ammon, we are nothing as to ourselves. We are ever grateful for the grace of God the Father and our Savior Jesus Christ. As our empathy increases, so will our gratitude and our love for our Heavenly Father and our Savior.

CHRIST ON THE CROSS

While on the cross, the Lord spoke seven times. Each time He spoke carries a great message to us from which we can learn.

- "Father, forgive them, for they know what they do" (Luke 23:34).
- "Verily I say unto thee, To day shalt thou be with me in paradise" (Luke 23:43).
- "Woman, behold thy son. Behold thy mother" (John 19:26–27).
- "My God, my God, why hast thou forsaken me?" (Matthew 27:46).
- "I thirst" (John 19:28).
- "It is finished" (John 19:30).
- "Father, into thy hands I commend my spirit" (Luke 23:46).

1. Father, forgive them, for they do not know what they do.

The Savior had suffered in Gethsemane. He had gone through the trumped-up charges in the trial, which was illegal on many counts. He was spit upon. He was mocked. He was scourged. He was reviled on the cross by those who said to Him, "Thou that destroyest the temple, and buildest it in three days, save thyself. If thou be the Son of God, come down from the cross" (Matthew 27:40). The scribes and elders mocked him: "He saved others; himself he cannot save. If he be the King of Israel, let him now come down from the cross, and we will believe him. He trusted in God; let him deliver him now, if he will have him: for he said, I am the Son of God" (Matthew 27:42–43).

Luke 23:34 is clarified in the Joseph Smith Translation: "Father, forgive them; for they know not what they do (Meaning the soldiers who crucified him)" (Luke 23:34, footnote c; from Joseph Smith Translation, Luke 23:35). The Roman soldiers had little knowledge of Christ and His role. They were raised within a different society and culture with different values and beliefs. Can you imagine the transcendent love that our Savior had for all mankind, as evidenced by His forgiveness and compassion even at this moment? There was no hatred in His soul. He never did lash out at His tormentors. Only forgiveness could come from His soul and be spoken from His lips. He was their only way, and they did not understand or believe He was the promised Messiah. The ever-loving Christ did what only He could do: pray for those who did not understand what they were doing. "Father, forgive them, for they do not know what they do." It has been said, "After all that has been preached, we need but repent and forgive one another." Surely this is the essence of a Christlike life, for all of the attributes of the divine nature of Christ are found within repentance and forgiveness—faith, virtue, knowledge, temperance, patience, brotherly kindness, godliness, charity, humility, diligence (D&C 4:6; see also 2 Peter 1:5–7). These divine qualities of Christ will lead us to forgive others in all things. Forgiveness empowers us with freedom. There are no grudges. Vengeance flees from our souls. We are doing the most Christlike thing mortal man can do. Only Christ can forgive sins, but we can forgive others and ourselves, not only because it is a commandment but also because it brings true joy and happiness. You feel good. I am grateful for those who have forgiven me, but I must confess the joy of this doctrine and principle is in forgiving others.

2. Verily I say unto thee, To day shalt thou be with me in paradise.

Salvation was accomplished through the Lord Jesus Christ. "For God hath not appointed us to wrath, but to obtain salvation by our Lord Jesus Christ" (1 Thessalonians 5:9; see also Romans 1:16; 2 Timothy 2:10; 3:15; Hebrews 9:28; Omni 1:6; Mosiah 3:12, 17–18; 5:8, 15; Alma 34:6, 34).

In regard to this statement made by Christ, the Prophet Joseph Smith taught that Jesus was saying, "This day thou shalt be with me in the world of spirits" (*Teachings of the Prophet Joseph Smith* [Salt Lake City: Deseret Book, 1938], 309). We note that the Savior taught that He would teach in the world of the spirits. "By which also he went and preached unto the spirits in prison" (1 Peter 3:19; see also D&C 138:8). The Lord in His altruistic fashion was seeking to give comfort to this man who surely wondered about his fate. We need not judge him or anyone. Yet surely he would go to the spirit world, where he could be taught, yet judged according to those in the flesh (see 1 Peter 4:6). As always, the Savior was giving the man on the cross hope as only Christ could give.

3. Woman, behold your son. Behold your mother.

Our Savior's love was ever extended to His mother throughout His life. "Now there stood by the cross of Jesus his mother, and his mother's sister, Mary the wife of Cleophas, and Mary Magdalene. When Jesus therefore saw his mother, and the disciple standing by, whom he loved, he saith unto his mother, Woman, behold thy son! Then saith he to the disciple, Behold thy mother! And from that hour that disciple took her unto his own home" (John 19:25–27). Elder James E. Talmage, in his landmark work writing about Jesus the Christ, makes special mention of the possible relationship between the Savior and John: "From the fact that John mentions the mother of Jesus and 'his mother's sister' (19:25) and omits mention of Salome by name, some expositors hold that Salome was the sister of Mary the mother of Jesus; and therefore the Savior's aunt. This relationship would makes James and John cousins to Jesus" (James E. Talmage, *Jesus the Christ* [Salt Lake City: Deseret Book, 1915], 521).

The use of the word *woman* is a term of endearment, reverence, dignity, and respect. There is also a possible connection with the term *woman* as noted in Genesis: "And I will put enmity between thee and the woman, and between thy seed and her seed; it shall bruise thy head, and thou shalt bruise his heel" (Genesis 3:15). Moses in the Pearl of Great Price is more specific: "And I will put enmity between thee and the woman, between thy seed and her seed; and he [Christ] shall bruise thy head, and thou [devil] shalt bruise his heel" (Moses 4:21).

Christ on the cross was making sure that His beloved mother was cared for and that all would be well with her. This statement is transcending when we understand the great concern in a most compromised state that the Lord was ever thinking about His mother. Is it possible to repay our mothers? I think the debt is too high. One of the ways, which I can still hear ringing inside my soul, is shown through the words from my mother when I would ask her want she wanted for Mother's Day, her birthday, and Christmas: "Oh Ed, just be a good boy." And so this was my goal, to be a good boy. Our concern for our mothers is ever present in our minds, but there comes a time of separation. In this separation, we need to make sure they are cared for in every way. The tenderness of our Savior is ever the example for us.

4. My God, My God, why have you forsaken me?

"Now from the sixth hour there was darkness over all the land unto the ninth hour. And about the ninth hour Jesus cried with a loud voice, saying, Eli, Eli, lama sabachthani? That is to say, My God, my God, why hast thou forsaken me? Some of them that stood there, when they heard that, said, This man calleth for Elias" (Matthew 27:45–47).

Why at this moment does it seem as if God the Father has left the Savior alone? The Savior clearly felt abandoned. The Father knew that His Son had to suffer and sacrifice for all mankind. Thus He withheld His power so that justice might be fulfilled. Knowing our beloved Father, I can feel the pain and sorrow He had for His Son. I suggest it was more difficult for Him to observe the suffering of His Son than we could imagine.

I vividly remember my mother expressing these words: "Oh, Ed, I wish I could be sick for you." This is not a fleeting wish. This is the ultimate expression of love. Father knew what was best for all of His children, and thus He allowed His Only Begotten Son to finish what He was ordained to do. His love for His Son never wavered, because God knew the beginning from the end. Remember, the Savior had power within Himself, yet He suffered. The "grace of the Holy Messiah, who layeth down his life according to the flesh, and taketh it again by the power of the Spirit, that he may bring to pass the resurrection of the dead, being the first that should rise" (2 Nephi 2:8). The Lord had to suffer to pay the debt so that justice would be satisfied (see Mosiah 15:9). He also suffered like no other, so He would know how to succor us in our trying times (see Alma 7:11–12). The Lord reminds us, "He that ascended up on high, as also he descended below all things, in that he comprehended all things, that he might be in all and through all things, the light of truth" (D&C 88:6). Because of this, the Lord knew how to respond to the Prophet Joseph in his darkest days:

> If thou art called to pass through tribulation; if thou art in perils among false brethren; if thou art in perils among robbers; if thou art in perils by land or by sea;
>
> If thou art accused with all manner of false accusations; if thine enemies fall upon thee; if they tear thee from the society of thy father and mother and brethren and sisters; and if with a drawn sword thine enemies tear thee from the bosom of thy wife, and of thine offspring, and thine elder son, although but six years of age, shall cling to thy garments, and shall say, My father, my father, why can't you stay with us? O, my father, what are the men going to do with you? and if then he shall be thrust from thee by the sword, and thou be dragged to prison, and thine enemies prowl around thee like wolves for the blood of the lamb;
>
> And if thou shouldst be cast into the pit, or into the hands of murderers, and the sentence of death passed upon thee; if thou be cast into the deep; if the billowing surge conspire against thee; if fierce winds become thine enemy; if the heavens gather blackness, and all the elements combine to hedge up the way; and above all, if the very jaws of hell shall gape open the mouth wide after thee,

> know thou, my son, that all these things shall give thee experience, and shall be for thy good.
>
> The Son of Man hath descended below them all. Art thou greater than he?" (D&C 122:5–8)

Why all this suffering? "Know thou, my son, that all these things shall give thee experience, and shall be for thy good" (D&C 122:7). All of us will suffer to one degree or another, and with the eyes of the Lord we can see if we choose: "All these things shall give thee experience, and shall be for thy good."

The Savior had to suffer for all. The Lord had to be bruised for our sakes. It was part of the plan: "Yet it pleased the Lord to bruise him; he hath put him to grief; when thou shalt make his soul an offering for sin he shall see his seed, he shall prolong his days, and the pleasure of the Lord shall prosper in his hand. He shall see the travail of his soul, and shall be satisfied; by his knowledge shall my righteous servant justify many; for he shall bear their iniquities. Therefore will I divide him a portion with the great, and he shall divide the spoil with the strong; because he hath poured out his soul unto death; and he was numbered with the transgressors; and he bore the sins of many, and made intercession for the transgressors" (Mosiah 14:10–12).

And thus we see that in being alone, the Lord was able to pay the ultimate price. I would suggest at that moment when the Father withheld His power and presence from His Beloved Son that He was literally suffering with Him. Yet the Father suffered it to be so that the plan of redemption might be fulfilled.

It is easy to say, yet hard to experience. The law is clear, but the experience is sometimes horrific as Christ suffered in the Garden and on the cross, as Joseph pleaded in Liberty Jail, the prophets Jeremiah (see Jeremiah 12:1) and Habakkuk (see Habakkuk 1:1–2) lamented, and as Alma and Amulek cried out, "How long shall we suffer these great afflictions, O Lord?" (Alma 14:26). And this is the lesson we are taught so that the law of opposition we may understand, but more important, we must experience the mentoring and training of the heart, and sometimes we must walk the path seemingly alone for a time. This requires that we must suffer, else we cannot really understand. We *must* go through these trials and tribulations of suffering and pain, else we will never truly come to appreciate and understand the feelings and pain of others when we seek to help them in their hour of need.

And we will. Pain is part of the law of opposition and part of the school of mortality. Pain is in everyone's life with varying degrees—life-threatening or overwhelming, disruptive or nagging. Pain is there. We all want to be able to understand pain, learn from pain, and be able to cope with the pain so that we might endure all things to prove ourselves worthy of the presence of our Heavenly Father. This is so easy to say and yet hard to endure.

My own family faced opposition, like so many others have. The situation was so unexpected and had such tragic results. It happened in October of 1986. I was, at the time, serving as a mission president of the England London South Mission. President Wendall Ashton—my dear and beloved friend who presided with his sweetheart, Belva, over the London England mission with headquarters in Hyde Park—had invited our family to a special youth morning-side with President Monson. We were all excited and looked forward to the day.

Prior to the meeting, there was a short time we met with President Monson and other leaders. President Ashton's secretary rushed up to me and said, "President, you have an urgent call from the States." I took the call in the room and learned that Cory, our son who was attending his senior year of high school in Provo, had been in a serious car accident and was in a coma. Upon hearing the news, President Monson quickly took his airline ticket out of his pocket and gave it to my wife, Pat, and then told his traveling companion to take her home to Utah on the next flight. (You could exchange tickets back in the 1980s). President Monson then turned to me and said that I might need to go home if things did not improve shortly. In shock, we all agreed, and Pat was off for the States.

The following day, the report was worse, and so Traci and Tricia, our youngest daughters, and I hurried back to Provo. When we arrived at the hospital, I offered prayer and pleaded with the Lord for our beloved son. The answer came the next morning. Cory was returning to his Heavenly Father. I remember my sweetheart holding his hand while the life-support systems were turned off and his hand turned cold. Cory Matthew Pinegar then passed on to the other side. Ever the servant, President Monson had called several times to get a report on Cory's condition. When hearing of his passing, President Monson called, expressed his sorrow, and asked how he might help. I asked if he would speak at his funeral, and he responded with loving kindness: "I hoped you would ask." At the funeral, President Monson spoke with great empathy and power. He said, "Don't ask why. That is a negative comment. He had his mission call early and is transferred to the spirit world, where a great deal of work in going on." And then he smiled and said, "I can see him with his new companion, Elder LeGrand Richards—that would be a great twosome." We all smiled and laughed. It brought joy to a somber family. Then with the power of the greater priesthood—even the priesthood of the Son of God, which we call Melchizedek—he bestowed an apostolic blessing upon our family and spoke of how we would be healed by the enabling power of the Atonement and would carry on in serving the Lord in England.

We returned to England with the pain of a lost loved one. I felt as if my entire body had been ripped from its moorings. My entire soul, it seemed, was wrenched in pain. My body and mind were racked with sorrow. Flesh of my flesh, my beloved son with such a bright future, was dead. I felt so weakened. I wondered how I could ever preach and teach with power to inspire the missionaries. I had lost my dad when I was a twelve-year-old boy, but this was a profoundly different experience. Was this opposition too much for me to handle? And then the miracle happened. The power of the Atonement entered into my being and our family's, and the pain was swept away. There were moments of tenderness when our thoughts would turn to our son, but we were healed. We knew that he was happy serving his mission in the spirit world.

When I spoke with the missionaries the following week of our return, they were amazed. Greater power was in my soul. Inspiring words came by the power of the Holy Ghost. The Lord in His goodness through a living prophet had made me into something I cannot describe save it was an instrument to do His work. I knew who I was serving and who was helping me at every turn. The Lord and His goodness are ever present as He succors and blesses His children.

I also testify that President Monson is a saint of the highest order, a prophet who speaks for God and leads the kingdom of God on the earth, even The Church of Jesus Christ of Latter-day Saints. He, like Christ, whom he follows, is the example that we can all trust, for he is a man of God, walking in the Lord's ways and keeping His commandments. In many cases of difficult opposition, the Lord provides an angel, even a messenger of light and truth, to help us through our trials and tribulations, and often it is another mortal. In the great rescue effort, the Lord has asked us through His prophet to be the angels of mercy. We are to be the Lord's representatives. We become the nurturers in the strength of the Lord. When we go through specific trials, the knowledge and feelings gained often become the power of our ability to help others.

It was in the pain of this great trial of losing a son that the supernal knowledge and power of the infinite Atonement came to me. Its enabling power is real. I felt it. I know it works. I know I was healed from my grief and sorrow. I now preach and teach with greater faith, conviction, and power, all through the goodness and mercy of God. There is a difference in my heart. I am more grateful to my Father and my Savior. I acknowledge my nothingness and joy in my dependence upon the strength of the Lord in my life. My empathy and compassion have increased. I am now better able to help those who are struggling. I never would have been able to understand and appreciate their sorrow or grief if I had not known and been healed myself. The pain of opposition was the requirement for me to suffer so I could appreciate more the Atonement and the life of my beloved son. Pain resolved to peace, and broken heartedness to joy. Only through suffering can we grow.

Having said all this, I have learned that in our suffering, the pain will pass in time. Time is our ally. But the greatest power is the healing power of our Savior. I have quoted Alma 7:11–12 many times for the purpose of showing that the Lord has suffered so He would know how, according to the flesh, to succor His people. There is pain and sorrow in death, disabilities, and all manner of afflictions, but there is also sorrow for the struggling child, the wayward friend, and the disbelieving soul. It is trials such as these that I have seen cause many parents to struggle for years pleading with the Lord to send an angel to help. Day after day their prayers ascended to heaven. Finally in tears and desperation they cried out, "Father, you sent Alma an angel!" They were desperate. They couldn't handle it alone. They were pleading for help. Their faith was on trial, and then the transcending moment occurs when the Lord says with a soft whisper to their minds, "He is my son too." Then they knew, like they had always known, that God our Father is there and hears their prayers. Peace entered their souls. They remembered, "For my thoughts are not your thoughts, neither are your ways my ways, saith the Lord. For as the heavens are higher than the earth, so are my ways higher than your ways, and my thoughts than your thoughts" (Isaiah 55:8–9). And then another scripture entered their souls, "Trust in the Lord with all thine heart; and lean not unto thine own understanding. In all thy ways acknowledge him, and he shall direct thy paths" (Proverbs 3:5–6). I know, like we have always known, that the goodness of God and His tender mercies will be there for us at the right time and the right way so that we will not only grow and overcome our trials but also be nurtured and blessed in the perfect way of the Lord. Remember, we must experience the pain to know the joy.

5. I Thirst.

The Savior was offered different kinds of drinks while He was on the cross: vinegar with gall (a bitter plant used to numb the pain) or wine with myrrh (has many uses, from anointing oil to precious gifts, but in this case it was to produce insensibility as a pain killer). He was first offered one of these two drinks, which He tasted and then refused. Surely the Lord knew the effects of the drink and did not partake. The second offering of vinegar, which they put upon hyssop (a plant used for ritual cleansing), He finally put to His lips. There is no doubt that the Savior was thirsty, and yet He had a greater thirst that the Psalmist recorded:

"As the hart panteth after the water brooks, so panteth my soul after thee, O God. My soul thirsteth for God, for the living God: when shall I come and appear before God?" (Psalm 42:1–2). We thirst after righteousness and will be filled with the Holy Ghost. The Lord sought to come unto His Father. The Lord taught, "In the last day, that great day of the feast, Jesus stood and cried, saying, If any man thirst, let him come unto me, and drink" (John 7:37). Could our Savior have been thirsting for His Father? David said as he sought favor with the Lord, "I remember the days of old; I meditate on all thy works; I muse on the work of thy hands. I stretch forth my hands unto thee: my soul thirsteth after thee, as a thirsty land. Selah" (Psalm 143:5–6).

Selah is used often throughout the book of Psalms. The meaning is obscure and there is a great amount of disagreement among the scholars. The Psalms were normally performed musically with voice and instruments such as harps. *Selah* always appears after a period, and then simply the word *Selah*, period. Which simply meant to the musicians "pause." It was like a rest sign we would use in music today. A definition that seems to be most acceptable as the word is used in Psalms is to pause to ponder and meditate about what has just been said. David is telling the Lord that he is reaching out to God, not only reaching but thirsting after Him, and then using a metaphor: even as a thirsty land seeketh rain so as to exist. In the Sermon on the Mount and at the temple, the Lord said, "And blessed are all they who do hunger and thirst after righteousness, for they shall be filled with the Holy Ghost" (3 Nephi 12:6).

Whether it be physiological or metaphorical, both definitions are true, for He did thirst and He did desire to come to His Father. Is not this our yearning in our hearts? The essence of everything in the gospel and kingdom of God is to help us return to our Father. This is what life is all about—that we "may dwell with God in a state of never-ending happiness. O remember, remember that these things are true; for the Lord God hath spoken it" (Mosiah 2:41). Everyone is different, and it is hard to relate some of the most tender feelings I have for my Heavenly Father. He is real. I know Him. I talk with Him. I seek to please Him. I want to be good. I desperately want to hear that He is pleased with me. I fall short. Yet I try hard. I know He loves me and cares personally about me and my life. He feels this way about all His children because He has all power, all wisdom, and all knowledge and only seeks the welfare of His children—their immortality and eternal life—because He is our Father and He loves us completely.

6. It is finished

"Now there was set a vessel full of vinegar: and they filled a sponge with vinegar, and put it upon hyssop, and put it to his mouth. When Jesus therefore had received the vinegar, he said, It is finished: and he bowed his head, and gave up the ghost" (John 19:29–30). Thus the prophecy was fulfilled, "They gave me also gall for my meat; and in my thirst they gave me vinegar to drink" (Psalm 69:21). The Greek word for finished is *tetelestai*. This wonderful word means "paid in full, and with full effect and ongoing." This perfectly describes the infinite and enabling power of the Atonement: it is constant, continuous, and ever present in our lives.

"It" is finished refers to the Atonement, which the Son was required to do at the request of His Father.

The following scriptures speak of the Savior's fulfilling this great commandment.

"Behold I have given unto you my gospel, and this is the gospel which I have given unto you—that I came into the world to do the will of my Father, because my Father sent me. And my Father sent me that I might be lifted up upon the cross; and after that I had been lifted up upon the cross, that I might draw all men unto me, that as I have been lifted up by men even so should men be lifted up by the Father, to stand before me, to be judged of their works, whether they be good or whether they be evil—And for this cause have I been lifted up; therefore, according to the power of the Father I will draw all men unto me, that they may be judged according to their works" (3 Nephi 27:13–15). This expression of the "good news" of the gospel of Jesus Christ contains so many points of light that enhance our understanding.

- The Lord came to do the will of the Father. He was ever the obedient Son.
- The Father sent Him on this errand of mercy to redeem the world.
- He was sent to atone for all as described, being "lifted up upon the cross."
- This empowering act of love is what has drawn us to Christ through gratitude.
- The Father, who has all power, literally resurrects through His Son His children to stand before His Son to be judged.

"And as many as have received me, to them have I given to become the sons of God; and even so will I to as many as shall believe on my name, for behold, by me redemption cometh, and in me is the law of Moses fulfilled" (3 Nephi 9:17). The Savior teaches that He fulfills the law of Moses. It is interesting to note that the Lord uses the words *received me*. These words connote the power that comes from receiving: "And also all they who *receive* this priesthood *receive* me, saith the Lord; for he that *receiveth* my servants *receiveth* me; and he that *receiveth* me *receiveth* my Father; and he that *receiveth* my Father *receiveth* my Father's kingdom; therefore all that my Father hath shall be given unto him" (D&C 84:35–38; emphasis added). There is power in receiving.

I repeat a previous paragraph concerning the doctrine of receiving, "*To receive* indicates acknowledgment and acceptance of knowledge, a gift, or a blessing from a giver. To receive the infinite Atonement with all the associated ordinances, covenants, and principles, we must accept them and act upon them, else we have not truly received. Receiving acknowledges that those things we have accepted are true. To *receive* the Atonement means taking it into our soul. This includes that the temple ordinances are received and faithfully honored. We start to receive the blessings of the Atonement as we begin to appreciate the suffering of our Savior—and gratitude is born."

Paul surely explained our dependence upon God and our Savior. "But God commendeth his love toward us, in that, while we were yet sinners, Christ died for us. Much more then, being now justified by his blood, we shall be saved from wrath through him. For if, when we were enemies, we were reconciled to God by the death of his Son, much more, being reconciled, we shall be saved by his life. And not only so, but we also joy in God through our Lord Jesus Christ, by whom we have now received the atonement" (Romans 5:8–11). It was God's love that gave us His Son (see John 3:16). Even though we were unworthy through our sins, His love was constant and complete. We were vindicated and made acceptable to our Father through His Beloved Son. When we were separated from God because of our fallen state and our individual sins, He was ever anxious and pleased that His Son would be bruised for us, even die for us. We were saved by the life of God's Only Begotten Son, for in His Son's death and Atonement we live. And we rejoice for the goodness of God and our Savior.

> Grace be to you and peace from God the Father, and from our Lord Jesus Christ, Who gave himself for our sins, that he might deliver us from this present evil world, according to the will of God and our Father. (Galations 1:3–4)

> Jesus saith unto him, I am the way, the truth, and the life: no man cometh unto the Father, but by me. (John 14:6)

> Behold, I am he who was prepared from the foundation of the world to redeem my people. Behold, I am Jesus Christ. I am the Father and the Son. In me shall all mankind have life, and that eternally, even they who shall believe on my name; and they shall become my sons and my daughters. (Ether 3:14)

These beautiful and salient scriptures make it clear that the phrase "It is finished" refers to Christ and His mission as the Anointed One. His mission was to redeem the world, to suffer for our sins, and to provide the way back to the Father by the power of the resurrection. The infinite Atonement was the essence of the plan of redemption. This was the culminating event that made possible the work of the Father and the Son, "For behold, this is my work and my glory—to bring to pass the immortality and eternal life of man" (Moses 1:39).

In Gethsemane, the suffering began; on the cross, it continued; and from the Garden Tomb, it was completed and glorified the Father with the Resurrection of His Beloved Son.

7. Father, into thy hands I commend my spirit.

Again a prophecy was fulfilled when the Savior said, "Into thine hand I commit my spirit: thou hast redeemed me, O Lord God of truth" (Psalm 31:5). The suffering and sacrificing part of the Atonement is finished with the Savior's suffering on the cross, thus His death completes the infinite sacrifice and the enabling power of the Atonement, which will empower His Resurrection. The soldiers pierce His side, fulfilling the prophecy, "Yea, a spear shall pierce through him to the wounding of thine own soul also" (Joseph Smith Translation, Luke 2:35). Isaiah spoke of this very deed: "But he was wounded for our transgressions, he was bruised for our iniquities" (Isaiah 53:5). It is noted by many scholars that the original Hebrew for the word wounded read "pierced" for our transgressions. The Lord is literally surrendering His spirit unto His Father. They are one in all things. They are united in purpose, cause, and action. The Lord has finished and now awaits the additional work the Father yet requires of His Son, for He is in the hands of His Father, which surely connotes the instrumentality of God being expressed though His Only Begotten Son.

He died, the great Redeemer died. Our Elder Brother, the Only Begotten of the Father in the flesh, the Savior and Redeemer had completed His suffering and sacrificing so that we might have everlasting life. And because of this, what shall we do? I cannot suggest what is proper or expected us individually. The Atonement is personal for each of us. We each should have in our minds what gratitude has prompted us to do. May we each make those commitments, go forward in faith, and assist the Lord in bringing souls to Him so that they too may have everlasting life. If we believe, it is the least we can do.

UPHEAVALS OF THE EARTH—THE VEIL IS RENT

All the upheavals of the earth were expressed at the death of the promised Messiah. "And, behold, the veil of the temple was rent in twain from the top to the bottom; and the earth did quake, and the rocks rent" (Matthew 27:51). The renting of the veil in particular had great significance. In Mosaic times only the high priest was allowed to go through the veil into the "holiest" place, the Holy of Holies. Symbolically it was the presence of God in the tabernacle and later in the temple. The veil precluded all others from entering. When the Lord and Savior offered His infinite sacrifice, the way opened for us, *through Him*, to enter that holiest of chambers, for "the veil of the temple was rent in twain from the top to the bottom" (Mark 15:38). This passage has great implications to each of us: we may now enter the Holy of Holies if we are worthy, through Christ's sacrifice.

Jesus Christ is often called our Great High Priest, for He has made it possible for us to enter into the presence of God. As the Apostle Paul wrote, "Seeing then that we have a great high priest, that is passed into the heavens, Jesus the Son of God, let us hold fast *our* profession" (Hebrews 4:14; emphasis added). Paul, also in his Epistle to the Hebrews, further clarifies this doctrine: "Having therefore, brethren, boldness to enter into the holiest by the blood of Jesus, By a new and living way, which he hath consecrated for us, through the veil, that is to say, his flesh; And *having* an high priest over the house of God" (Hebrews 10:19–21; emphasis added). Christ is the way to the Father. It is "through" Him that we can return to His presence. "Jesus saith unto him, I am the way, the truth, and the life: no man cometh unto the Father, but by me" (John 14:6). We now see the significance of "through the veil, that is to say, his flesh." Christ the Lord and His infinite Atonement can bring us into the presence of the Father.

Because of the Savior's Atonement, we no longer live in fear, for a way has been provided for us to repent and return to the presence of God. "These are they who are just men made perfect through Jesus the mediator of the new covenant, who wrought out this perfect atonement through the shedding of his own blood" (D&C 76:69). We become bold, rather than hesitant or fearful, because of our faith in Jesus Christ. We come into His holy house by the power and blessings of His Atonement. The new and living way is through the greater priesthood, and the law of Moses, which the Lord fulfilled, no longer restricted the fulness of the gospel. "And my Father sent me that I might be lifted up on the cross; and after that I had been lifted upon up upon the cross, . . . even so should men be lifted up by the Father" (3 Nephi 27:14). The Lord has ordained, set apart, and sanctified the way for us to pass through the veil, which was rent by His flesh. Thus we see the significance of the statement of our Savior, "I am the way, the truth, and the life: no man cometh unto the Father, but by me" (John 14:6). And, "For it is expedient that there should be a great and last sacrifice; yea, not a sacrifice of man, neither of beast, neither of any manner of fowl; for it shall not be a human sacrifice; but it must be an infinite and eternal sacrifice. Now there is not any man that can sacrifice his own blood which will atone for the sins of another" (Alma 34:10–11). These words bring great meaning to the connection of the enabling power of the Atonement and the holy endowment and how we symbolically enter into the holiest of sanctuaries, through Christ, into the presence of the Lord God our Father. Our Heavenly Father seeks that all of His children, through His Beloved Son, may return to His presence and enjoy the blessings of exaltation. This is the purpose of the temple, the At-one-ment—to be "brought back into the presence of" or to be "one with." The Atonement is the enabling power of the endowment, which Brigham Young describes: "Your *endowment* is, to receive all those ordinances in the House of the Lord, which are necessary for you, after you have departed this life, *to enable you to walk back to the presence of the Father*" (quoted in John A. Widstoe, *Discourses of Brigham Young* [Salt Lake City: Deseret Book, 1954], 416).

With the additional quaking of the earth, darkness prevailed during the last moments of His death: "Now from the sixth hour there was darkness over all the land unto the ninth hour" (Matthew 27:45). And in addition "the sun was darkened" (Luke 23:45). And on the American continent, the prophet Samuel declared, "Yea, at the time that he shall yield up the ghost there shall be thunderings and lightnings for the space of many hours, and the earth shall shake and tremble; and the rocks which are upon the face of this earth, which are both above the earth and beneath, which ye know at this time are solid, or the more part of it is one solid mass, shall be broken up; yea, they shall be rent in twain, and shall ever after be found in seams and in cracks, and in broken fragments upon the face of the whole earth, yea, both above the earth and beneath. And behold, there shall be great tempests, and there shall be many mountains laid low, like unto a valley, and there shall be many places which are now called valleys which shall become mountains, whose height is great. And many highways shall be broken up, and many cities shall become desolate" (Helaman 14:21–24). And all this came to pass as described in 3 Nephi 8.

What does all this tumult and commotion of the earth symbolize? The Lord repeatedly warned the people on this continent of the forthcoming judgment at the time of the Lord's Crucifixion (see 1 Nephi 12:4–6; 19:10–14; 2 Nephi 26:3–4). The judgments of God will be fulfilled. This just judgment came upon the wicked: "It is because of their iniquity and abominations that they are fallen! . . . To hide their iniquities and their abominations from before my face, that the blood of the prophets and the saints shall not come any more unto me against them. . . . And many great destructions have I caused to come upon this land, and upon this people, because of their wickedness and their abominations" (3 Nephi 9:2, 5, 12). There were three days of darkness because the Son of God was not here on the earth. Surely all this was the prophesied sign of the death of Savior of the world. The Lord reminds us that these things were done "unto the fulfilling of the prophecies of many of the holy prophets" (3 Nephi 10:14). The light and life of the world was gone for three days. "And it came to pass that thus did the three days pass away. And it was in the morning, and the darkness dispersed from off the face of the land, and the earth did cease to tremble, and the rocks did cease to rend, and the dreadful groanings did cease, and all the tumultuous noises did pass away" (3 Nephi 10:9). Why? Because God's Almighty Son had returned as the resurrected Lord— "King of Kings and Lord of Lords" (Revelation 19:16). And in all this we come to understand that the greatest event in the history of mankind had been completed—the infinite and eternal Atonement of the Lord Jesus Christ, which empowered His glorious Resurrection.

Chapter 8

The BURIAL and RESURRECTION

We read, "And after this Joseph of Arimathaea, being a disciple of Jesus, but secretly for fear of the Jews, besought Pilate that he might take away the body of Jesus: and Pilate gave him leave. He came therefore, and took the body of Jesus. And there came also Nicodemus, which at the first came to Jesus by night, and brought a mixture of myrrh and aloes, about an hundred pound weight. Then took they the body of Jesus, and wound it in linen clothes with the spices, as the manner of the Jews is to bury. Now in the place where he was crucified there was a garden; and in the garden a new sepulchre, wherein was never man yet laid. There laid they Jesus therefore because of the Jews' preparation day; for the sepulchre was nigh at hand" (John 19:38–42; see also Mark 15:43–47; Luke 23:50–56; Matthew 27:57–60).

Joseph of Arimathaea and Nicodemus, though members of the Sanhedrin, who were righteous and noble followers of Christ, laid the Savior to rest. They were men of power, prestige, and wealth, and were taking a great risk in their support for and love of Jesus. Indeed, they fulfilled the prophecy that, the Messiah would be "with the rich in his death" (Isaiah 53:9) because it was a new tomb cut from the rock. Yet possibly a great meaning is the true meaning of rich: "Seek not for riches but for wisdom; and, behold, the mysteries of God shall be unfolded unto you, and then shall you be made rich. *Behold, he that hath eternal life is rich*" (D&C 11:7; emphasis added). In eternal life we are with our beloved Savior and our Heavenly Father. Mary Magdalene and the other Mary were also there at the sepulcher. The Jews, fearing the disciples would steal away the body, "went, and made the sepulchre sure, sealing the stone, and setting a watch" (Matthew 27:66). And the guards stood watch over the tomb.

As my thoughts turn to Joseph of Arimathaea and Nicodemus, I am filled with gratitude for their goodness in laying to rest our beloved Savior. Surely there was risk and possible persecution involved. They were noble and gracious as converts of the Lord. As I sit here in the quietness of the morning, I am compelled to offer a prayer of gratitude for Joseph in providing a place for our Savior's body to rest prior to His triumphal Resurrection. Surely our Heavenly Father was pleased with their graciousness and kindness to His Son.

The Savior had been laid to rest, and the magnificent, infinite, and eternal suffering and sacrificing portion of the great Atonement had been finished. The Resurrection is the culminating event of Atonement in that it allows us to return to our Father. It is about returning clean, pure, and holy, without spot, to the God that gave us life. It is about overcoming death and sin.

> For as death hath passed upon all men, to fulfil the merciful plan of the great Creator, there must needs be a power of resurrection, and the resurrection must needs come unto man by reason of the fall; and the fall came by reason of transgression; and because man became fallen they were cut off from the presence of the Lord.
>
> Wherefore, it must needs be an infinite atonement—save it should be an infinite atonement this corruption could not put on incorruption. Wherefore, the first judgment which came upon man must needs have remained to an endless duration. And if so, this flesh must have laid down to rot and to crumble to its mother earth, to rise no more.
>
> O the wisdom of God, his mercy and grace! For behold, if the flesh should rise no more our spirits must become subject to that angel who fell from before the presence of the Eternal God, and became the devil, to rise no more.
>
> And our spirits must have become like unto him, and we become devils, angels to a devil, to be shut out from the presence of our God, and to remain with the father of lies, in misery, like

> unto himself; yea, to that being who beguiled our first parents, who transformeth himself nigh unto an angel of light, and stirreth up the children of men unto secret combinations of murder and all manner of secret works of darkness.
>
> O how great the goodness of our God, who prepareth a way for our escape from the grasp of this awful monster; yea, that monster, death and hell, which I call the death of the body, and also the death of the spirit.
>
> And because of the way of deliverance of our God, the Holy One of Israel, this death, of which I have spoken, which is the temporal, shall deliver up its dead; which death is the grave.
>
> And this death of which I have spoken, which is the spiritual death, shall deliver up its dead; which spiritual death is hell; wherefore, death and hell must deliver up their dead, and hell must deliver up its captive spirits, and the grave must deliver up its captive bodies, and the bodies and the spirits of men will be restored one to the other; and it is by the power of the resurrection of the Holy One of Israel. (2 Nephi 9:6–12)

The miracle of the suffering Christ through the Atonement has made possible the forgiveness of our sins. This is more than we can comprehend, but we can still be grateful. Likewise the miracle of the Atonement empowered the Resurrection, and though the power and workings of the Resurrection is beyond the comprehension of the mortal mind, we can again be grateful. Last, the Atonement makes possible our immortality and eternal life. It too is incomprehensible; yet again we can be grateful. Gratitude dwells in our hearts, because we understand and appreciate what our circumstances would be without the Atonement. This knowledge of our helplessness without Christ helps us be drawn through gratitude to our Lord and Savior. The power and majesty of God and His Beloved Son transcend our capabilities as mortals. It is through the Resurrection that our spirit and body are reunited. "For man is spirit. The elements are eternal, and spirit and element, inseparably connected, receive a fulness of joy; and when separated, man cannot receive a fulness of joy" (D&C 93:33–34).

President Gordon B. Hinckley said regarding the Resurrection:

> Of all the victories in human history, none is so great, none so universal in its effect, none so everlasting in its consequences as the

> victory of the crucified Lord who came forth in the Resurrection that first Easter morning.
>
> We laud the captains and the kings, we praise the nations that are victorious against oppressors. We appropriately build monuments to remember their sacrifices and their triumphs over the forces of oppression. But great and important as are these achievements, none can compare with the victory of the lonely, pain-racked figure on Calvary's cross who triumphed over death and brought the gift of eternal life to all mankind. (Gordon B. Hinckley, "Empty Tomb Bore Testimony," *Ensign*, May 1988)

We see the typifying of Christ, His Atonement, and the promise of the Resurrection throughout the scriptures.

Paul makes the great comparison to baptism and the newness of life. "Therefore we are buried with him by baptism into death: that like as Christ was raised up from the dead by the glory of the Father, even so we also should walk in newness of life. For if we have been planted together in the likeness of his death, we shall be also in the likeness of his resurrection" (Romans 6:4–5). The scriptures not only typify of Christ in all things but also testify of Christ in all things. When we see any name or title that speaks of Christ, the Messiah, the Holy One of Israel, our Redeemer, our Savior, it should connote in our minds the length and breadth of the Atonement and all it entails—from the suffering and sacrificing Christ to the glorious empowering Resurrection of Christ, which opened the way back to the presence of our Father.

Our Savior teaches clearly the doctrine of the Resurrection. "Jesus said unto her, I am the resurrection, and the life: he that believeth in me, though he were dead, yet shall he live: And whosoever liveth and believeth in me shall never die. Believest thou this?" (John 11:25–26). This question is given to all of us. Do we believe? A resounding yes echoes from our hearts as with a sound of a trump. Because we believe, "we talk of Christ, we rejoice in Christ, we preach of Christ, we prophesy of Christ, and we write according to our prophecies, that our children may know to what source they may look for a remission of their sins" (2 Nephi 25:26). We look to Christ in all things that we might have everlasting life (see John 3:36).

Our Savior also states that He had the power given Him of God to do all things. "Jesus answered and said unto them, Destroy this temple, and in three days I will raise it up. Then said the Jews, Forty and six years was this temple in building, and wilt thou rear it up in three days? But he spake of the temple of his body" (John 2:19–21). They could not make the connection that He really was speaking of His body. The Jews could not believe, especially the Sadducees, because they did not believe in the Resurrection. The disciples also struggled with this doctrine. After it has happened, we all have a more complete perspective. It was after the Resurrection that His disciples remembered this scripture (see John 2:22). We all can see except those who do not believe in the testimonies of others, and in this they too will struggle with the doctrines of Christ and His literal Resurrection. We stand in awe of the power of Almighty God and our beloved Savior.

Lehi reminds his children, as well as us, that through the grace of Lord the Resurrection will take place and we will see God again. "Wherefore, how great the importance to make these things known unto the inhabitants of the earth, that they may know that there is no flesh that can dwell in the presence of God, save it be through the merits, and mercy, and grace of the Holy Messiah, who layeth down his life according to the flesh, and taketh it again by the power of the Spirit, that he may bring to pass the resurrection of the dead, being the first that should rise" (2 Nephi 2:8). Lehi is speaking and blessing his children for the last time. This is the last thing he wanted them to know. It is a message of our total dependence upon the grace of Christ. Lehi's son Jacob taught, "Wherefore, beloved brethren, be reconciled unto him through the atonement of Christ, his Only Begotten Son, and ye may obtain a resurrection, according to the power of the resurrection which is in Christ" (Jacob 4:11). It is a message of hope in Christ. Oh, the goodness of God in making possible the Resurrection unto a newness of life. And this was done by the power of the Atonement of Christ.

THE GARDEN TOMB—THE RISEN LORD

We read, "In the end of the sabbath, as it began to dawn toward the first day of the week, came Mary Magdalene and the other Mary to see the sepulchre" (Matthew 28:1). We then read, "For two angels of the Lord descended from heaven and came and rolled back the stone from the door, and sat upon it. And their countenance was like lightning, and their raiment white as snow; and for fear of them the keepers did shake, and became as dead men. And the angels answered and said unto the women, Fear not ye; for we know that ye seek Jesus, which was crucified. He is not here; for he is risen, as he said. Come, see the place where the Lord lay. And go quickly, and tell his disciples that he is risen from the dead; and, behold, he goeth before you into Galilee; there shall ye see him: lo, I have told you" (Matthew 28:2–5, footnotes 2a, 3a, 5a; from Joseph Smith Translation).

The two Marys and other women were drawn to the tomb. "They remembered His words [Christ's word that He would rise on the third day; see Luke 24:7], and returned from the sepulchre, and told all these things unto the eleven, and to all the rest. It was Mary Magdalene, and Joanna, and Mary the mother of James, and other women that were with them, which told these things unto the apostles. And their words seemed to them as idle tales, and they believed them not. Then arose Peter, and ran unto the sepulchre; and stooping down, he beheld the linen clothes laid by themselves, and departed, wondering in himself at that which was come to pass" (Luke 24:8–12). The Savior had risen.

On the way to tell the disciples, the women saw the Savior. "Jesus met them, saying, All hail. And they came and held him by the feet, and worshipped him. Then said Jesus unto them, Be not afraid: go tell my brethren that they go into Galilee, and there shall they see me" (Matthew 28:9–10). The Apostles had a hard time believing. "And she [Mary] went and told them that had been with him, as they mourned and wept. And they, when they had heard that he was alive, and had been seen of her, believed not. After that he appeared in another form unto two of them, as they walked, and went into the country. And they went and told it unto the residue: neither believed they them" (Mark 16:10–13).

Though the Gospels of Matthew, Mark, and Luke are synoptic, the exact accounts are different in the records. Mark records that Mary Magdalene, Mary the mother of James, and Salome had come to anoint the Savior's body with sweet spices and were even discussing how they would roll back the stone. The stone was gone, and the angel who was in the sepulcher informed them that Christ had risen and to go and tell His disciples to go to Galilee and to see Him there. These sister disciples were always the ones who "waited" upon the Lord. The Gospels record that many women came to the sepulcher and appeared as if all were waiting upon the Lord. Ever the saints, the sisters were there seeking to help. It is interesting that the record of Mark makes special reference to the fact, "Now when Jesus was risen early the first day of the week, he appeared first to Mary Magdalene, out of whom he had cast seven devils" (Mark 16:9). Matthew simply indicates that the Savior met "them" as the sisters were on their way to tell the disciples. It is evident that the sisters saw the Savior first because they had come to serve the Lord.

We should note that throughout the Savior's life, He was indeed deferential to the sisters. He was not affected by the ways of the culture of His day and was ever thoughtful and kind to all women. It was as if He was trying to teach the brethren who were steeped in tradition the elevated role of womanhood in the perfect plan of exaltation.

The Savior finally appears to His Apostles, and we read, "Jesus himself stood in the midst of them, and saith unto them, Peace be unto you" (Luke 24:36). They were afraid, and the Savior said, "Why are ye troubled? and why do thoughts arise in your hearts? Behold my hands and my feet, that it is I myself: handle me, and see; for a spirit hath not flesh and bones, as ye see me have. And when he had thus spoken, he shewed them his hands and his feet" (Luke 24:38–40). The Gospel of John records the Savior's words: "As my Father hath sent me, even so send I you. And when he had said this, he breathed on them, and saith unto them, Receive ye the Holy Ghost: Whose soever sins ye remit, they are remitted unto them; and whose soever sins ye retain, they are retained" (John 20:21–23). It is noted that the Lord said, "Receive ye the

Ghost," and so they did. They were given the blessing of the Holy Ghost.

Thomas was not present with the other Apostles, and when he heard the news of Jesus's Resurrection, he said, "Except I shall see in his hands the print of the nails, and put my finger into the print of the nails, and thrust my hand into his side, I will not believe. And after eight days again his disciples were within, and Thomas with them: then came Jesus, the doors being shut, and stood in the midst, and said, Peace be unto you. Then saith he to Thomas, Reach hither thy finger, and behold my hands; and reach hither thy hand, and thrust it into my side: and be not faithless, but believing. And Thomas answered and said unto him, My Lord and my God. Jesus saith unto him, Thomas, because thou hast seen me, thou hast believed: blessed are they that have not seen, and yet have believed" (John 20:25–29). This was a great teaching moment for those who exercise faith, that they might believe without having a sure knowledge, for in doing so they will be blessed. John concludes his Gospel with these stirring words: "And many other signs truly did Jesus in the presence of his disciples, which are not written in this book: But these are written, that ye might believe that Jesus is the Christ, the Son of God; and that believing ye might have life through his name" (John 20:30–31).

INSTRUCTIONS FOLLOWING THE LORD'S RESURRECTION

The Savior was "seen of them forty days, and speaking of the things pertaining to the kingdom of God" (Acts 1:3), of which we do not have a full record of all that transpired. What happened during the forty-day ministry? John said, "And there are also many other things which Jesus did, the which, if they should be written every one, I suppose that even the world itself could not contain the books that should be written" (John 21:25).

The Lord stated during this time, "But ye shall receive power, after that the Holy Ghost is come upon you: and ye shall be witnesses unto me both in Jerusalem, and in all Judaea, and in Samaria, and unto the uttermost part of the earth" (Acts 1:8). The Lord then ascended into heaven. There are many apocryphal writings related to this forty-day ministry, which have not been canonized; suffice it to say, the Apostles and disciples fulfilled their commission to go "into all the world, and preach the gospel to every creature" (Mark 16:15–16; see also Matthew 28:18–20; Luke 24:47–48; John 21:15–17; Acts 1:4–5).

The significant events of our Savior's life following the Resurrection were to make sure that His disciples knew He was the resurrected Christ and they needed to testify of Him to all the world. This is because the disciples were given the charge to preach and teach of Christ and His atoning sacrifice and Resurrection so that all may know whom to look to regarding their salvation.

It was at this time following the Resurrection that Peter and other disciples went fishing. As they came to the shore, the Lord feeds them and teaches them for the third time He had been with them since He had risen. The Lord taught them the requirements to feed His sheep (see John 21:15–17).

While serving as president of the England London South Mission (1985–88), we had the privilege of having Elder Russell M. Nelson of the Quorum of the Twelve Apostles come and give a fireside. We were to pick up Elder Nelson at the Heathrow airport in London. We arrived early and were excited and anxious to have him come and be with us and teach the Saints in England. As it came time for his plane to land, an announcement came over the loud speakers: "Flight such and such has been diverted to an airport north of London due to fuel issues." I quickly went to the desk and said, "Where is this airport?" I was told the mileage. It was totally out of range to pick him up and make it to the fireside. I was sick. Over two thousand Saints would be at the Crawley Stake Center for the fireside. I prayed. I went and pleaded with the clerk at the desk. He smiled and said he was sorry. I said, "There is an Apostle of the Lord on that plane, and he needs to be in Crawley to speak." Again "I am sorry" was his only response. I pleaded with the Lord to intervene somehow. It is now getting to be one hour before the fireside. I went to the clerk and said, "Why don't they land at Gatwick?" Gatwick was only a few minutes from the Crawley Stake Center. He reminded me that he was merely relaying the message from the air controller to the people at Heathrow. Within a minute or so, an announcement of Elder Nelson's flight was made that the plane had again been diverted, and this time to the Gatwick airport. I couldn't believe it. A miracle. I called the stake center and told them to send a car to Gatwick to pick up Elder Nelson. Meanwhile, I drove on the edge of the M-25 from Heathrow to the Crawley exit. I hurried to the stake center, and just as I pulled in the little driveway, a car with Elder Nelson pulled in behind us. I jumped out with my sweetheart and opened his door. He smiled and asked if we had waited long. I smiled and said everything was fine. The fireside started a few minutes late, but we were all relieved and thankful for his save arrival and were spiritually fed.

As we drove home after the fireside to our home in Cobham, I related the story to Elder Nelson. He had been calm and full of faith, merely asking the Lord to get him down so he could deliver the message the Lord wanted us to hear. Then he said, "When we touched down at Gatwick for fuel, I went to the flight attendant and mentioned that I had to deplane here. They said I couldn't." He then said to the flight attendant, "You don't understand. I have to get off here." They then checked with the captain, who said, "We cannot open the baggage area to get your bags. You have to stay on the plane." Elder Nelson said, "I have no bags, simply my carry-on." The pilot shrugged and told the crew to let him off. He walked in to the terminal and the car was waiting—miracles at every turn so the Lord's servant could bless our lives.

When we got home, Elder Nelson was invigorated and, due the time change, was not tired at all, so he suggested we have scripture time. We sat around the table, with finger food and treats made by my sweetheart, Pat, and searched the scriptures for a couple of hours. This was one of the things he taught us that night. Now to the teachings of our beloved Savior.

He said, "Peter was asked if he loved the Lord. The conversation between the Savior and Peter is recorded in John 21:15–17:

> "So when they had dined, Jesus saith to Simon Peter, Simon, son of Jonas, lovest thou me more than these? He saith unto him, Yea, Lord; thou knowest that I love thee. He saith unto him, Feed my lambs. He saith to him again the second time, Simon, son of Jonas,

> lovest thou me? He saith unto him, Yea, Lord; thou knowest that I love thee. He saith unto him, Feed my sheep. He saith unto him the third time, Simon, son of Jonas, lovest thou me? Peter was grieved because he said unto him the third time, Lovest thou me? And he said unto him, Lord, thou knowest all things; thou knowest that I love thee. Jesus saith unto him, Feed my sheep."

Going on, Elder Nelson asked, "Why would the Lord ask Peter three times?" In the Greek, the word *love* as a verb has three forms: *agapao*, which is the perfect love of God; *phileo*, which is brotherly or reciprocating love; and *erao*, which is physical love. When the Lord would express love in the form of *agapao*, Peter would answer with *phileo*, which is not enough love to truly feed the Lord's sheep. So the Lord asked again, and finally the third time the Lord uses the *phileo*, and Peter was grieved because of being asked three times. This teaches us a great principle about loving. Our love must be complete, perfect, and unconditional for all mankind because that is the way the Lord's disciples are known (see John 13:34–35). Indeed, we must have charity—the pure love of Christ, which never fails. We show our love to the Lord by loving and serving everyone (see Matthew 25:40). We show our love by keeping the commandments (see John 14:15).

Elder Nelson taught so clearly that the love necessary to feed His sheep is a godlike love, or else it will not be strong enough to give us enough of a motive to care for our fellowmen. Needless to say, we taught this to our wonderful missionaries, just as a prophet of God had taught us.

This commission to Peter from the Lord to feed His sheep is a commission to all. Peter was the chief Apostle. He was to direct the great work of salvation, but the Lord wanted him to know that a greater love is required in order to continually search out for the lost and weary. Brotherly love is not enough. It must be a selfless, godlike love that is constant and never-ending. This is what the work of the Lord's disciples is all about—lifting others and helping them come unto Christ. In the other Gospels, the Lord is giving them the mandate to take the gospel to all the world, as we shall see. This is missionary work. This is perfecting the Saints, and that refers to here and now and to those on the other side of the veil, where the great Apostle Peter is preaching today. It was following this exchange that the Lord foretold of Peter's martyrdom: "Verily, verily, I say unto thee, When thou wast young, thou girdedst thyself, and walkedst whither thou wouldest: but when thou shalt be old, thou shalt stretch forth thy hands, and another shall gird thee, and carry thee whither thou wouldest not. This spake he, signifying by what death he should glorify God. And when he had spoken this, he saith unto him, Follow me" (John 21:18–19).

The Savior's prophetic words speak of Peter's death. As John recorded this, Peter had probably been martyred. The Lord made known to Peter that in his service of the Master, he too would be required to seal his testimony with his blood. Peter, ever the enthusiastic and devoted defender of the gospel of Jesus Christ, was fearless and faithful as he followed the Savior. Peter was so strengthened by the Holy Ghost that he became like unto the Lord. The Lord had promised them, "He that believeth on me, the works that I do shall he do also; and greater works than these shall he do; because I go unto my Father" (John 14:12). Luke records this magnificent Apostle's works when he was endowed with power and the Holy Ghost. "Insomuch that they brought forth the sick into the streets, and laid them on beds and couches, that at the least the shadow of Peter passing by might overshadow some of them. There came also a multitude out of the cities round about unto Jerusalem, bringing sick folks, and them which were vexed with unclean spirits: and they were healed every one" (Acts 5:15–16).

The Apostles were then instructed to meet with the Savior: "Then the eleven disciples went away into Galilee, into a mountain where Jesus had appointed them. And when they saw him, they worshipped him: but some doubted" (Matthew 28:16–17). Were there more people than the eleven disciples in the presence of the Lord? Thomas had already seen the Lord, so this does not refer to him in this instance. The word *some* indicates more than one. As we look at the translation, we may learn some insights. The use of the word *doubt* here should not be considered unbelief, but as some lexicons state several meanings of the use of this Greek word, it is more like a hesitation or "am I really experiencing this," which is totally understandable. The disciples were amazed. So another reading of this verse could simply be "they worshipped him: but some hesitated." This is a natural expression for seeing a resurrected being. They were simply a little reluctant.

The Lord then gives the great commission to His remaining Apostles: "And Jesus came and spake unto them, saying, All power is given unto me in heaven and in earth. Go ye therefore, and teach all nations, baptizing them in the name of the Father, and of the Son, and of the Holy Ghost: Teaching them to observe all things whatsoever I have commanded you: and, lo, I am with you alway, even unto the end of the world. Amen" (Matthew 28:18–20). Mark records, "And he said unto them, Go ye into all the world, and preach the gospel to every creature. He that believeth and is baptized shall be saved; but he that believeth not shall be damned" (Mark 16:15–16). The Savior was received into heaven, and "they went forth, and preached every where, the Lord working with them, and confirming the word with signs following" (Mark 16:19–20). Luke records concerning their duty: "And that repentance and remission of sins should be preached in his name among all nations, beginning at Jerusalem. And ye are witnesses of these things. And, behold, I send the promise of my Father upon you: but tarry ye in the city of Jerusalem, until ye be endued with power from on high. And he led them out as far as to Bethany, and he lifted up his hands, and blessed them. And it came to pass, while he blessed them, he was parted from them, and carried up into heaven" (Luke 24:47–51).

The Lord has given the commission to take the gospel to all the earth, to every nation, kindred, tongue, and people. We have that same commission today, from the nearly ninety thousand missionaries preaching the gospel to all fifteen million members and "member missionaries." I shall never forget the inspiring story of successful missionaries teaching and assisting in the conversion process, and even the greater power of member missionaries sharing the gospel.

My dear friend Stan Collins told me of an experience where such zeal of a new convert blessed the lives of many. He said, "Eddie, sit down. I have to tell you a miraculous story."

He had my attention, for no one could tell a story like Stan. Now, mind you, we were both over fifty-five at the time. He began, "When I was back on my mission, we were surrounded by the Great Lakes. The humidity was high, and the temperatures were low in the winter (-30 degrees). We would knock on a few doors, go warm up in the nearest little store, and then go out again. We did this over and over until we had to stop at 9:30 p.m. Most of the time our hands were so cold we could hardly make a fist to knock on the doors.

"It was our last time out, and we thought we might just as well go back to our apartment, but we decided to do one more door. The Spirit is always in charge. We knocked, and a young mother came to the door. I guess we looked like two frozen icebergs because she said, 'Get in here before you freeze to death out there.' And so we went in and sat down. While we got warmed up, she asked us a question. 'What are two young kids doing knocking on doors in the dead of winter at this time of the night?' We told her we were missionaries for the Lord Jesus Christ. We had a message of the gospel of Jesus Christ that could bring happiness into the lives of her and her family. The family was golden. The Spirit was strong. They loved us, and we loved them. Six weeks later, they were baptized. I was transferred a couple of weeks after and have never heard from them until last week. It has been over thirty-five years."

A woman had called on the phone and asked if Elder Collins was in. (There are five Elder Collins who were missionaries in that family, all them magnificent too.) Stan asked which one, and she said that he would be really old. Stan smiled and said that was surely he. She told him who she was, and it didn't ring a bell. She lamented the fact and said, "You mean to tell me you have forgotten the cold night of -30 when we let you in our house and you taught us the gospel?" The bell rang inside his head, and he remembered and expressed great love and joy for her calling.

Then she said, "I thought it would be good to give you a follow-up report on your missionary efforts that cold night. We've been missionaries too. When we were converted, we were so excited, we visited with both sides of the family. Our testimonies were firm in the Lord. Our joy was full, and we wanted those we loved to enjoy the gospel of Jesus Christ as we did. We brought both of our families into the Church. All the sons and some of the daughters have gone on missions. The convert baptisms of their family members, including those being born into the Church, were over one thousand people." She cried. Stan cried, and as he told me the story, I cried. We hugged and felt the joy for all of Heavenly Father's children who came unto Christ. The story didn't end there. The family came out to see him about ten years later and said that the number had risen to two thousand. The missionaries introduced the spark of the gospel, but the members spread the flame. The results were brand-new converts with the power of the Holy Ghost that assisted in bringing more members of their families into the kingdom of God. That same fire was given to their extended families, and all were converted and became member missionaries of the Lord, happy in assisting others to come unto Christ.

Many new converts are fearless. They have the fire of the gospel deep within their souls. They have partaken of the Atonement. They are alive in Christ. Their testimonies are bubbling over, and they seek opportunities to bear witness of their newfound truths of the gospel of Jesus Christ. They can be our examples as they are anxious to share the gospel with their immediate families and all their friends. Remember that the Lord will help you, just like He helped them. This is why we seek to assist others to come unto Christ. This is why we seek to bring people into the waters of baptism. This is why we share the gospel. People's lives are changed, and the blessings bring joy and happiness to their souls forever. This should inspire us to do all we can to help others find peace and rest here and in the hereafter while we share the gospel of Jesus Christ with them. The time is now because the Lord is hastening His work. We are the ones to testify of Christ and His infinite Atonement and stand as witnesses at all times and in all places. As our souls are filled with gratitude for the Lord's atoning sacrifice, sharing the gospel will become the consequence of the love of God in our hearts.

Having given His disciples their commission to take the gospel to all the earth, the Savior then returned and taught His disciples concerning the kingdom of God "and, being assembled together with them, commanded them that they should not depart from Jerusalem, but wait for the promise of the Father" (Acts 1:4). We note that the Lord said, "I send the promise of my Father upon you" (Luke 24:49). Surely this is in reference to the transcending blessing of the endowment when the Savior reminds them to "tarry ye in the city of Jerusalem, until ye be endued with power from on high" (Luke 24:49). In *Joseph Smith's Commentary on the Bible*, the Prophet suggests this is a reference to "the endowment" and not to their receipt of the Holy Ghost, which they had already received—though the Holy Ghost makes the promises of the endowment efficacious (Joseph Smith and Kent P. Jackson, *Joseph Smith's Commentary on the Bible* [Salt Lake City: Deseret Book, 1994], 143).

I try to imagine being in the presence of the Savior and not only being given the charge to go into all the world but also being endowed with power from on high and then personally taught at the Master's feet. The thrill of it all surpasses my ability to literally visualize it. As I now think of it, I have come to realize that whether by the Lord's voice or the prophet's voice, it is the same (see D&C 1:38). We all have the blessing to be endowed with power from on high when we receive our temple blessings. We all have been given the charge to take the gospel to every nation, kindred, tongue, and people. This is not all the Lord has promised. "And whoso receiveth you, there I will be also, for I will go before your face. I will be on your right hand and on your left, and my Spirit shall be in your hearts, and mine angels round about you, to bear you up" (D&C 84:88). The Lord, the Holy Spirit, and the angels of God will assist us in this work, provided we work with all our heart, might, mind, and strength. This work is for the dedicated and devoted disciples of Christ. Yes, the Lord loves us and gives all of the blessings He has given other disciples who go forth to proclaim His gospel. I am eternally grateful to my Savior and His constant care for His disciples.

Going on, the disciples were then endowed with power and the Holy Ghost. We learn from the great dedicatory prayer of the Kirtland temple, "And do thou grant, Holy Father, that all those who shall worship in this house may be taught words of wisdom out of the best books, and that they may seek learning even by study, and also by faith, as thou hast said; *and that they may grow up in thee, and receive a fulness of the Holy Ghost*, and be organized according to thy laws, and be prepared to obtain every needful thing" (D&C 109:14–15; emphasis added). We have the privilege to receive of the fulness of the Holy Ghost in the Lord's holy house.

The Apostles were empowered. They were no longer without all the blessings and power of God to do the work of the Lord. And they did it with the power and authority of God. "And they worshipped him, and returned to Jerusalem with great joy: And were continually in the temple, praising and blessing God" (Luke 24:52–53). The Apostles then inquired of the Savior, "Lord, wilt thou at this time restore again the kingdom to Israel? And he said unto them, It is not for you to know the times or the seasons, which the Father hath put in his own power. But ye shall receive power, after that the Holy Ghost is come upon you: and ye shall be witnesses unto me both in Jerusalem, and in all Judaea, and in Samaria, and unto the uttermost part of the earth. And when he had spoken these things, while they beheld, he was taken up; and a cloud received him out of their sight" (Acts 1:6–9). These were the last things the Savior apparently taught His Apostles prior to His Ascension.

These last moments with His Apostles were essential to their work in building up the kingdom of God, most particularly the instructions, "Tarry ye in the city of Jerusalem, until ye be endued with power from on high" (Luke 24:49). They were in need of their higher blessings of the greater priesthood in order to carry the work forward and fulfill their roles as Apostles. Elder McConkie spoke on this issue when he said,

> It is common in Christendom to suppose that Jesus here commanded His apostles to tarry in Jerusalem until the promised gift of the Holy Ghost was received, which gift would constitute an endowment of power from on high. Perhaps the statement can be so used, for certainly the disciples were marvelously and powerfully endowed when the Holy Spirit came into their lives on the day of Pentecost (Acts 2). But from latter-day revelation we learn that the Lord had something more in mind in issuing this instruction. In this dispensation, after the elders had received the gift of the Holy Ghost and as early as January, 1831, the Lord began to reveal unto them that he had an endowment in store for the faithful (D&C 38:22; 43:16), "a blessing such as is not known among the children of men" (D&C 39:15). In June, 1833, he said: "I gave unto you a commandment that you should build a house, in the which house I design to endow those whom I have chosen with power from on high; For this is the promise of the Father unto you; therefore I command you to tarry, even as mine apostles at Jerusalem" (D&C 95:8–9; 105:11–12, 18, 33).
>
> Thus the Apostles—or any ministers or missionaries in any age—are not fully qualified to go forth, preach the gospel, and build up the kingdom, unless they have the gift of the Holy Ghost and also are endowed with power from on high, meaning have received certain knowledge, powers, and special blessings, normally given only in the Lord's Temple. (Bruce R. McConkie, *Doctrinal New Testament Commentary* [Salt Lake City: Deseret Book, 1965], 1:859)

The Apostles were empowered to do the Lord's work.

Speaking of the temple and its blessings, we learn an insight to these blessings as we read in Acts following their endowments. In Acts 1:3 we read an interesting phrase: "To whom also he shewed himself alive after his passion by *many infallible proofs*, being seen of them forty days, and speaking of the things pertaining to the kingdom of God" (Acts 1:3; emphasis added). The Greek word translated as "infallible proofs" in Acts 1:3 is a derivative of *tekmerion*, which means "a sure sign," "a mark," or "a token" (see W. E. Vine, Merrill F. Unger, and William White Jr.,*Vine's Complete Expository Dictionary of Old and New Testament Words* [Nashville, TN: Thomas Nelson, 1996]). This surely sheds light on what the Apostles were receiving while they tarried in Jerusalem. They had received their endowments with all the ordinances, covenants, signs, and tokens. The blessing of the holy endowment and sealing ordinances are the blessings of exaltation. And with the prophets of old, we likewise can partake of these transcending blessings today through our faithfulness.

Surely we now see how the Lord felt about His disciples being endowed with power from on high. This was and is imperative for us to not only *become* but also be given the power *to do*. From the *Encyclopedia of Mormonism*, we learn, "An Endowment generally is a gift, but in a specialized sense it is a course of instruction, ordinances, and covenants given only in dedicated temples of The Church of Jesus Christ of Latter-day Saints. The words 'to endow' (from the Greek *enduein*), as used in the New Testament, mean to dress, clothe, put on garments, put on attributes, or receive virtue. . . . The Prophet Joseph Smith taught that these were 'of things spiritual, and to be received only by the spiritual minded' (*TPJS*, p. 237). The Endowment was necessary, he said, to organize the Church fully, that the Saints might be organized according to the laws of God, and, as the dedicatory prayer of the Kirtland Temple petitioned, that they would 'be prepared to obtain every needful thing' (D&C 109:15). The Endowment was designed to give 'a comprehensive view of our condition and true relation to God' (TPJS, p. 324), 'to prepare the disciples for their missions in the world' (p. 274), to prevent being 'overcome by evils' (p. 259), to enable them to 'secure the fulness of those blessings which have been prepared for the Church of the Firstborn' (p. 237)" (Alma P. Burton, "Endowment," in *Encyclopedia of Mormonism*, ed. Daniel H. Ludlow 5 vols., 1992, 1:454–55).

The endowment given through the greater priesthood will help us come to know God the Father and our Savior, the mysteries (doctrinal truths) of the kingdom of God, and the power of godliness. Indeed, we will be empowered to become more like our Savior Jesus Christ and go forward to do His work. This was evidenced by the work of the Apostles on the day of Pentecost.

Chapter 9

The DAY *of* PENTECOST

PENTECOST, THE FIFTIETH DAY, was called the Harvest Festival or Feast of Weeks. Tradition speaks of it being fifty days following the giving of the Ten Commandments and that Pentecost was fifty days following the Resurrection, which would put it seven to ten days after the Ascension of our Savior. Some say that it was started in the upper room where the Lord's Supper was first given. The Lord had given His Apostles the Holy Ghost previously: "And when he had said this, he breathed on them, and saith unto them, Receive ye the Holy Ghost" (John 20:22). The Lord also stated that the Holy Ghost could not dwell with them until He was glorified (see John 7:39). The day of Pentecost arrived, and the Apostles' hearts were of one accord. They were unified. They were one. And they were gathered in one place. We learn from this situation that the blessing of unity and oneness makes the presence of the Holy Ghost possible. "And they were all filled with the Holy Ghost, and began to speak with other tongues, as the Spirit gave them utterance" (Acts 2:4). And they had all things in common: "And all that believed were together, and had all things common; and sold their possessions and goods, and parted them to all men, as every man had need" (Acts 2:44–45).

It is only when we are one, unified, and have no contention among us, with kindness and love abounding toward all men, that the Holy Spirit can be present and truly abound with us. This was the case following the Savior's visit to the Nephites: "And it came to pass in the thirty and sixth year, the people were all converted unto the Lord, upon all the face of the land, both Nephites and Lamanites, and there were no contentions and disputations among them, and every man did deal justly one with another. And they had all things common among them; therefore there were not rich and poor, bond and free, but they were all made free, and partakers of the heavenly gift" (4 Nephi 1:2–3). And they were happy because the love of God did dwell in their hearts. These feelings I have felt in the temple, in special family gatherings, and in private moments of prayer and pondering. Missionaries throughout the world will testify of the outpouring of the Holy Spirit as it directs everything they do. The Spirit is the key to missionary work as it is the key to spirituality. Where would we be without the blessings of the Holy Ghost—miserable at best?

And even in the days of the Prophet Joseph, we find like situations, "Nevertheless, in your temporal things you shall be equal, and this not grudgingly, otherwise the abundance of the manifestations of the Spirit shall be withheld" (D&C 70:14). The disciples, having been empowered and blessed with the power of the Holy Ghost, were to go about building up the kingdom of God. And so should we.

Chapter 10

IN CONCLUSION

REMEMBERING IS THE KEY

With the thoughts of gratitude for our beloved Savior streaming through our minds, what can we do to retain these feelings? And then how will we act because of those feelings?

In response to such questions, we read, "And again I say unto you as I have said before, that as ye have come to the knowledge of the glory of God, or if ye have known of his goodness and have tasted of his love, and have received a remission of your sins, which causeth such exceedingly great joy in your souls, even so I would that *ye should remember, and always retain in remembrance*, the greatness of God, and your own nothingness, and his goodness and long-suffering towards you, unworthy creatures, and humble yourselves even in the depths of humility, calling on the name of the Lord daily, and standing steadfastly in the faith of that which is to come, which was spoken by the mouth of the angel" (Mosiah 4:11; emphasis added).

The word *remember* or a form of the word occurs frequently throughout the scriptures (over 110 references appear in the Book of Mormon and Doctrine and Covenants alone). We have made covenants with our Heavenly Father and our Savior to remember. It seems as though the power to do good and be good is tied to our ability to remember. The ability to keep sacred things in our minds is part of our covenants—to remember, to bear in mind, to keep in our mind, to recall and retain, and to think back upon these things, so that we might remember the goodness of God and keep the commandments.

President Spencer W. Kimball stated, "When you look in the dictionary for the most important word, do you know what it is? . . . 'Remember' is the word" ("*Circles of Exaltation*," address to religious educators, BYU, 28 June 1968, 8.) Why would President Kimball state that? I would suggest that it is because remembering is the only way we can move ourselves into action. If we do not remember, we will not act upon the truths we have come to understand and appreciate. Remembering and feeling gratitude work hand in hand to help us express thanksgiving for our beloved Savior and His atoning sacrifice. Remembering important principles and experiences is vital to our spiritual well-being. We recall what Enos said concerning his celebrated conversion experience in the forest: "The words which I had often heard my father speak concerning eternal life, and the joy of the saints, sunk deep into my heart" (Enos 1:3). That act of remembering led to a life-changing transformation and a legacy of the power of prayer. We also recall what Alma the Younger said when he was struggling in the depths of darkness to find spiritual deliverance: "I remembered also to have heard my father prophesy unto the people concerning the coming of one Jesus Christ, a Son of God, to atone for the sins of the world" (Alma 36:17). Again, that act of remembering proved to be decisive in Alma's spiritual recovery and vitality.

The scriptures teach the principle of *remembering* again and again. Remembering is a dynamic spiritual process of bringing key things to mind on a continual basis to cultivate "a godly walk and conversation" (D&C 20:69). Remembering will help us to align ourselves to the will of God to become, on a daily basis, more and more like Him. Thoughts lead to action; thus remembering in a faithful and obedient way leads to living in a faithful and obedient way.

In all this remembering, we should ponder and meditate often to be sure that our lives reflect our Master. Some of the things we can ponder and pray about could include the following:

- The goodness and mercy of God our Father and our beloved Savior Jesus Christ.

- The infinite and eternal Atonement of our Savior.
- The importance of feasting upon the word of God.
- The doctrines, principles, commandments, covenants, and ordinances of the gospel of Jesus Christ, and how we might live and appreciate them.
- The importance of building up the kingdom of God while we serve one another.
- The importance of praying always and doing as Jesus would do.

The ability to always remember these things is key to have the enabling power of the Atonement to assist us by the power of the Holy Ghost. Forgetting is the heart of the problem, as we learned from the Nephites:

> And thus we can behold how false, and *also the unsteadiness of the hearts* of the children of men; yea, we can see that the Lord in his great infinite goodness doth bless and prosper those who put their trust in him.
>
> Yea, and we may see at the very time when he doth prosper his people, yea, in the increase of their fields, their flocks and their herds, and in gold, and in silver, and in all manner of precious things of every kind and art; sparing their lives, and delivering them out of the hands of their enemies; softening the hearts of their enemies that they should not declare wars against them; yea, and in fine, doing all things for the welfare and happiness of his people; yea, then is the time that they do harden their hearts, *and do forget the Lord their God*, and do trample under their feet the Holy One—yea, and this because of their ease, and their exceedingly great prosperity.
>
> And thus we see that except the Lord doth chasten his people with many afflictions, yea, except he doth visit them with death and with terror, and with famine and with all manner of pestilence, *they will not remember him.*
>
> O how foolish, and how vain, and how evil, and devilish, and how quick to do iniquity, and how slow to do good, are the children of men; yea, how quick to hearken unto the words of the evil one, and to set their hearts upon the vain things of the world!
>
> Yea, how quick to be lifted up in pride; yea, how quick to boast, and do all manner of that which is iniquity; and how slow

> are they to remember the Lord their God, and to give ear unto his counsels, yea, how slow to walk in wisdom's paths! (Helaman 12:1–5)

And thus we see that we should earnestly seek to remember those things that pertain to eternal life and righteousness so that we stay on the straight and narrow path.

It is well to remain aware of the consequences of forgetting:

- We separate ourselves from God.
- We become subject to the devil.
- We become carnal, sensual, and devilish.
- We become worldly and seek the vain things of the world.
- We become prideful and fall away.

Let us guard against forgetfulness. Let us quicken our minds to a remembrance of the things of the Lord, for it is only through remembering that our faith and our hope are nurtured. Here is an observation from President David O. McKay concerning our obligation to avoid forgetting at all costs:

> Husbands, remember the covenants you have made to your wives. Do not permit our affections to be led away from the mother of your children. Mothers, do not forget that you owe something to your children and to your husband. (President David O. McKay, *Conference Report*, October 1955, Afternoon Meeting, 129–30)

Elder Neal A. Maxwell counseled us with the following words:

> Remembering and counting our many blessings can humble us by reminding us of all the reasons we have to be thankful to God; not just today's reasons, but those relating to all our yesterdays. Each week a sincere partaking of the sacrament can become part of this very process. We partake "in remembrance," so that we may "always remember" what Jesus has done for us (3 Nephi 18:11; Moroni 4, 5).
>
> If we fail to stir remembrance of blessings received, the human tendency is to say, in effect, whether to one's God or to one's fellows, "What have you done for me lately?" Indeed, prophets of the Lord have asked directly whether their people had "sufficiently retained in remembrance" His deliverances and blessings

> (Alma 5:6–7). It is best to cultivate our "remembering" capacity now and to be guided accordingly, since at judgment day we will have "perfect remembrance" (Alma 5:18). The important theme of remembrance occurs in one form or another in the Old Testament well over two hundred times. It appears in the Book of Mormon dozens of times, too. This parallelism is to be expected, since the Israelites in Palestine observed the law of Moses and the Nephites kept it "strictly" for many years (see Mosiah 13:30; Alma 30:3). Wherever the gospel is, there too is the call to remembrance. (Neal A. Maxwell, *A Wonderful Flood of Light* [Salt Lake City: Bookcraft, 1990], 51)

Let us therefore supplant our forgetting with Spirit-induced remembering, our lapses of goodness with a surge of loving-kindness, and our omissions with a genuine devotion to God as we remember His beloved Son and His atoning sacrifice.

Remembering is the key—remembering the gift of our beloved Savior and all that He has done for us. What shall we do to remember the suffering and sacrificing Christ? What can we do to always remember Him and keep His commandments, which He has given us? The Lord's plan has reminders built into it to help us remember. It is through the sacrament when we covenant weekly to remember Him. We lay upon an altar, the sacrament table, the emblems of our beloved Savior.

Then the sacramental prayer teaches us the profound significance of remembering:

> O God, the Eternal Father, we ask thee in the name of thy Son, Jesus Christ, to bless and sanctify this bread to the souls of all those who partake of it, that they may eat *in remembrance* of the body of thy Son, and witness unto thee, O God, the Eternal Father, that they are willing to take upon them the name of thy Son, and always *remember him* and keep his commandments which he has given them; that they may always have his Spirit to be with them. Amen. (D&C 20:77; emphasis added; see also D&C 20:79; Moroni 4:3; Moroni 5:2)

The Savior reminds us, "But the Comforter, which is the Holy Ghost, whom the Father will send in my name, he shall teach you all things, and bring all things to your remembrance, whatsoever

I have said unto you" (John 14:26). Remembering takes effort, and it is helpful to form a plan, else we shall forget. The following will help your planning to be successful:

- Plans to remember our Savior and His infinite Atonement so we will be obedient and keep the commandments.
- Plans for ways to avoid, overcome, and resist temptation.
- Plans to organize every needful thing—prioritize those things that matter most.
- Create a gratitude journal to stay in remembrance of your blessings. Count your blessings day by day. When we remember our blessings, we are filled with gratitude, and we will remember our Savior and Heavenly Father and all that They have done for us. This process of counting is an important part of remembering, for it keeps us tuned to our dependence on the Lord and prevents us from becoming too proud and self-sufficient. A notation entered into our gratitude journal every day will preserve this precious attitude of gratitude: thanksgiving for the people we love, the goodness of God, the marvels of His creation (animals, plants, rivers and streams, mountains and valleys, the stars in the heavens—reminders of the magnificent gift of the Creation and the power and glory of God), even inventions that the Lord has inspired mankind to produce to make life better (cars, planes, boats, farm equipment, medical devices, technology). You can view everything as a gift of God. All things can turn us to God if we have but eyes to see and hearts that feel.
- Make a plan for small reminders—a penny in your shoe, a bell, a key word or phrase, memos, posters, signs—to stir the mind to remember that which is vital. I remember wearing a penny in my shoe for several years, and it was a continual reminder, for I could always feel it and my mind was constantly being turned to remember to be good.

In all this we must understand that the opposite of remembering is forgetting—allowing the goodness, beauty, and vitality of the gospel to slip from our minds and hearts.

Moses, who received the Ten Commandments directly from the Lord for the people of Israel—those mighty and thundering exhortations given to remember—recorded, "Only take heed to thyself, and keep thy soul diligently, lest thou forget the things which thine eyes have seen, and lest they depart from thy heart all the days of thy life: but teach them thy sons, and thy sons' sons" (Deuteronomy 4:9). And furthermore: "Take heed unto yourselves, lest ye forget the covenant of the Lord your God, which he made with you" (Deuteronomy 4:23).

The Book of Mormon is a chronicle of both remembering and forgetting, of light and darkness, of joy and anguish of the soul. When the people remembered the Lord and kept His commandments, they prospered. But when they forgot, they suffered a speedy and painful decline: "Thus we see how quick the children of men do forget the Lord their God, yea, how quick to do iniquity, and to be led away by the evil one" (Alma 46:8).

Remembering to be grateful can be the catalyst for doing good, and good is the state of being from which springs happiness and joy. President Henry B. Eyring assures us of the following:

> And so the remembrance King Benjamin urged upon us can be ours. Remembrance is the seed of gratitude, which is the seed of generosity. Gratitude for the remission of sins is the seed of charity, the pure love of Christ. And so God has made possible for you and me this blessing, a change in our very natures: "And the remission of sins bringeth meekness, and lowliness of heart; and because of meekness and lowliness of heart cometh the visitation of the Holy Ghost, which Comforter filleth with hope and perfect love, which love endureth by diligence unto prayer, until the end shall come, when all the saints shall dwell with God. (Henry B. Eyring, *To Draw Closer to God: A Collection of Discourses* [Salt Lake City: Deseret Book, 1997], 80)

To remember means more than just recollecting a thought periodically. It means to always have the principle, doctrine, and covenant in our minds. In remembering, we should think, ponder, and meditate upon the things of the Lord, and in particular our covenants. This is a key point in living the gospel: "For as he thinketh in his heart, so *is* he" (Proverbs 23:7; emphasis added). The process of thinking and mental exertion (part of exercising faith) is the beginning of gaining the vision, the desire, and the ability to live the gospel through our words and actions.

The catalyst for the transition from thoughts to desire to action is enhanced when we understand the gospel, appreciate the Lord's blessings, and feel gratitude for His atoning sacrifice. As we follow this process, we will find that we indeed always remember the Lord and His Atonement—and that our remembrance translates into action and goodness. The question, at that point, is one of initiative and self-mastery: Will we in fact remember the goodness and mercy of God and our dependence upon the Lord and His infinite and eternal Atonement?

As mentioned previously, when we liken the word of God to our lives, we see that the sacramental prayers command us to *remember* the Lord's sacrifice of His body and His blood on our behalf. We are commanded to remember Him always and keep His commandments. Doing so brings to us the magnificent blessing of having His Spirit to be with us always. It is in this sacred moment of partaking of the sacrament each week that we renew all of our covenants. The key to living these covenants is to *remember.*

This treatise on remembering is born of gratitude. And when we remember, our hearts are *filled* with gratitude. Gratitude and remembering are both symbiotic and synergistic—they feed off each other and work together. The entire purpose of this book is to encourage each of us to increase in our gratitude and thanksgiving for the goodness of our Father and our beloved Savior's atoning sacrifice. Gratitude is the great catalyst to change to keep us on the straight and narrow path so that we may enter into our Lord's rest. Then the time will come when we become more like Him. Our actions will flow from who we are and who we have become, not necessarily from the lists we have made but rather from what our hearts have become—even a new heart the Lord will give the house of Israel: "A new heart also will I give you, and a new spirit will I put within you: and I will take away the stony heart out of your flesh, and I will give you an heart of flesh. And I will put my spirit within you, and cause you to walk in my statutes, and ye shall keep my judgments, and do them" (Ezekiel 36:26–27). With the love of God in our hearts, we will be the Lord's people. A happy people with no contention but a oneness brought about by the infinite Atonement of Christ the Lord (see 4 Nephi 1:15–16).

The hope of the resurrection and coming into the presence of our Father and our Savior, along with being with our families, is a driving force in my life. Heavenly Father and our Savior repeatedly mention and teach of our promised blessings that are given to us. It seems at every turn when a doctrine is preached, a promised blessing is pronounced upon the faithful. I will quote just a few.

> Always remember him and keep his commandments which he has given them; that they may *always have his Spirit to be with them.* (D&C 20:77)

> I would desire that ye should consider on the blessed and happy state of those that keep the commandments of God. For behold, they are blessed in all things, both temporal and spiritual; and if they hold out faithful to the end they are received into heaven, that thereby *they may dwell with God in a state of never-ending happiness.* O remember, remember that these things are true; for the Lord God hath spoken it. (Mosiah 2:41; emphasis added)

> Wherefore, ye must press forward with a steadfastness in Christ, having a perfect brightness of hope, and a love of God and of all men. Wherefore, if ye shall press forward, feasting upon the word of Christ, and endure to the end, behold, thus saith the Father: *Ye shall have eternal life.* (2 Nephi 31:20)

> And again, verily I say unto you, if a man marry a wife by my word, which is my law, and by the new and everlasting covenant, and it is sealed unto them by the Holy Spirit of promise, by him who is anointed, unto whom I have appointed this power and the keys of this priesthood; and it shall be said unto them—Ye shall come forth in the first resurrection; . . . and shall be of full force when they are out of the world; and they shall pass by the angels, and the gods, which are set there, to their exaltation and glory in all things, as hath been sealed upon their heads, which glory shall be a fulness and a continuation of the seeds forever and ever. *Then shall they be gods, because they have no end; therefore shall they be from everlasting to everlasting, because they continue; then shall they be above all, because all things are subject unto them. Then shall they be*

gods, because they have all power, and the angels are subject unto them. (D&C 132:19–20; emphasis added)

These are just a few glorious scriptures to teach an eternal principle about the goodness of God, and His desires are always to bless His children with everything He has if they will but keep His commandments. Everything is made possible by the grace of God, and our judgment is up to us according to our works and the desires of our hearts, which are recorded in the book of life (see D&C 128:6–7; Alma 5:58; Revelation 20:12).

When coming into the presence of our Father, surely we will feel His loving arms around us, embraced by His perfect love. I seek to embrace my Heavenly Father and my Savior and express in Their presence the gratitude I feel for all They have done, ever hoping that I have pleased my Father and my Savior. I look forward to holding my son again after nearly thirty years since his call to the spirit world and to thanking my mother, as well as hoping for approval that my life was acceptable to her. I pray that my father, who had waited fifty-two years for my mother, was prepared and ready for that joyful reunion. I think of the sociality that we will enjoy, "that same sociality which exists among us here will exist among us there, only it will be coupled with eternal glory, which glory we do not now enjoy" (D&C 130:2). Having the joy and rejoicing with our families—surely this will be a time of rejoicing. Just imagine meeting all of the prophets that have become dear friends as we have read about their lives over and over again in the scriptures. And to think I can call them by their first name. Oh how I love the prophets and those who have brought the word of God to us. I can't wait to thank the writers of the Book of Mormon, especially Mormon for his great abridging of this most perfect of all books, and, of course, our beloved Prophet Joseph, who translated it by the gift and power of God. They all suffered so much to bring this record to us. And they have exhorted us to read and ponder it so we can liken it to our lives, and thus we can live by every word that proceedeth forth from the mouth of God and not stand under condemnation for treating it lightly.

The resurrection and eternal lives are real.

The Lord, having done all things necessary for our redemption by accomplishing the infinite Atonement, requires us to repent and have a softened heart. The suffering in Gethsemane and on Golgotha's hill requires of us repentance to fully accept His atoning sacrifice. Only through repentance can we receive His ultimate gift of the Atonement, including eternal life. Only through repentance can we be made clean through the blood of the Lamb of God.

I, with my heart softened and broken and my spirit contrite, seek to repent. Jesus is the promised Messiah, the Savior and Redeemer of the world—Christ the Lord. He suffered for us. He sacrificed for us. He lived for us. He has sought to bring us everlasting life if we will but receive His ultimate gift—the infinite Atonement. It is this gift, when understood and appreciated, which will exalt us. It is this gift that will nurture and strengthen us. It is this gift that provides for everything that relates to returning to the presence of our Father—for Christ is the only way. He is the way, the truth, and the life. He is our friend who died that we might live. As Paul reminds us, "And that he died for all, that they which live should not henceforth live unto themselves, but unto him which died for them, and rose again" (2 Corinthians 5:15). We now, having received the magnificent Atonement into our lives, we should live for Christ. And let it be said of us, "You have in all things lived outside yourself in charity."

ABOUT THE AUTHOR

Ed J. Pinegar is the author of over sixty nonfiction books and audio tapes—most recently *The Temple: Gaining Knowledge and Power in the House of the Lord* and the bestselling Christmas story *The Christmas Code*. He has taught part time at the BYU College of Religion for nineteen years and full time at the Orem institute for ten years. He has also taught early morning seminary for five years and as a volunteer teacher at the Provo MTC for ten years. He has served in many positions of leadership in The Church of Jesus Christ of Latter-day Saints, including bishop, stake president, mission president, and president of the Provo MTC and Manti Temple. He and his wife, Pat, are parents of eight, grandparents of thirty-eight, and great-grandparents of twenty-two. Ed and his wife live in Orem, Utah.

SCAN TO VISIT

WWW.EDJPINEGAR.COM

0 26575 17659 9